Classics and Colonialism

Classics and Colonialism

Edited by
Barbara Goff

Duckworth

First published in 2005 by
Gerald Duckworth & Co. Ltd.
90-93 Cowcross Street, London EC1M 6BF
Tel: 020 7490 7300
Fax: 020 7490 0080
inquiries@duckworth-publishers.co.uk
www.ducknet.co.uk

A catalogue record for this book is available
from the British Library

ISBN 0 7156 3311 2

Typeset by e-type, Liverpool
Printed and bound in Great Britain by
CPI Bath

Contents

Contributors

Felix Budelmann is a lecturer in Classical Studies at the Open University. He is the author of *The Language of Sophocles: Communality, Communication and Involvement* (Cambridge 2000) and the co-editor of *Homer, Tragedy and Beyond: Essays in honour of P.E. Easterling* (London 2001).

John Gilmore is a lecturer in the Centre for Translation and Comparative Cultural Studies and the Centre for Caribbean Studies at the University of Warwick. His many publications on the literature, history and culture of the Caribbean include *The Poetics of Empire: A Study of James Grainger's The Sugar-Cane* (Athlone Press, 2000), which explores the function of Grainger's imitation of Vergil in this important early Caribbean poem. Current projects include a full-length study of Francis Williams and a collection of translations from eighteenth-century Latin verse by British authors.

Barbara Goff is Senior Lecturer in Classics at the University of Reading. Most of her publications concern Greek tragedy, particularly Euripides, but her most recent book is *Citizen Bacchae: Women's Ritual Practice in Ancient Greece* (University of California Press, 2004). She is currently working on a co-authored book on Oedipus and Antigone in dramas of the African diaspora.

Emily Greenwood is a lecturer in Greek Literature and Classical Studies at the University of St Andrews. She has written articles on Greek historiography and the reception of classics in the Caribbean, and is currently preparing a book on Thucydides.

Lorna Hardwick teaches at the Open University, UK, where she is Professor of Classical Studies and Director of the Research Project on the Reception of Classical Texts. Recent publications include *Translating Words, Translating Cultures* (Duckworth, 2000) and *New Surveys in the Classics: Reception Studies* (Oxford University Press, 2003). She is currently working on the relationship between classical receptions and broader cultural shifts.

Contributors

Thomas Harrison is Rathbone Professor of Ancient History and Classical Archaeology at the University of Liverpool and specialises in Greek history and historiography. His publications include *Divinity and History: the Religion of Herodotus* (Oxford, 2000) and *The Emptiness of Asia: Aeschylus'* Persians *and the History of the Fifth Century* (Duckworth, 2000).

Phiroze Vasunia is Assistant Professor of Classics at the University of North Carolina at Chapel Hill. He is the author of *The Gift of the Nile: Hellenizing Egypt from Aeschylus to Alexander* (Berkeley 2001) and numerous other publications on the ancient world. Among his research interests is the relationship between colonialism, imperialism, and classics.

Introduction

Barbara Goff

The essays that make up this book represent the proceedings of a one-day conference entitled 'Classics and Colonialism' which took place in May 2001 at the Institute of Classical Studies in London.[1] The conference as a whole was conceived as a response to the movement in literary and cultural analysis which is known as postcolonialism, and these essays investigate a selection of the ways in which the projects of the British Empire have been furthered or undermined by a cultural politics focused on the classics. I propose in this Introduction to discuss the nature of postcolonialism, and then to ask why *classics* and colonialism counts as a topic, and why the work collected here does not simply come under the rubric of 'the classical tradition'. I shall then indicate what other work has been undertaken in this field, before briefly introducing the chapters that make up this volume.

Postcolonialism?

Postcolonialism – an expansive and generous term which I shall try to explain more closely in what follows – has advanced through the academy in the last decade or so with remarkable speed and ease. Such is the rapid turnover in contemporary theoretical discourse, indeed, that it is already possible to announce 'the end of' postcolonialism, as does Bart Moore-Gilbert in 1997: 'There must be a suspicion that the postcolonial "moment" has been and gone' (185).[2] Oddly enough, the end of feminism has also been announced, even though, as is all too clear, women globally are still subordinate to men in a variety of ways. Postcolonialism strikes me as being similar to feminism not only in these premature reports of its demise. Feminism, as a political stance and a critical practice, wishes to transform the world as well as the text; and within the realm of the text, it wishes not only to find new things to say about existing topics but also to make new topics emerge. So too the impetus behind much of postcolonialism is both political and cultural. In terms of politics, real and radical changes have overtaken the world since the independence movements of the mid-twentieth century; and in terms of culture, one of the changes is the emergence of new literary voices within previously colonised countries. As a critical practice, postcolonialism, in its response to these changes, has the capacity to transform what we study as well as how we study, and thus to modify our understanding of the world we live in.

Given these multiple determinants, what can be meant by 'postcolonialism'? We should perhaps start further back, with 'colonialism' itself and indeed 'imperialism'. Despite the possibility of differentiating between these two movements, they are closely connected and in this Introduction will be used almost interchangeably. Imperialism, according to Edward Said, is 'the practice, the theory, and the attitudes of a dominating metropolitan centre ruling a distant territory', while 'colonialism, which is almost always a consequence of imperialism, is the implanting of settlements on distant territory' (1993: 8). 'Postcolonialism' is then 'post' in at least two senses: first, it only arises as an analytic enterprise in the wake of the independence movements of the middle of the twentieth century, once the colonised have managed to dismiss their erstwhile overlords; secondly, because of its position in the aftermath of independence movements, postcolonialism is 'post' in that its focus is inclined to be cultural rather than immediately political or economic, and it tends to examine not so much the imposition of external force as the responses to that force. Such responses may include compliance or negotiation as well as resistance.[3] As Ania Loomba writes, 'post' is 'temporal, as in coming after, and ideological, as in supplanting' (1998: 7). Postcolonialism attends especially to the new voices that emerge within colonised cultures in the wake of imperial domination, but it is also interested in the metropolitan societies, and particularly in how their cultural products are formed by their implication in imperial dominance. Again in Said's words, postcolonial analysis seeks 'to show the dependence of what appeared to be detached and apolitical cultural disciplines upon a quite sordid history of imperialist ideology and colonialist practice' (1993: 47). The present collection spans these various aspects of postcolonialism in that, within its overall focus on the British Empire, it includes analyses of texts produced in countries both metropolitan and colonised, and its historical range extends from the eighteenth to the twenty-first century.[4]

Since the term 'postcolonialism' covers so many bases, it is hard to give a definition as such.[5] Ashcroft et al. began the process of defining in 1989: 2 with 'to cover all the culture affected by the imperial process from the moment of colonization to the present day'. Gilbert and Tompkins (1996: 2) quote a more focused, but still very broad account: 'a politically motivated historical-analytic movement [which] engages with, resists, and seeks to dismantle the effects of colonialism in the material, historical, cultural-political, pedagogical, discursive and textual domains'.[6] Slightly less ambitious is the account given by Moore-Gilbert (1997: 12) which holds postcolonialism to be the 'analysis of cultural forms which mediate, challenge and reflect upon the relations of domination and subordination ... between (and often within) nations, races and cultures, which characteristically have their roots in the history of modern European colonialism and imperialism'. All of these formulations weight cultural analysis at least equally with political, and indeed literary works have been particularly targeted by postcolonial analysis ever since the formative study by Said, his *Orientalism* of 1978.[7] His subsequent work (*Culture and Imperialism*, 1993) maintains this position when it argues that 'cultural forms as the novel ... were immensely important in the formation of imperial attitudes, references, and experience ... [the novel] is *the* aesthetic object whose connection to the expanding societies of Britain and France is particularly interesting to study' (1992: xii). Other scholars have taken up the theme, claiming that literature is at the centre of gravity of the imperial project because it offers a way to the 'hearts and minds' of all imperial subjects, in metropolis or colony alike. Thus Ashcroft et al. write in their seminal work of 1989 of the 'cultural hegemony' of the colonisers persisting among the colonised even when the political and economic hold over the colonised country has to all appearances given way. Boehmer explains her critical stance (1995: 5): 'empire is approached as in the main a textual undertaking – as are the movements which emerged in opposition to empire'. The literature which is produced as part of the response to empire, by colonised or coloniser, is characterised by new themes and preoccupations: Walder (1998: x) for instance cites 'history, language, race, gender, migration and cultural exchange', while Boehmer finds 'identity' to be a term of overriding importance (1995: 8). The emphasis in both the literature and the criticism is often on a hybridity of experience, on the impossibility of recapturing a single essence after the enforced cultural mingling that is the fruit of empire. This emphasis can be read both in the new literatures produced within e.g. Africa and India, and in the metropolitan writings that tackle imperial themes. Thus postcolonial literature is often recognised by its focus on displacement, in tales of exile and deracination; by its interrogation of the notion of identity; and by its deliberate impurity of language, genre and/or style.

The success of postcolonialism may perhaps be measured not only by the vast quantity of literature from former colonies that is now extremely influential in the metropolis and beyond, but also by the number of new understandings of canonical metropolitan texts that have been generated. It is no longer appropriate to account for e.g. British Romanticism without an acknowledgement of the emergent British Empire, or to ignore e.g. Caribbean writing in departments of English. But as I indicated at the outset, there are problems attendant on this success. Despite the apparent hegemony of literary study within postcolonialism which I have just sketched, there have in fact been repeated disputes over whether imperial domination should be understood primarily in cultural or in political forms: should postcolonial analysis concentrate its firepower on 'text' or on 'history'?[8] This conflict is recognisable within the humanities as being a version of a longstanding debate between the formalists and the materialists, and remains, recognisably, difficult. Leela Gandhi writes that postcolonialism is situated 'somewhere in the interstices between Marxism and postmodernism/poststructuralism. It is, in a sense, but one of the many discursive fields upon which the mutual antagonism between these competing bodies of thought is played out' (1998: 167). Within postcolonialism this disagreement is often described in terms of 'theory' and 'criticism', terms which in this context have particular significances. 'Postcolonial theory' is usually identified with the names of Edward Said, Gayatri Spivak and Homi Bhabha, and exhibits affiliations with the 'high theory' of Derrida, Lacan and Foucault. 'Theory' in this context privileges the concepts of language, desire, identity, power and knowledge, which it takes to be both central to understanding of human enterprises, and, correspondingly, beyond the reach of empirical or positivist discourse. 'Criticism', in this debate, is more inclined to stake its claims on the grounds of class, race and gender, to espouse political and economic tools of analysis, and to concentrate on the particularities of literary works. It is important to note, however, that there is no very clear agreement among participants in the debate about where to draw the precise lines that demarcate their various areas of activity, and that a tendency to polarise the differences between the two camps sometimes reduces the debate to a simplified version of itself.[9]

'Postcolonial theory' came under particular attack from Aijaz Ahmad's *In Theory: Classes, Nations, Literatures* (1992), which argues that postcolonial theory is just another manifestation of the West's 'will to power'. Not only are the writings from former colonies which are most studied and fêted those which respond to Western texts, and which are in English, but the 'theorists' themselves are likely to be domiciled in the West and indeed inside Western academe.[10] Ahmad concludes that this 'new' field of enquiry simply reproduces the old relations between the centre and the periphery, the coloniser and the colonised. He urges that the study of postcolonial relations have recourse to Marxist economic and political analysis, rather than to the terms of cultural and literary criticism. There is, of course, a certain irony in thus theorising a critique of theory,[11] and while Ahmad's intervention is clearly important, other practitioners who also criticise the theoretical tendency within postcolonialism make different points which may be more relevant to the project in hand here. Some critique the habit within postcolonial theory of homogenising all the societies it discusses, without making proper differentiations among them. Dennis Walder, for instance, notes that postcolonial analysis can be too totalising and generalising (1998: xi) and suggests that for writers at least, 'postcolonial' is a 'questionable' and even 'irritating' label (1998: 1). Walder recommends a return to the text (1998: xi) – a move away from overarching theories in favour of the specificity of particular works and the way that these engage, each at its own particular point in the relations with the processes of colonisation and decolonisation, with the themes of e.g. exile, migration and identity. In this he is also following e.g. Elleke Boehmer, who describes her *Colonial and Postcolonial Literature* (1995) as an attempt 'to introduce more texts and contexts into the discussion of colonial and postcolonial issues' (8) rather than as yet another theoretical overview. Given that these 'critics' are implicitly 'theorising' about what the postcolonial enterprise should be, it is clear that the different categories cannot be kept strictly apart from one another. As Loomba notes, 'economic plunder, the production of knowledge and strategies of representation depended heavily on one another' (1998: 97). Within the terms of the debate, however, we may say that the position of the present collection is allied to 'criticism' rather than to 'theory', and to literature and culture rather than to history and politics.

Classics and colonialism?

Given that postcolonialism is itself not an untroubled practice, exhibiting stories of both success and failure, why should classics as a discipline or as an intellectual enterprise take an interest in it? One answer might be in terms of the ability of classics to participate in the general discourse of the humanities; classics cannot easily ignore an important critical development in the humanistic disciplines any more than it could, finally, ignore feminism, structuralism or even the New Criticism. (I speak, of course, not for the whole of the classical establishment, some of which does indeed ignore lots of things, and quite successfully.) Another answer would stress survival; in a context where – at least in Britain – institutions of higher education compete for humanities students, teaching in classics could, perhaps, address new audiences if it gave new accounts of itself.[12] But another important answer, it seems to me, is that classics has a stake in postcolonial analysis because the discipline has played an active role both in imperialist and colonialist movements and in the opposing movements of resistance. The history of the discipline has been intimately connected with the processes of empire at many levels, and it cannot come to historical self-consciousness without attention to these connections. As I hope to show later in this Introduction, classicists are already investigating these connections in some areas, but the specific postcolonial context is only infrequently acknowledged. It seems timely, then, to consider what fresh insights may be produced by a postcolonial focus on the discipline of classics.

This collection as a whole offers new analyses of various kinds of material, but let me begin by adducing two examples of my own, which I shall sketch out as representative anecdotes rather than as fully-fledged discussions. My examples are both 'Greek', but within this field they give an idea of the range of ways in which classics can intersect with imperial practices. One cultural phenomenon which represents this intersection is the Elgin Marbles.[13] The occasion of their acquisition by Lord Elgin, in the early years of the nineteenth century, was afforded by a clash between the nascent British and French empires, both bent on acquiring the materials of a 'classical heritage' from other empires whose star was definitely on the wane. As Browning writes, '[Elgin] found himself in a position of unexampled opportunity, since after the defeat of the French fleet by Lord Nelson in the battle of the Nile in August 1798 the Sultan looked to Britain to protect the Ottoman Empire against the French' (1987: 23-4).[14] The French, meanwhile, in the person of Napoleon, had extracted from Italy 'all the valuable Statues – Sixty-two choice pieces from the Vatican alone – among which are the torso Apollo of Belvedere, Laocoon, Meleager, etc – besides the best from the other Museums – Most of the best pictures are also at Paris …'.[15] Thus William Richard Hamilton, Elgin's private secretary (later Under Secretary of State for Foreign Affairs) writing to Elgin in 1799.[16] Nor were the French efforts confined to Italy: Cook recounts that the French Ambassador in Constantinople instructed his draughtsman: 'Take away everything you can. Do not neglect any opportunity to remove everything in Athens and its neighbourhood that is removable' (1984: 55). Hamilton clearly sees the inter-imperial dimension of his activities when he writes:

> He [Elgin] had … an example before him, in the conduct of the last French embassy sent to Turkey before the Revolution. French artists did

then remove several of the sculptured ornaments from several edifices in the Acropolis, and particularly from the Parthenon ... other objects from the same temple were conveyed to France, where they ... occupy conspicuous places in the gallery of the Louvre. And the same agents were remaining at Athens during Lord Elgin's embassy, waiting on the return of French influence at the Porte to renew their operations.

> *Memorandum on the Earl of Elgin's Pursuits in Greece*
> (London: W. Miller, 1811)

In a miniature (and much less brutal) version of the later 'scramble for Africa', Britain and France vie with each other in a scramble for the classical heritage. By acquiring this heritage, the contemporary empire would announce its claim to be the new heart and centre of Europe, a centre which proclaimed not only its cultural identity with the ancient version of Europe but also its new ability to reach beyond itself and engage with foreign lands and other empires.

One obvious objection to the argument here is that Elgin did not act initially as a representative of the British government, although he was at the time Ambassador to the Sublime Porte of Turkey. Although he acquired the Marbles in a private capacity, however, they swiftly became a matter for national attention. The Commons debate of 7 June 1816 over the purchase of the Marbles for the nation, while making evident the possibilities for considerable disagreement over the morality of the case, turns frequently on the stature of Britain with respect to the rest of the world. Mr Croker, speaking for the purchase, offers grounds on which the Marbles might develop British standing in the world, noting political as well as artistic benefits: 'the possession of these precious remains of ancient genius and taste would conduce not only to the perfection of the arts, but to the elevation of our national character, to our opulence, to our substantial greatness'.[17] Those on the other side of the debate were also placed to appeal to 'national honour' and the 'jealousy' of other nations (Hitchens 1987: 129, 135). Hamilton had already pointed to a possible connection between the Marbles on one hand, and British national physique and character on the other:

> it may not be too sanguine to indulge a hope, that, prodigal as Nature is in the perfections of the human figure in this country, animating as are the instances of patriotism, heroic actions, and private virtues, deserving commemoration, sculpture may soon be raised in England to rival the ablest productions of the best times of Greece.
> *Memorandum on the Earl of Elgin's Pursuits in Greece*
> (London: W. Miller, 1811)

The 'Report of the Select Committee of the House of Commons on the Earl of Elgin's Collection of Sculptured Marbles' (quoted in Hitchens 1987) envisages a different kind of continuity between Greece and Britain:

> ... if it be true, as we learn from history and experience, that free governments afford a soil most suitable to the production of native talent, to the maturing of the powers of the human mind, and to the growth of every species of excellence ... no country can be better adapted than our own to afford an honourable asylum to these monuments.

Here, the Marbles in their search for 'asylum' are assisted by the political excellence of Britain.

As Christopher Hitchens has argued (1987), the Marbles became a figure for nineteenth-century British patriotism, and we may see them eventually becoming such for imperialism. By the end of the century, the argument for retaining the Marbles, and against restoring them to Greece, has shifted:

> What cannot the platform-Pharisee say of Gibraltar, Malta, India, Burma, Hong Kong, the Cape, Canada, New Zealand, Australia, IRELAND? Will not every imaginable motive cry aloud in his Pecksniffian bosom to purge himself of all this perilous stuff till England, denuded of every possession which God and her forefathers gave her, shall stand up naked and not ashamed in the midst of a Salvation Army clamour – clothed only in self-righteousness and self-applause and the laughing stock of the whole world? This is the logic of 'giving back the Elgin Marbles'.[18]

The argument has in fact advanced to the point where it takes on the contours of a wholesale defence of the Empire. Imperial identity, history and the acquisition of the Marbles underwrite each other, and possession of the classical heritage is almost effortlessly transformed into a metonym for other kinds of possession. Even in the twentieth century, in the aftermath of the Second World War, when the return of the Marbles was mooted as a sign of the renewal of relations between Britain and Greece, it was conceived partly as a means of diverting Greek attention from the British presence in Cyprus (Greenfield 1995: 66-7).

Despite this background, the Elgin Marbles seem to be a topic on which classicists have on the whole preferred to write with an artistic rather than a political focus. Remarkably, neither Jenkyns (1980) nor Turner (1981) makes the connection between the Marbles and imperialism, choosing rather to concentrate on the aesthetic issues generated by the arrival of the sculptures.[19] Similarly muted in the secondary literature is my second example of the intersection between classics and colonialism, namely the role of the classics within education in Africa of the colonial and postcolonial period. The issues raised here are different from those involved with the Marbles, if only because the Marbles emerge from a competition among European powers managing a nascent imperialism, while in Africa there is a binary relationship of domination and subordination between coloniser and colonised, articulated partly in the cultural and educational fields.

The role of classics within colonial and postcolonial African education has been varied and often contradictory. In some parts of colonial Africa, the classical curriculum of the metropolitan countries was imported wholesale into their colonies, so that African students were set to work learning the Greek and Latin languages even when the language of instruction was not the native tongue, but rather French or English. This could have varying effects: one source reports that 'this multiplicity of tongues ... gives the African scholar an outlook on languages differing altogether from that of his schoolboy British contemporary. Latin is simply one more language. Greek, to the Africans who reach Greek, is simply another ... '.[20] There were more obviously negative effects as well. The classics could be criticised as part of the 'bookishness' that was said to deform African education and that was seen as the antithesis to the 'practical' or 'technical' education which gained ground over the course of the late nineteenth and early twentieth centuries.[21] The dead languages were, furthermore, vulnerable to the perception that they were part of the imposition of 'Western civilisation' and the consequent downgrading of any African tradition. Latin and Greek were therefore multiply ripe for rejection in plans of reform consequent on independence; thus Moumouni writes (1968: 167):

> The teaching of dead languages ... is a 'luxury'. They are supposedly indispensable for the stereotype of a 'cultivated man', which springs no doubt from historical conditions peculiar to France ... It 'looks well' to be able to quote Sophocles, Homer, Euripides, Plato or Socrates in Greek or Cicero, Plutarch, Caesar or Seneca in Latin, even if in reality one has retained nothing of the positive content of their works ... It may be desirable ... that specialists ... of Greek, Latin, or Greek and Roman civilisation and history be able to read original documents. But the study of these languages, in what concerns us Africans, cannot conceivably be thought of as essential to everyone ... Latin and Greek teaching cannot apply except to a very tiny minority of future specialists.

Moumouni writes of Francophone Africa, but his arguments are represented within Anglophone countries too.

Still other relationships between Africans and the classics were
possible. In South Africa the classics, along with much else, were
completely denied to native Africans. Despite this discriminatory structure, white scholars could find in classical culture a position from which
to articulate a modicum of dissent from the apartheid ideology; thus
Simon Davis, in an inaugural address of 1953 (just before the passing of
the Bantu Education Act) reminds his audience that 'In the study of
race relations in the ancient world, our own world can learn much from
the attitude of the ancients, whose ultimate criterion for citizenship
was not colour but status'.[22] Political reform in South Africa, when it
came, had little time for classics, and since the abolition of apartheid
and advent of democracy the requirement of Latin for the university
study of Law has been dropped, with predictable results on the numbers
studying classics throughout the system. There is now in South Africa
a move to develop instead ways of teaching Latin to people whose first
tongue is an African language (Claassen 1992 and 1998).

Elsewhere in contemporary Africa, there developed a quite different
institution in which Africans can be seen to assert an independent claim
to classical culture, rather than having it either imposed on or withheld
from them. In 1981 Malawi opened the Kamuzu Academy, in which
Latin, Ancient History and Greek were the core subjects studied by all
pupils. 'Five forty-minute lessons a week in each language for four
years' ensure that 'boys and girls from village primary schools' can 'get
along in Latin and Greek' (McKechnie 1992: 142). McKechnie, who
praises the Academy's pedagogical success, also situates the whole
undertaking precisely in the context of neo-colonialism (1992: 143):

> And the point to remember is that the whole enterprise is a political mani-
> festo as well as an educational one. Donors (UN, governments and NGOs)
> are important in Malawi and the Malawi government puts a good deal of
> effort into working together with them ... But in the educational field
> donors prefer to support technical programmes consisting of training in
> agriculture, engineering or other practical fields that will offer a short-
> term economic payoff. The choice of Classics, which donors will not
> support, is a commitment to a larger and longer-term vision that involves
> Malawi's taking of a place in the international community that it chooses
> for itself rather than one prescribed by donors' views of what a black
> African country should have.

'Classics' is still opposed to the practical or the technical, but in the
changed context the stakes are perhaps even higher.[23]

Classics in the education of Africans, as a contested inheritance from the days of colonialism, has been and remains a highly contentious issue – and in this respect alone we can see a connection to the Elgin Marbles where there may be no other. An obvious question, nonetheless, emerges from my two examples: are they connected in the meaningful fashion which would allow us to develop a discourse titled 'classics and colonialism'? For instance, surely the first topic could be satisfactorily dealt with as part of the history of the British Museum, or of sculpture, and the second as part of the history of Africa, or of education. The answer to this objection is, of course, yes; both topics do form parts of other histories and have dimensions other than the ones that I concentrate on now. But both topics also constitute an important part of the history of imperialism and colonialism, in that they represent the ways in which empire is maintained, developed, and questioned in the cultural field. That these topics can still generate passion and dissent is perhaps another sign of their imperial origins – and the strangeness and inappropriateness of the juxtaposition, between African education and ancient Greek sculpture, offers us one way to measure the power of empire to make connections where there were none before.[24] Both items in the juxtaposition involve a cultural politics of imperialism, focused on the classical heritage, and together they go a long way towards demonstrating that classics has been bound up with the processes of empire – and vice versa – and not, in Said's words, a 'detached and apolitical cultural discipline' (1993: 47).

If we accept that there *is* a story to be told here about the cultural politics of colonialism, we could then ask why *classics* should be the medium of the connection. Would not another literature or culture have served as well? Could we not write a book about e.g. Shakespeare both in the high culture of early imperial London and in colonial Africa? The answer is again yes, to an extent it would, and we could. But there is an argument to be made that classics is preselected as the vehicle of these imperial combinations by its role in Europe as the common coin of the educated metropolitan elite.[25] Latin and Greek language and culture were so inseparable from the elite's vision of itself that they become inseparable from the vision of the imperial role, and they could wield a more extensive influence than e.g. Shakespeare because they could connect European elites which otherwise were divided by national languages. The role of classics in elite culture also predisposes it in another way to be closely connected with imperial projects: because classics bears with it the weight of tradition and authority, it can easily be pressed into service as a *sign* of tradition and authority in general. As such, classics can either be wielded over subjected groups, or contested by them as part of a wider resistance. We shall see versions of both these possibilities in this collection.

The classical tradition?

Since I have begun to specify some of the links between the discipline of classics and the practices of colonialism, it would be fair to ask at this point what the difference is between this project and the kind of work that is already being done on the classical tradition. In other words, why is doing 'classics and colonialism' not the same as simply doing a version of 'the classical tradition'? The answer, I think, lies in the force of the metaphors used to discuss 'tradition'. Etymologically the word has to do with 'handing down', and 'handing down' must to some extent be a peaceful process attended by goodwill. Studies of 'the classical tradition' often make much of the vocabulary of 'inheritance', 'heritage' and even 'legacy', terms which attest both to the willed activity of the past within the now, and to the receptivity of the present. Richard Jenkyns' *The Legacy of Rome* (Oxford, 1992), for instance, begins by recounting the history of previous publications which were also titled *The Legacy of Rome* (1921, edited by Sir Richard Livingstone, and 1981, edited by Sir Moses Finley), and thereby doubles or triples the testamentary metaphor. Another recent and well-received collection is titled *Roman Presences: Receptions of Rome in European Culture 1789-1945*. Although the essays in this collection range widely in terms of approach, style, and ideological engagement, and are often well aware that what is at stake is '*uses* of the past both public and also more personal' (Edwards 1999: 4, my emphasis), it is nonetheless possible to read a play on the title metaphor in formulations like 'the studies offered here explore a number of the sometimes strange and unexpected places where Roman presences have manifested themselves in recent times' (Edwards 1999: 5). My disagreement is not so much with the essays in either this collection or Jenkyns (1992), as with the general understanding indicated by the metaphor in the titles.

An alternative to this rather irenic sense of process is suggested at the close of the previous section: classics as an inheritance that is contested, fought over by those who want to share it out differently as well as by those who want none of it. In the context of colonialism, this means that classics may be invoked by writers in colonised countries, as well as by those in the metropolis, with a range of gestures of appropriation. This is a situation slightly different from the one suggested in, for instance, the 'Introduction' to Wyke and Biddiss, which suggests that 'classical antiquity ... has been most regularly deployed to bolster a supposed cultural elite of white males and to marginalize or silence whatever that imagined community came to fear as its Other' (1999: 13). I am sketching a situation in which various groups, not only a cultural elite, can have recourse to the notion of antiquity and can shape it to their own quite diverse ends. To use a mechanical and overly simple metaphor: much work on the classical tradition envisages the classical object – Greece or Rome and their various cultural products literary and artistic – as *pushing* its way through time to a contemporary period, under its own steam. Another way to look at the process is to imagine the object *pulled*, by forces not itself, which deploy it – the classical object – for their own purposes.

In the first, 'pushing' scenario, the classical object is likely to exist in a relatively conflict-free zone, where, if it has escaped destruction by war or like disaster, the only mishaps that befall it are to be temporarily lost or misunderstood. Its survival is ultimately guaranteed by its own inherent qualities, because it is endowed with enough beauty, truth, and general importance to enable it to set its own agenda. This beauty and truth remain the same at all times, and set the object apart from the various contexts in which it may find itself. Thus Jenkyns (1992: 2) categorises the varieties of influence a classical object may wield – constitutive, auxiliary and decorative[26] – without noting the possibility that the object exerting the 'influence' may itself be altered by the situations in which it fetches up. 'Influence' is a one-way street. Likewise, when his work has to account for the variety of ways in which Vergil and the *Aeneid* appear in modern critical discourse, it ensures that both remain fundamentally transcendent by explaining that 'For such variety of interpretation there are two causes. The first is simply that Vergil is a towering genius, and through the ages people have wanted to have him on their side ... ' (1992: 17).[27] The value of the classics, or at least of some of them, is that they manage to remain outside historical process.

In the second, 'pulling' model, the classical object, far from dictating its own terms, may be put to work in the service of various projects, and may become a counter in conflicts not of its own making. This version of the classical tradition is well represented by Christopher Stray's magisterial work *Classics Transformed*. Although the book concentrates on the role of classics and the Latin and Greek languages in education, its overall cultural understanding of 'classics' can be applied to other circumstances, since its argument is that classics has represented, for British society, a political struggle continued by cultural means (Stray 1998: 29):

Nineteenth-century English classics were a central resource for the self-recognition and social closure practised by an assimilated noble-bourgeois elite ... education became a crucial status marker, providing the means to distinction and social exclusions ... this use of education was characteristic of the emergence of successive bourgeois groups through the century, each seeking distinction in relation to its perceived superiors and inferiors.

Here classics is, quite clearly, a counter in a conflict ultimately determined from elsewhere.

In the educational context of more recent times, as Stray emphasises, classics has increasingly seen itself as embattled and under threat – correctly! – and therefore the discourses which surround it are more inclined to show awareness of socio-economic pressures. An interest in the intersections between classics and colonialism would, I think, similarly have to recognise these pressures and to privilege the second 'pulling' model. It would also have to note that accurate accounts of the fate of classical objects, if such exist, are likely to combine both models. Turner, writing on the Greeks among the Victorians, demonstrates how the critics who acclaim their objects' ability to 'push' are in fact themselves doing the 'pulling'. For instance, about British histories of Athens he observes (1981: 189):

Such favourable commentary [as that of Zimmern in 1911] on the Athenian political experience ... would have seemed nothing less than impossible a century earlier ... The movement of thought from the strictures of [nineteenth century writers] to the effusion of Zimmern is in part the story of the transformation of commentary on Athenian politics from a stronghold of conservative polemic into a model of liberal political development and behavior. But it is also the story of the transformation of British political thought itself.

One of the important aspects of histories of Athens in this account, then, is their relationship with the history of Britain, and with the shifts in British politics.

Classics and *colonialism*?

This collection of essays does not, of course, come into being in a vacuum. Other studies which have begun to trench on the relations between classics and colonialism, and thus implicitly to answer in the affirmative the questions above of whether there is such a topic and whether we should be interested in it, are alive to the possibilities of contestation and to the model of the troubled inheritance. We may usefully date the beginning of this process to Martin Bernal's *Black Athena* (1987 – the second volume appeared in 1991), which has generated considerable controversy within the discipline of classics as well as elsewhere. Bernal's overall thesis, much simplified, is that the Greeks themselves acknowledged their cultural borrowings from places like the Near East and Africa, especially Egypt, but that their version of their hybrid identity was superseded, in the discourse of nineteenth-century classical scholars, by the 'Aryan Model' which claimed Greece as the pure source of Greekness.[28] The nineteenth-century classicists' view of Greece, according to Bernal's investigation, was contaminated by racist prejudices that prevented those scholars from giving an accurate account of Greek history and its connections to ancient African and Semitic cultures. Bernal is not very explicit about the connection with colonialism,[29] but it is arguable that the same attitudes which could denigrate the cultural achievements of e.g. Africa and Asia, as part of a project of celebrating Greece and Europe, could also underpin the actual physical interventions by nineteenth- and twentieth-century Europeans into other lands and other societies.

The *reception* of *Black Athena*, moreover, cannot be understood without invoking some dimensions of the history of empire and its aftermath. The book is controversial because, as some commentators have noted, it has become caught up in the 'culture wars' of the USA that postdate the end of the Cold War. Bernal himself writes that 'the collapse of European communism ... meant that the American right-wing lost much of its left-wing target and began to pay more attention to the so-called "culture wars" ... in the nineteen nineties they [the wars] became central' (1997: 68). Wim van Binsbergen goes further, setting these 'culture wars' in a racial context, when he claims (1997a: 43) 'after the end of the Cold War, the American Black population and their socio-cultural aspirations were pressed into service by the dominant right-wing community in order to constitute one of their much needed enemies within, now that the major external enemy, communism, had dissolved'. This specifically North American context is crucial for understanding *Black Athena*'s popularity particularly among Afrocentrists – whether we understand by that term 'African and African-American ... authors seeking to overcome the exclusion to which they and their ancestors have been subjected by the past few centuries' or alternatively the *'extremist variant* [original italics] ... which claims that European, North Atlantic and increasingly global civilisation sprang uniquely from Africa' (van Binsbergen 1997b: 220). The opposition to *Black Athena* among classicists rightly concentrates on its various failures in accuracy and shortcuts in original research, but some classicists also adduce their unease with versions of the Afrocentric project: 'to the extent that Bernal has contributed to the provision of an apparently respectable underpinning for Afrocentric fantasies, he must be held culpable, even if his intentions are honorable and his motives are sincere' (Lefkowitz and MacLean Rogers, 1996: 20; see also Lefkowitz 1996). Since both the 'aspirations' and the 'fantasies' of African-Americans are conditioned by their position within a society to which their ancestors were exported as slaves, it is the diaspora to the States, consequent on the exploitation of Africa by the European empires, that partly determines both sides of this modern debate about ancient Greece.

Bernal's work has generated very mixed reactions within classics; of the numerous collections that have responded to *Black Athena* one is largely hostile and others, more favourable overall, still sound warning notes. Van Binsbergen, however, seems to me to set Bernal's work in its proper context when he writes: 'Whatever error has crept in is more than compensated by his scope of vision which made him realise that, inside as well as outside scholarship, creating a viable and acceptable alternative to Eurocentrism is the most important intellectual challenge of our time' (1997: 64). Bernal's project thus provides what is probably the largest useful context in which to site the present collection. Other work, however, has already taken up the challenge of rethinking the ancient world in the postcolonial terms offered to us by contemporary analysis. Thus Burton (1995), for instance, seeks to shift the terms in which we may account for Hellenistic poetry, and more specifically for Theocritus. She tracks a move away from notions of 'elitism, aestheticism, and irony', with 'realism and romanticism' as optional extras, in the understanding of Hellenistic poetry, towards an exploration of that poetry's 'engagement with issues linked to mobility, colonialism, and immigration' (1995: 1). Theocritus' 'urban mimes' – *Idylls* 2, 14 and 15 – are singled out as prime examples of the 'representation of the experiences of urban Greeks in a mobile Hellenistic world' characterised by the 'cultural dislocation' that arose from the movement of peoples consequent on Alexander's territorial acquisitions.

Burton traces these overall themes through the specificities of the poems she selects. Her reading of *Idyll* 15, the journey of the two Syracusan women to Arsinoe's Adonia in Alexandra, focuses on the women's maintenance of their identity in the face of potential threats from Egyptians and non-Dorian Greeks alike (13-14). She goes on to suggest that the symposium in *Idyll* 14 engages with similar issues. The symposium is no longer a forum in which aristocratic Greeks reinforce their class identity by establishing solidarity at both a local community and a wider international level (1995: 23). Instead, it provides a setting in which the 'dislocated' Greek males of the Hellenistic period could 'restore their sense of self-identity and community by participating in such institutions' (1995: 24-5). The story of *Idyll* 14, however, addresses the issue of mobility and isolation precisely by showing the symposium to fail, at the moment when Aeschinas strikes his girlfriend Cynisca and the other male guests at the party reject him. He ends by planning to enlist as a mercenary soldier in Ptolemy's employ, thereby committing himself to a life of absolute mobility and exchanging the failed sympotic community for the military unit. Burton demonstrates, for Theocritus' poetry at least, the value of an approach which can be broadly characterised as 'postcolonial' in that it focuses on the difficulties of mobility and migration in colonised and colonising societies.

My third example of previous work on 'classics and colonialism' is an area in which classicists of varying ideological allegiance have been quick to see the connections, namely in the nineteenth-century deployment of the Roman empire as a paradigm, whether positive or a negative, for the British.[30] Vance (1997) shows very clearly how Rome's 'rich, unstable ambiguity' (223) allowed the eternal city to be mobilised on both sides of the debate about the viability of British imperialism, but also stresses that the analogy with Rome provoked anxiety about where the Empire might be heading. If Rome fell, could Britain be far behind? Macaulay's famous fantasy suggested so, in its invocation of a time 'when some traveller from New Zealand shall, in the midst of a vast solitude, take his stand on a broken arch of London Bridge to sketch the ruins of St Paul's' (quoted in Jenkyns 1980: 52). But Rome presented a corrective to British ambitions in other ways too. The ancient city was acknowledged as having extended a common citizenship, and thus a 'sense of common identity and common purpose' (Vance 1997: 233) throughout her subject peoples, and this was a thing that imperial Britain was unwilling, perhaps even unable to do. As Majeed (1999) points out, in the case of India at least, this divergence between Roman and British policies was explained quite simply in terms of 'race' or 'colour' (1999: 105). Nineteenth- and early twentieth-century colonialist writers explained that the 'backwardness' of subject peoples was something with which the Romans did not have to contend (apparently), and so the British Empire was left with a 'modern problem' (1999: 105) for which Rome could provide no solution.

There was another tremendous difficulty inherent in wielding ancient Rome as an exemplar or legitimating precedent for the British Empire, and that was the fact that Rome had colonised Britain. This part of the British past, if plugged into the British present, would indicate not only that the British Empire might come to an end but also that the colonised people might eventually overtake the colonisers. Vance's account of Millais' painting 'The Romans Leaving Britain' (1865) shows one way of dealing with the historical reality of a colonised Britain. The 'tender regret of the departing Roman' and the 'sombre strength' of the British woman serve to distinguish the painting by softening 'the implied colonial relations of exploitation or one-sided gratification into one of partnership'. This achievement of an equality, or at least a reciprocity, between the Roman coloniser and the British colonised served not only as 'a mode of national face-saving' but also as a 'model of justification for Britain's contemporary overseas involvements' (1997: 200). Much less encouraging conclusions, however, also remained to be drawn from the history of a colonised Britain. Writing of India, Majeed (1999: 108) shows how 'identity with Imperial Rome is divided in that Roman Britain becomes too close for comfort to colonised India itself. As Imperial Britain is identified with Imperial Rome, ... there is also a threatened identity between colonised Britain and colonised India.' Both ancient Rome and contemporary India, finally, have 'the fearsome capacity to assimilate British national identity on different levels'.

If we take a representative text, which could be paralleled elsewhere, from the interwar period (soon after the Empire reached its territorial peak, but also when the ideologies underpinning it began to implode) we can see that classicists themselves were well aware of the pleasures and pitfalls of the Roman analogy. J. Mackail, addressing the Midland Institute of Birmingham, on 23 February 1925, on the topic of 'The Place of the Classics in Imperial Studies' contends that mother-country and dominions share the 'common parentage of the Graeco-Roman civilisation', and thus can insist that 'a common historical past' gives rise to the community which binds 'a nation or ... an empire'; it provides 'the sense of common pursuits and interest, of mutual understanding and mutual goodwill' (1925: 219). Classical civilisation is here deployed to give cheerful coherence to an assemblage of peoples which – even if we concentrate on the 'white' countries of the Empire, as Mackail seems tacitly to do – might not easily attain it otherwise. Within this Graeco-Roman parentage, however, there are at least two parents, and it turns out that 'Greek history is the history of one long failure to create and establish an empire' (1925: 222), contrasting implicitly with both Rome and Britain. Mackail subtly extends the connotations of his 'common parentage' metaphor when he further defines an 'empire' as 'that is to say, an organic Commonwealth of

States or Nations' (222). 'Organic', resonating with the imagery of nature and growth in 'parentage', might be opposed to e.g. 'the use of force'; and sure enough, it is the Romans who provide the alternative to the Greeks' rather ineffectual brilliance. 'Step by step, slowly, patiently, and inflexibly, the constructive Latin genius, backed by the disciplined power of Rome, spread throughout the Mediterranean world first the aim, then the accomplished fact, of a single and inclusive Imperial citizenship' (1925: 224). The account of this achievement is, naturally, followed by a list of the causes of Rome's decline, which include malaria as well as 'a mysterious loss of intellectual and moral fibre' (1925: 226).

A new note is then sounded, in the specific problem faced by the British Empire but not the Roman. This problem is 'friction and clash of interests between self-governing, proud, largely independent communities within the Empire' (1925: 226). For Mackail, I would venture, such communities are composed of white persons; for the British Empire a few years later, they were also, and more troublingly, composed of Indians and Africans. Greece did not have this problem because she had no empire; Rome was free of it because she 'deprecated[ed], guarded[ed] against, and even on occasion forcibly repress[ed] the growth of separatist national feeling' (1925: 227). In fact, such feeling was a symptom of the end of empire: 'it was not until the fabric of empire had become loosened ... that there was any movement towards national separation, or the creation of distinct states within the Empire' (1925: 227). At this point, where the experience of antiquity and that of modernity diverge so notably, Mackail's text gives up, and reverts to platitudes about what can be learnt from antiquity. We have seen this impasse, where Rome runs out of solutions for Britain, in Majeed, and the difficulty may be recognised in Jenkyns (1980) as well, which closes with an uncharacteristically short chapter on 'Empire and War'. But what did have to be learnt, by British people in the early part of the twentieth century and subsequently, is, precisely, the phenomenon of postcolonialism: the adjustments to be made to independence for the former colonised and to the necessary forging of new relations between centre and periphery. In this process, as in the earlier process of empire-building, classical models are called upon to play a various but persistent part.

*

The papers gathered here offer a series of case studies in the way that classics has been mobilised in the service or otherwise of British imperialist projects. Within this broad consensus there is considerable divergence of subject matter. Harrison's essay treats of versions of the

Athenian empire, Vasunia's of India, Greenwood's of classical education in the Caribbean, Gilmore's of a black Caribbean neo-Latin poet. Hardwick writes on classics in postcolonial literature generally while Budelmann supplements her analysis with a detailed treatment of Greek tragedy in West African adaptations.

Thomas Harrison's chapter, 'Through British Eyes: the Athenian Empire and Modern Historiography', is the only one to concentrate on an ancient empire, but he shows how assessments of the Athenian empire in the nineteenth and twentieth centuries were largely shaped by the emerging consensus about rationales for the British Empire. Citing in particular the work of Said on the ideological underpinnings of the British Empire, he then suggests that the Athenian empire was similarly prepared for and buttressed in the ideological field, and proposes that we look more carefully for an 'Athenian imperial ideology' in areas like tragedy, art, and the 'proto-imperial' ventures of the sixth and early fifth centuries.

For Phiroze Vasunia in 'Greater Rome and Greater Britain', the invocation of the Roman empire in colonised India was a way to negotiate the 'contradictions of liberal empire'. He makes the important point that the Roman example is mobilised not only by British apologists for empire (who mostly also happen to be classicists) but also by the opponents of empire both in Britain and in India itself – the latter group notably including Gandhi.

In '"We Speak Latin in Trinidad": Uses of Classics in Caribbean Literature' Emily Greenwood studies the place of classics in Caribbean education, with especial reference to the leading politicians of independence and to writers like Walcott and C.L.R. James. Significantly, she does not devote a great deal of time to delineating the ways in which classics has been on the 'wrong side' of 'racial, imperial and political oppositions', but instead concentrates on two strategies of reading deployed by Caribbeans in their relations with classics: formulating interpretations independent of European colonialist scholarship, and appropriating ancient Greece by mapping the Aegean onto the Caribbean sea.

John Gilmore's chapter, 'The British Empire and the Neo-Latin Tradition: the Case of Francis Williams,' is more specific than these last two in that it takes on the remarkable Latin poem of 1759 by Francis Williams, arguably the 'earliest black writer from anywhere in the English-speaking Atlantic world'. Gilmore's approach is to reconsider the extraordinary achievement Williams' poetry might represent by setting it firmly in a context where Latin is a familiar mode of expression for denizens of the Caribbean. He examines the neo-Latin verse of *white* Creoles, noting the ways it deals with its colonial identity, before moving on to look at the ways in which Williams' poem also engages with the issue of colour: 'Williams is unusual because he is black, not because he is a Caribbean poet writing in Latin.'

The chapter by Lorna Hardwick, 'Refiguring Classical Texts: Aspects of the Postcolonial Condition', introduces explicitly the topic of classical literature as it is 'refigured' in postcolonial contexts. The paper ranges over a variety of national literatures and theatres, including the African, Caribbean, Irish and Scots. The focus throughout is on the 'double perspective' afforded by classical texts, their potential to be either 'repressive or liberating'; the paper concludes that in the postcolonial context, classical literature itself has undergone the experience of being 'released from oppressive constraints' and 'freed to assume new identities'.

Felix Budelmann investigates a particular case of postcolonial refiguration. In 'Greek Tragedies in West African Adaptations' Budelmann notes that Greek tragedy has 'caught the imagination of a range of West African writers over the years' and asks both what makes Greek tragedy attractive to West African dramatists, and what the new plays offer to audiences and readers interested in the ancient plays. He explores various reasons for the appeal of Greek tragedy in this context, including its potential to be a vehicle of protest; its wealth of myth and ritual; and its usefulness as a means to thinking about dramatic form.

From these brief sketches of the essays gathered here a few consistent themes emerge. Education in classics, for both colonisers and colonised, is important for more than one paper, as is its salutary lesson of the fall of empires. The common coin of the elite which I adverted to earlier is shown to be common coin for members of the non-elite too. Several authors also share a desire to bring into focus little- or lesser-known texts that become newly significant as part of the intersection between classics and colonialism. And to reiterate: none of these essays dwells on the ways in which classics has been used to impress colonised peoples with a sense of their own inferiority.[31] Very few even dilate on the polar tendency to articulate protest by means of classical models. Rather, they foreground the pliability of the multifarious classical heritage and the diverse roles it may play in a postcolonial world. In this focus they point beyond themselves to the possibility of further work on the connections that they make.

Notes

1. The chapters in this book concentrate on the British Empire; the conference itself ranged somewhat more widely and although very lively and productive, was correspondingly less clearly focused. My thanks are due to all

those who participated in the conference and who helped behind the scenes, and to those involved in the publication of this collection.

2. See the opening pages of Moore-Gilbert 1997 for an excellent account of the success of postcolonialism.

3. Some critics define postcolonialism only as *resistance* to empire, and therefore include such writers as Césaire and Fanon, who write before independence, among postcolonials (but not, for instance, apologists for empire whenever they write). See on these definitions also Hardwick in this collection. It is helpful to remember that as a discipline which has changed the face of the humanities, postcolonialism definitely arose in the period 'post'.

4. To exhaust our stock of preliminary definitions, let us also note that neo-colonialism, or neo-imperialism, is generally taken to refer to the continuation of foreign domination by other means, as when the oil companies, mining outfits and banana enterprises remain in control long after the colonial troops and police have departed. It can also refer to corrupt and anti-democratic practices by the indigenous elites who may take over in the wake of colonialism.

5. Gilbert 1999: 1 suggests that the term is really too large for usefulness. There have been innumerable debates over the exact meaning of the word; Loomba 1998 devotes the first twenty pages of her work to the history of such attempts. The debates over whether there should be a hyphen after 'post' or not fortunately now appear almost antediluvian. See Gandhi (1998: 3-4).

6. They quote from Alan Lawson, 'Comparative Studies and Post-colonial "Settler" Cultures', *Australian-Canadian Studies* 10.2 (1992), 153-9.

7. Again, see the first chapter of Moore-Gilbert for an account of various kinds of imperialist and anti-imperialist writing that emerge before the codification of postcolonialism as an academic discipline.

8. See on the two sides to this debate e.g. Loomba 1998: 69-94 and 94-103 and Gandhi 1998: 141-66.

9. See Moore-Gilbert 1997 passim for the necessary corrective to this tendency.

10. See Gandhi 1998: 54-63 on the postcolonial intellectual.

11. Gandhi 1998: 56 writes that 'while Ahmad's claim [that shifts in governance affect more people than shifts in critical methodologies] is incontestable in itself, his objections take a disablingly prejudicial turn when he begins to treat all postcolonial theorising and practice as purely recreational'.

12. Classics is not known for its ability to engage the attention of minority students, but some American classicists have told me that they are able to attract African-American and Asian-American students if they make it clear that the class will read e.g. Fugard's and Brathwaite's versions of *Antigone* as well as Sophocles'.

13. It has recently become more acceptable to call them the Parthenon Sculptures, but in fact the Act of Parliament by which the sculptures were acquired for the nation stipulates that they be called 'The Elgin Marbles'. See Hitchens 1987: 57.

14. In the Commons debate on the possible purchase of the Marbles, Mr Hammersley, against the purchase, notes that 'the Turkish government [of Greece] was in a situation to grant any thing which this country might ask, on account of the efforts which we have made against the French in Egypt. It thus appeared that a British ambassador had taken advantage of our success over the French to plunder the city of Athens' (Hansard, 7 June 1918, quoted in Hitchens 1987: 132).

15. Mr Banks in the Commons debate of 7 June 1816, speaking for the purchase, notes that 'there was nothing like spoliation in the case, and that it bore no resemblance to those undue and tyrannical means by which the French had obtained possession of so many treasures of art' (Hansard, quoted in Hitchens 1987: 130).

16. Quoted by Hitchens 1987: 40.

17. Hansard, 7 June 1816, quoted in Hitchens 1987: 134.

18. James Knowles, 'The Joke About the Elgin Marbles', *The Nineteenth Century*, March 1891. A later proposal to return them, in 1983, was characterised in the *Times* as 'post-imperial conscience' (Greenfield 1995: 72). The *Times* is right, even if for the wrong reasons. Unfortunately, this proposal formed part of a Bill to offer the Trustees of the Museum greater powers of disposal in general; and those who followed politics in Britain at that time will be under no illusion that this was anything other than a plan to sell off yet more bits of the national property.

19. See e.g. Turner 1981: 44-6.

20. Parliamentary Papers Command 6655, *Report of the Commission on Higher Education in West Africa*, 1945, 12.

21. See e.g. Wise 1956, who writes from within the controversy, and for a wider ideological understanding of it, see King 1971.

22. Simon Davis, 'The Study of the Classics: Inaugural Address Delivered at Pietermaritzburg 1st October 1953', 11.

23. There are of course problems attending the development of this Academy, as with many other initiatives by 'Life President' Banda. The Academy was linked to reports of financial corruption, and its role as 'Eton in the bush' may not have been most conducive to producing either the leaders or the society that Malawi most needs. See e.g. *Malawi News Online* 29, 5 July 1997, *Electronic Mail and Guardian*, 27 July 1997.

24. I realise that this argument about imperial connections is threatened by a *reductio ad absurdum* in which everything is connected to everything else just by virtue of being inside the British Empire. I would counter the *reductio* by observing that my examples come into being already potentially connected by virtue of their joint origin within the field of classics; but it is empire that allows the classics to play the particular roles that I am here investigating, and which therefore elaborates further connections.

25. On this role, see especially Stray 1998 and Waquet 2001. In this volume, Greenwood and Gilmore explore the role of classics in Caribbean education.

26. 'Constitutive' means that the classical source is the basis of or necessary condition of the subsequent work; 'auxiliary' that it is not necessarily the basis, but affords support and coherence; 'decorative' that it provides an elegance of surface, a pretext or a starting-point that could almost equally well have come from elsewhere.

27. The second reason, presented alas with rather less panache, is that 'there is indeed something protean about his poetry' but nonetheless, 'the hard truth is that one could get him more badly wrong than Dante or Milton' (1992: 17).

28. The secondary literature on Bernal's book is already considerable. See e.g. Levine 1989, Lefkowitz 1996 and Lefkowitz and MacLean Rogers 1996, and Van Binsbergen 1997.

29. See e.g. the introduction to Volume I, 1987: 26-32, where 'racism' is the term of analysis, and imperialism or colonialism as such is not invoked.

30. See also Vasunia in this collection, and, with different emphases, Harrison.

31. This may perhaps even be considered a deficiency in a volume with this title.

Through British Eyes: The Athenian Empire and Modern Historiography[1]

Thomas Harrison

The study of the history of the Athenian empire of the fifth century might fairly be said to reduce to a single question: the popularity of the Athenians' rule with her allies or subjects, or – to put it another way – whether the Athenians' intentions were opportunistic or benign, whether indeed Athens' empire was an empire at all.

Even such a simple question may elicit a variety of answers, of course. 'Benign for whom?', we may ask. For the allies or for the Athenians? For all the allied cities, or only some?[2] A range of different evidence can be introduced: revolts, garrisons, cleruchies, tribute, all present their own difficulties. Then we can split the atom of the Greek *polis*, and see divisions within the allied cities, the poor craving for Athens to ensure democracy, the rich pleading with their Athenian friends to mitigate it.[3] (There is a whole sub-class of questions then on Thucydides, whether 'his picture of the empire is borne out by other evidence' and so on.) If we have any sense, we realise also that even that pattern was not a clear-cut one, that day-to-day circumstances – the presence of an Athenian or Spartan army on your doorstep – may have made a crucial difference, that the rhythm of revolts was dictated by the progress of the Peloponnesian war, or of the 'First Peloponnesian war', as much as by 'pure' ideological allegiance. We also realise that there may have been a chronological shift, that an alliance founded for altruistic reasons – the eradication of the Persian threat in the Mediterranean – may have developed organically into something quite different, Athenian rule in her own interests, reinforced by compulsion. This transition is dated by the 'harshness of tone' of Athenian decrees[4] – and it is these, their dating and significance, which have been the focus of much of the most important recent scholarship on the Athenian empire.[5]

We end up then with a very complex answer, but an answer, nonetheless, to a straightforward question. This approach to the Athenian empire can be described – in a phrase used both by Moses Finley, in a famous article, and by Russell Meiggs – as the 'balance-sheet' model.[6] The presumed disadvantages to the allies or subjects of Athens (tribute, garrisons, the loss of military autonomy and so on) are set against the advantages (enhanced trade, military security) that may have made up for the loss of political freedom. The term 'balance-sheet' was used by Finley and Meiggs of tangible benefits and disadvantages. As Finley himself acknowledged, however, it can apply also to other, more intangible phenomena.[7] On the one hand, did the allies feel a sense of community (derived either from religious ritual or from perceived kinship)? On the other hand, were the Athenians motivated simply by greed or by a benevolent sense of mission to their subordinates? This broader approach was pursued with particular panache by W.G. Forrest. In an article on 'Aristophanes and the Athenian empire', he detected such a 'mission civilisatrice' beneath the oath sworn by the Athenian generals of 439/8, 'to do and advise and say only what is good for the people of Samos'.[8] 'Did the men who swore that oath have their tongues in their cheeks, all of them?', wrote Forrest. 'Or did one or two of them have a tear in their eye?'

What I would like to do in the following pages is not to look at the work done within this overall framework but rather to address the framework itself – and to suggest that the questions being asked of the 'Athenian empire' are very far from being inevitable.

We may observe, first, the significant coincidence that the term 'balance-sheet' is one frequently used in the context of the British Empire, in contemporary discussions of the profitability of the Empire for Britain or in subsequent considerations of the good or harm done by Britain to her colonies.[9] It is a model that was born out of a debate (from the late nineteenth century onwards) as to whether the Empire could be justified in terms of its good works or good intentions. 'We can point without cheap pride', wrote Sir Edward Grigg (in explaining the British Empire, as an 'unrepentant Englishman', to Americans), 'to railways and telegraphs, to canals and irrigation schemes, to the extinction of much cruelty, to the protection of the weak against the strong, to the establishment of a fairer incidence of taxation, to the maintenance of security on coast and frontier, and of a peace unknown to India through all the preceding centuries.'[10] A rather harsher example of the argument of the balance-sheet (and for a British classicist somewhat closer to home) can be found in Evelyn Baring, Lord Cromer's 1910 Classical Association Presidential Address, in which he put his received knowledge of ancient empires alongside his hands-on experience of administering a modern one. [11] Though the British, Cromer acknowledges, may have made their share of mistakes in India, 'not a word of reproach can be breathed against the spirit which has animated their rule' (1910: 70-1). He goes on to tell a story to illustrate his point:

> A wealthy young Bengali, who was disclaiming against the British government, and expressing his wish that they should be expelled from India, was asked what he would do if, as the result of the anarchy and confusion which would ensue, his personal property was confiscated. 'What should I do, sir?' was his reply; 'I should apply to the High Court'. British ideas of justice had so unconsciously penetrated into his mind that he could not conceive a condition of affairs which involved the possibility of the supremacy of the law being attainted.

Lest we suppose that more established or professional scholars might somehow be immune to such lofty attitudes we may point to similar observations by the Oxford ancient historian, Peter Brunt, in comparing Roman and British empires. Unlike the Romans, he observes, 'who had no curiosity in the past of their subjects', British philologists and archaeologists 'resurrected the Indian classics and the old glories of Indian civilization ... In much the same way ... European scholarship has been helping to recreate or create the past of Africa and therefore contributing to African nationalism' (1965: 127).

What is wrong with any of this? Bridges and telegraph poles are, in themselves, surely good things. (We may feel similarly positive about British ideas of justice or European scholarship.) The Athenians and British, even the Romans, may have been motivated – on occasion, at least, or in certain contexts – by a sense of duty or compassion. Forrest's observation of Athenian generals with tears in their eyes should perhaps ring alarm bells, however. Is it right to see the sense of mission, or good works, as mitigating empire, as if the popularity of the Athenians' rule could be measured on a simple scale of one to ten?[12] In other words, what the crude equation of the balance-sheet fails to register is the ambivalent reaction of those on the receiving end of such apparently straightforward beneficence; it also fails to appreciate the complex motivation and ideological grounding of the imperial 'aggressors'.

There is also clearly a danger here of taking Athenian, or British, claims at face value. (Forrest seems to have recognised this in talking – ironically – of the Athenians on Samos as carrying a 'White-Man's Burden' (1975: 27).) This danger exists even in the context of what might appear to be objective facts; highly charged Athenian claims may be seen, presented at face value, embedded in modern narratives. So, for example, at the outset of an important article which seeks to calculate 'The Size and Resources of Greek Cities' on the basis of the so-called Athenian Tribute Lists, Lucia Nixon and Simon Price assert that the Delian League was 'more or less a naval alliance, whose aims were to protect Greeks from Persians and to liberate Greeks under Persian domination' (1990: 138). Such a statement parallels Athenian claims – for example, those of the Lysianic funeral oration (2.56-8) or Isocrates' *Panegyricus* – too closely for comfort. Simon Hornblower was sceptical of the slogan of security from Persia in his 1983 introduction to *The Greek World*, but introduces another problematic benefit in its place: the Athenians' eradication of piracy. After summarising the evidence for economic coercion, administrative and political checks on autonomy, and juridical control, he then turns to the benign side of the empire: 'The positive advantages to the allies of subservience to Athens included security from Persia (a protection which was at most times no more than propaganda, and anyway covered only cities which were vulnerably placed) and from piracy.'[13] What might the allies have thought of the eradication of pirates? It is not mentioned in our sources, Meiggs adds, 'but they are unlikely to have protested, for the suppression of piracy would have been popular in the Aegean'. That surely depends on whether as an ally you were yourself deemed a pirate. Piracy, like terrorism, must surely be a convenient and adaptable label.[14] Moreover, the boast of the eradication of piracy – like the British claim of the eradication of Thuggee in India – seems to have been an element of Athenian imperial ideology.[15] The same pattern of behaviour is projected by Thucydides back on to the Athenians' mythological analogue, Minos (Thuc. 1.4-5.1).[16]

Another aspect of the modern treatment of Athenian imperialism also looks different in a comparative perspective. As we have seen, there is some limited room given in modern scholarship on the Athenian empire for a benign, self-sacrificing mission on the Athenians' part. In general, however, what we might term 'imperial ideology' has little place in most modern accounts. This is reflected in the usage of the term 'imperialism', interchangeable in an Athenian context with 'empire'[17] – or in Meiggs' placement of two chapters on 'Fifth and Fourth-Century Judgements' on the empire at the conclusion of his book rather than as an essential prelude to his treatment of the facts.[18] But the absence of imperial ideology from modern treatments is not simply a matter of unreflective practice. Rather the view has been explicitly enunciated that *there was no such thing as an Athenian imperial ideology*.

So, for example, Moses Finley began his 'balance-sheet' essay with a quotation from A.P. Thornton's 1965 *Doctrines of Imperialism*: 'Every doctrine of imperialism defined by men is a consequence of their second thoughts. But empires are not built by men troubled by second thoughts.'[19] This, Finley added, should be taken as an antidote to beginning with 'aims and motives and quickly sliding over to attitudes and theories of imperialism, thereby implying that the men who created and extended the empire also began with a defined imperialist programme and theories of imperialism'. In support of this, at the close of his essay, he cites the justification of empire put into the mouths of the Athenians by Thucydides (1.76.2):[20]

> We have done nothing extraordinary, nothing contrary to human practice, in accepting an empire when it was offered to us and then in refusing to give it up. Three very powerful motives prevent us from doing so – honour, fear and self-interest. And we were not the first to act in this way. It has always been a rule that the weak should be subject to the strong; besides we consider that we are worthy of our power.

Meiggs' view of the development of the Athenian empire might be described as a paraphrase of this passage. Unlike Finley, Meiggs sees an evolution in Athenian imperial ambitions, but his narrative is one in which Athenian self-justifications are again repeatedly embedded as historical fact (1972: 42-3):

> We can believe that Aristides had a shrewd idea of the benefits that a league under Athenian leadership could bring to Athens, but we should not be too cynical. Fear was one of the motives for the Athenian decision to accept the *responsibilities of leadership*, because Athens knew that she more than any other Greek state might have to face renewed attack from Persia; but there was also *pride and generosity* in the Athenian mood in 478. Later conditions should not be read back into the early years. It was the allies who had most to gain from Athenian leadership and from the start it was freely recognised by all that Athens was to lead and not merely join the alliance.

Finley, by contrast, has no truck with imperial ambitions in commenting on this passage:

> There is no programme of imperialism there, no theory, merely a reassertion of the universal ancient belief in the naturalness of domination ... . Athenian imperialism employed all the forms of material exploitation that were available and possible in that society. The choices were determined by experience and practical judgements, sometimes by miscalculations.[21]

Motives, it seems, can be taken for granted – a historical constant throughout antiquity.[22]

These two positions are obviously very different – Finley's strikingly cynical, Meiggs' more idealistic. They also have something in common, however. It was famously observed by J.R. Seeley (a professor of Latin at University College London before becoming Regius Professor of History at Cambridge) that the English had come to acquire their empire 'in a fit of absence of mind'.[23] They needed to wake up and work to maintain their position. 'The progress of Roman and British expansion' wrote James Bryce similarly, 'illustrates the remark of Oliver Cromwell that no one goes so far as he who does not know whither he is going' (1914: 9). The parallel between ancient and modern imperialism here should make us wary. Of course, though, empires do not come about by accident, but rather by a seemingly haphazard process of individual and collective effort, reinforced by and reinforcing a body of shared values, a 'structure of attitude and reference' in the phrase of Edward Said (1993: 73). Because the Athenians could not have conceived of the finished product of their empire at the outset, it should not be thought that they had *no* aims in mind, that the empire (in the phrase of Paul Veyne) fell into their arms without their wanting it (1975: 796). The theory of 'accidental imperialism' – like that of reluctance at every step fighting with a sense of duty – is itself an aspect of imperial ideology.[24] To talk of accidental imperialism, to encapsulate the process of imperial 'expansion' in such organic nominalisations except as a shorthand, or to assume a static, constant 'will to betterment' as a catch-all explanation, is not only to rob the Athenians of the responsibility for their actions but an abdication of the historian's responsibility to explain.[25]

There is something to learn here from more recent scholarship on the British Empire, with its focus not only on overt justifications of the imperial project but on its ideological underpinnings and reflections. 'For the enterprise of empire depends upon the *idea* of having an empire ...', in Edward Said's well-known formulation, 'and all kinds of preparations are made for it within a culture.'[26] Said and others have looked for the reflection and reinforcement of the 'structure of attitude and reference' of imperialism in such apparently unlikely places as Jane Austen's *Mansfield Park*. It is worth observing, however, that such a broader perspective easily predates Said. In his 1960 introduction to mid-Victorian imperialism, Bodelsen included not only active practical goals – 'the consolidation of the ties that bind colonies to the mother-country', that 'British movement which aims at preserving and consolidating the unity of the British empire' – but also the theories that underpin those (largely) practical programmes: 'aggressive Nationalism', Caesarism, 'doctrines about the function of the State, the theory of the civilizing mission, the system of ethics by which it has been attempted to justify conquest and the domination of the strong by the weak'.[27] A.P. Thornton, a regular point of reference in the 1978 volume on ancient imperialism to which Finley's essay was contributed, acknowledges at the outset that 'imperialism is less a fact than a thought' (1965: 2). In his discussion of 'doctrines of imperialism' he deals with, for example, public school education, 'a training for leadership more than intellectual brilliance', or with the 'ethical sanction' provided for empire by literature, for example for Rome by the *Aeneid* (1965: 30).

This is all well and good, it might be objected, but where are we to look, in the Athenian context, for evidence of this broader imperial ideology?

We should be looking, first, in the history of well-known events. In histories of the Athenian empire, it is rarely that much mention is made of a number of proto-imperial ventures in the sixth and early fifth centuries:[28] the Peisistratid interest in Sigeion, that of the Philaids in the Chersonese, or the curious and ultimately unsuccessful enterprises of Miltiades after Marathon (Hdt. 6.132; cf. 8.112.3). These ventures – undertaken by individuals, though with some state sanction, to establish family fiefdoms – precede the formal foundations of the Delian League; but they are surely connected to its rise.[29] We should also, however, look at types of material that are too easily seen as not on the syllabus: at Athenian art, at the traces of incipient Athenian imperialism in Herodotus' account of the Persian wars,[30] or at what we might call for convenience non-historical literary sources, such as Greek tragedy. Such material has, of course, been examined in this context: notably, in recent years, by Tonio Hölscher (1998), in the case of Athenian art, and by Sophie Mills (1997), in the case of Greek tragedy. This work, however, has not been integrated into conventional narrative treatments; arguably also, it has not always pushed its claims sufficiently.

Sophie Mills, for example, in her excellent discussion of Theseus and the Athenian empire, has shown how a number of strands of Athenian self-representation are to be found across Greek tragedy, Thucydides, and fourth-century authors such as Isocrates: Athens as the model and home of justice (the Athenians stooping to help suppliants), of intelligent and restless daring, but not overconfident *hybris*, of rigour tempered by sophistication, or of pious observance (ensuring the burial of the dead). In all these respects the standards the Athenians pursue are not ostensibly in opposition to those of other Greeks. Rather the Athenians consistently and doggedly champion Greek standards: they are in Mills' phrase 'super-Greeks'. Of the ideal image of Athens that emerges, she says (1997: 52):

> It is hard to believe that it could have been so prevalent and consistent in literature without having had some influence in real life, especially given that its fullest exposition is in the obviously educational, exhortatory genre of the funeral oration. I assume therefore that the funeral speeches contain an extreme and highly formalized version of an ideology which, in a less extreme form, pervades mainstream Athenian thought about Athens and Athenian identity. They both reflect and influence certain images of the city: there is no division between these two functions.

Mills' account brings out the power and grandeur of the Athenian image of Athens – something sometimes missing in relatively anodyne modern portrayals.[31] Nonetheless, there is arguably something passive and reflexive about the picture drawn, as shown by a concluding remark (1997: 84-5):

> The punishments of the wicked by Theseus or other Athenian representatives made a naturally attractive framework into which to fit much contemporary Athenian action. Even though most Athenians would have enjoyed the thought of their city's power, worked in the assembly and on the battlefield to retain it, and could perhaps have allowed on occasion that it was as great as the power of a tyrant, it is very doubtful that the majority of them would have been able to think that its possession was actually unjust. Ideological justifications, buttressed by what Athenians saw in the theatre, or heard at the *epitaphioi*, created a far more attractive way of looking at the empire which contributed to the well-being of all Athenians, materially and in less tangible ways.

Though Mills suggests that such images belong to real life rather than the secure preserve of literature, the emphasis here perhaps underestimates the degree to which they may have driven events; rather such images are seen as a kind of fragrant air-freshener to cover up Athenian bad consciences.

Art too may have played a more active role. The well-known pair of statues of the tyrannicides Harmodius and Aristogiton – set up in a prominent setting in the agora, next to the early meeting-place of the assembly – are referred to tellingly in the course of Aristophanes' *Lysistrata*. The chorus leader, enraged by the antics of Lysistrata and her colleagues, asserts that he will 'stand in arms by Aristogiton in the market place' (626 ff., tr. Halliwell). It has been suggested that the chorus might all have advanced at this moment with their hands raised in imitation of the statue group;[32] the passage then reflects the possibility that such images did not only reflect but also reinforced and formed Athenian attitudes.

Tragedy can also be used, finally, not only as a source for Athenian ideology but also to rewrite our core historical narrative. The tragedies discussed by Mills all date from the later part of the Athenian empire. How can we establish an earlier ideological underpinning to the empire except by extravagant extrapolation? In one passage of Aeschylus' *Persians* (the earliest extant tragedy, performed in 472, only a handful of years after the foundation of the Delian League), the chorus of Persian elders praise their former King Darius, in contrast to his son Xerxes, for his many conquests in the Greek world, all listed with great relish. At the end of this passage, we learn that Darius' conquests are the Athenians' gains at the time of the play's production. 'Now there is no doubt', they conclude, 'that through wars we are enduring the gods' reversal of our fortunes ...' (ll. 904-7). The ulterior dramatic motive of the list, it emerges, has been to tickle the Athenian audience's vanity. The passage has frequently been examined as evidence of which cities and islands may have joined the alliance by the date of the play. More can be gleaned from it, however: the fact that, so early in the history of the Athenians' empire, their hegemony is equated with that of the Persians, and that it is implicitly justified in terms of Athens' democracy, piety, bravery and so on.[33] In assessing the date at which the empire changed its character, this awareness of empire is quite as important as the tone of Athens' later imperial decrees.

One other important point emerges from this passage. Against the position that the Athenians had planned to coerce their allies from the outset, it has been argued that there is evidence of an idealistic attitude in the 470s. 'This [the notion of a cynical Athenian stance in the 470s]', according to Simon Hornblower, 'seems to ascribe too great a foresight to the Athenians of 478; and there is non-Thucydidean evidence that the mood at the outset was more idealistic than that' – in the form of the oath, sealed by the dropping of weights into the sea, 'a solemn act indicating intended permanence'.[34] The *Persians*, however, shows us that idealism and opportunism are *not incompatible*, that the empire was, even as early as 472, to this extent both opportunistic and benign.[35]

Beyond all of this – beyond, that is, the simple task of looking again at old texts, and the rather more complex task of eroding the sub-disciplinary boundaries that persist within 'classics' – we also perhaps need to ask different questions. To return to my opening caricature of modern scholarship, it is possible that we can never escape the question of the (un)popularity or harshness of the Athenian empire. Even were it necessarily desirable, Athens and her empire seem to attract a peculiar identification among modern scholars.[36] Pedagogically, moreover, it is perhaps a good question to ask: the facts that fill out the balance-sheet are ones that a student needs to know. (The approach adopted here could form a useful rhetorical twist to such a traditional model.) There are other questions, however, that deserve to be asked alongside this. There are, first, a number of possible side-angles that perhaps deserve more prominence: the relationship of democracy and empire; the effect of empire (and of the loss of empire) on the metropolis of Athens – a question with close parallels to recent treatments of the British Empire;[37] or the reflection of empire in public art. But there are still more questions to ask. We could, for example, put ourselves in the position of the Old Oligarch towards Athens – to try dispassionately to analyse how the empire (and democracy) operated on their own terms. We could also look at the mechanisms by which the empire came about (and indeed at the date at which it came about[38]) and those mechanisms by which it was maintained – not only practical methods of control, the gradual creation of an Athenian fleet, but also the creation, and the perpetuation, of the ideological conditions necessary for empire. If we were to ask a wider range of questions, we might receive different answers.

Notes

1. This paper forms a small part of an increasingly fantastic project: a study of the modern historiography of ancient empires (Near-Eastern, Athenian, Roman) across a long timescale and from a variety of national perspectives. My thanks to all who contributed to discussion at the conference, to other audiences at the Ancient History Seminar of the Institute of Classical Studies, London, and at the University of Glasgow, and especially to Jon Hesk.

2. See especially Robertson 1986; see also Quinn 1981.

3. The Ste. Croix question: de Ste. Croix 1954/5. Some consequent explorations: Bradeen 1960, Quinn 1964, Fornara 1977.

4. Contrast, however, Finley 1978: 103, despairing of the circular arguments by which certain phenomena were ascribed to early or late period in imperial development on the basis of their perceived harshness.

5. See also now, however, the refreshing perspectives of Kallet-Marx 1993, 2002 and Rood 1998.

6. Finley 1978, Meiggs 1972, ch. 14. As I heard Nirad Chaudhuri observe in a different context (British ideas of Hindu decadence) and of a different pairing (Winston Churchill and D.H. Lawrence), 'where these two agree, we have found, so to speak, the highest common factor of British opinion'.

7. Finley 1978: 121-2: 'I shall remain within my narrow framework, restricting "benefits", "profits", to their material sense, excluding the "benefits" (not unimportant) arising from glory, prestige, the sheer pleasure of power. I shall ignore also such side-benefits as the tourist attraction of every great imperial city.'

8. ML 56: 15-23 (according to Meiggs, 1972: 193, in a revival of earlier collective league language), with Forrest 1975. Cf. de Ste. Croix 1972: 44: the Athenians' 'deeply rooted belief in democracy and equality before the law made them concerned in principle to protect the mass of the people, however much they might on occasion sacrifice their principles to their own greed or desire for power and security. When an Athenian orator in the early fourth century claimed that the fifth-century Athenians had "kept their allies free from civil strife, not allowing the many to be kept in subjection to the few, but obliging them all to observe the principle of equality" (Ps.-Lys. II 55-6), it was not entirely an empty boast.'

9. Clark 1936, Kaye, in introduction to Kiernan 1995: 17. The term is also used in a 1928 Workers' Educational Association pamphlet on *Modern Imperialism* as the heading of a chapter arguing that the Empire was profitable for Britain.

10. Grigg 1924: 145-6; he begins his work with the bold statement that he speaks 'not as an apologist, but as one who holds for an article of reasoned faith that the British empire is justified by its works and needs no apologies. You may disagree ... But do not expect me to speak in any part but that of an unrepentant Englishman.' For a similar verdict in the Roman context, see Tenney Frank on the Augustan age, 1914: 353: 'Of far greater importance to the life of the empire than the occasional extensions of its limits was the orderly government now given it. The provinces especially profited by the responsible rule inaugurated by Augustus. With the *pax Romana* ended not only the ravages of civil war, and the irresponsible exactions of partisan leaders, but also the exactions of taxgatherers and of conniving governors, and the petty pilfering of the praetor's staff ... .' Ingeniously, the *pax Romana* is necessitated by the Romans' own acquisitiveness. See also Hammond 1948.

11. In addition to his 1908 *Modern Egypt*, Cromer also published two anthologies of translated Greek poetry, however.

12. So, e.g., Forrest concludes, 1975: 28, by judging the Athenian empire 'something like America's control of Western Europe, or Russia's of Eastern Europe; nothing like Britain's grip on her colonies or Rome's on her provinces. A firm control, but not readily defined.'

13. 1983: 30-1. He continues: 'There may even have been allies who, when they visited the buildings, like the Parthenon, on the Athenian Acropolis and its south slope, thought that their tribute had been splendidly, and not altogether selfishly, spent.' Contrast Hornblower 1991-6: 150, remarking that the claim concerning Scyros, though 'it may be tendentious, ... is a reminder that keeping the seas safe for commerce was no doubt seen as one of the functions and justifications of Athens' empire'. Contrast also Meiggs 1972: 69, bringing out the triumphalist potential of the episode inadvertently well in his reconstruction: 'but what left a greater impression was the recovery during the operation by Cimon of the bones of Theseus, which were solemnly brought back to Athens, a symbolic act which seems to have confirmed Athenian confidence in their growing naval power.'

14. The mention of piracy in contemporary sources in no way affects this: see especially *SIG* 37, 38 (= Fornara 1983 no. 63) with de Souza 1999: 26-30 (for a summary of the evidence). Plutarch's story of Cimon's expulsion of the Dolopians from Scyros, *Cim.* 8.3-7, is sufficiently tangled to allow of cynical interpretation.

15. The British in India eradicated suttee, human sacrifice, and they made war upon the 'Thugs, a ferocious species of armed robber which infested all the roads in many parts of empire': Grigg 1924: 143-4.

16. Thuc. 1.4-5.1; though see Hornblower 1991-6: 21-2.

17. E.g. Meiggs 1972 (though cf. p. 343 on 'Periclean imperialism'), Rhodes 1985: 2, for whom the 'nature of Athenian imperialism' reduces to the question of popularity, de Ste. Croix 1972: 44 (quoted below, n. 27). Contrast Veyne 1975.

18. Meiggs 1972, chs 21-2 (ch. 23 is an epilogue).

19. Finley 1978: 103 (the quotation is from Thornton 1965: 47).

20. In Finley's translation, 1978: 125-6.

21. Finley 1978: 125; cf. Finley 1973: 51-2.

22. Finley's approach is one generally shared by the other contributors to the 1978 collection of Garnsey and Whittaker: e.g. Brunt 1978: 161 ('Like all other peoples, the Athenians had been led to acquire their empire by considerations of security, profit and prestige' (1.76)), Griffith 1978: 127-8, 143 ('It is no accident, I suppose, that the Greeks had no word for imperialism'; contrast de Romilly 1963: 13), and above all Garnsey and Whittaker 1978: 4 ('So although we may feel in retrospect that actions ought to relate to a declared philosophy of conduct, in practice the information usually consists of either the pragmatic rationale of the frontiersmen, the men on the spot, for whom the action itself is sufficient without a clear policy, or ritual justifications and pretexts: claims of honour at stake, security at risk, necessary war measures and the "mission civilisatrice".'). Cf. also de Ste. Croix 1972: 44: 'The evidence is insufficient to enable us to decide how much exploitation and oppression took place in the Athenian empire. No doubt there was a good deal – imperialism is not a pleasant thing.'

23. Seeley 1886 (=1971): 8; for his parallel interest in Roman imperialism, see Seeley 1870. For Seeley, see Vasunia in this volume. Cf. Lord Rosebery's rectorial address at Glasgow in 1900 (quoted by Callander 1961: 24): 'Growing as trees grow, while others slept; fed by the faults of others as well as by the character of our fathers; reaching with the ripple of a resistless tide over tracts and islands and continents, until our little Britain woke up to find herself the foster mother of nations and the source of united empires. Do we not hail in this, less the energy and fortune of a race than the supreme direction of the Almighty? ...' For a variety of perspectives on this topos, see Arendt 1951: 132, Ferguson 1913: 38, Grigg 1924: 141-2 ('This absence of empire-building more than accounts for the extraordinary anomalies, which serve in the stead of political unity. The British Empire is a giant body, whose limbs are connected with it so loosely as to render it almost helpless ... ').

24. Cromer 1910: 24: Roman and British expansion 'was accompanied by misgivings, and was often taken with a reluctance which was by no means feigned'. Roman reluctance was 'constantly struggling both with national pride, which urged that these responsibilities should be assumed, and with fear of the consequences if some really efficient ruler were allowed to take in hand the task which Rome had declined.'

25. Jouguet 1928: 3; cf. de Romilly 1963: 59: [in the work of Thucydides] 'there is just this one fact, as if there were only one unchanging will – as if the whole of Athens were always imperialistic in its attitude, and always imperialistic in exactly the same way.'

26. 1993: 10. For a more recent example (with extensive bibliography), see Hall 2002.

27. 1960: 7. Contrast however, Hobson's famous formulation of imperialism as a 'conscious policy', 1905: 19, Ferguson 1913: 4 ('The policy by which a people or an autocrat acquires and maintains an empire, we call imperialism.' His purpose is to 'trace the development of the forms by which imperialism was obscured, evaded, and ultimately justified in Greece.')

28. See, however, Hornblower 1983a, Fornara and Samons 1991: 76-113, Mills 1997: 69, or Calame's hypothesis of reflections of Athenian territorial ambitions through myth, 1996: 223-7.

29. Further evidence of the scale of Athenian ambitions at this time can be found in the names given by Themistocles to his children: Asia, Hellas, Italia and Sybaris – in Hornblower's fine phrase, a 'gazeteer of Athenian fifth-century aspirations', 1983: 20.

30. See Fornara 1971, Stadter 1992, Moles 1996; contrast Meiggs 1972: 5: 'It would have been impossible for a man so clearly fascinated by the instability of prosperity and the danger of greatness not to have wondered what would follow Athens' spectacular rise to dominance. But Herodotus never reveals his feelings on these big issues.' Cf. Meiggs 1972: 375-6: 'there is little doubt that H admired Athenian leadership in literature and the arts; it does not follow, however, that he misunderstood or approved Athenian methods of controlling her allies'.

31. Contrast the unembarrassed perspective of Gillies; though he subsequently condemns the rigour with which Athens controlled her allies, 1786: 449-51, the fact e.g. that the empire was exercised over free cities only emphasises Athens' achievement (410): 'Our wonder will be justly increased if we consider that Athens obtained those immortal trophies, not over ignorant savages or effeminate slaves, but over men who had the same language and laws, the same blood and lineage, the same arts and arms, in short every thing common with the victors but their audacity and fortune.'

32. Henderson 1987: 154 (on 633-5); cf. Halliwell 1998: 119; cf. Sommerstein 1990.

33. See further Harrison 2000, ch. 10, Gow 1928.

34. Hornblower 1991-6: 144.

35. This is not, of course, to deny that there was any evolution in the nature of the Athenian hegemony.

36. See e.g. Bradeen 1960: 258 on de Ste. Croix and the popularity of the Athenian empire: 'Now the attraction here stems from the fact that most of us ancient historians have a sympathy for Athens and her Empire; no matter how impartial we try to be, our whole training as classicists, and possibly our political bent as well, incline us that way.'

37. See e.g. Hall 2002.

38. See e.g. Fornara and Samons 1991: 102: 'The conceptual error has been to consider the date 478/7 as the start of a new epoch – thereby encouraging the biological analogy holding that all things have a tender beginning (i.e. 478/7), grow to maturity (i.e. 450), and then old age (i.e. 425), instead of recognizing that the acquisition of empire was itself part of a larger sequence in which Athenian behavior had already become pronouncedly aggressive.' See also Fornara and Samons' hypothesis, 1991: 106, of the importance of prejudice against Asiatic Greeks.

2

Greater Rome and Greater Britain

Phiroze Vasunia

'Rome', Vladimir I. Lenin wrote in 1917, 'founded on slavery, pursued a colonial policy and achieved imperialism. But "general" arguments about imperialism, which ignore or put into the background the fundamental difference of social-economic systems, inevitably degenerate into absolutely empty banalities or into grandiloquent comparisons like Greater Rome and Greater Britain' (Lenin 1965: 82). Lenin was referring to the work of Sir Charles P. Lucas, *Greater Rome and Greater Britain*, which was published in 1912, and indirectly to essays by James Bryce (Viscount Bryce) and Evelyn Baring (the Earl of Cromer) that had appeared a few years earlier.[1] While Lenin found parallels between Britain and ancient Rome evasive, unhelpful, and self-promotional, intellectuals in Victorian and Edwardian England returned obsessively to such comparisons. An astounding range of writers, teachers, administrators, and politicians refer to the parallel between the two empires. A full list of figures would have to include Benjamin Disraeli, William Gladstone, Rudyard Kipling, Lord Curzon, Arthur Balfour, and Robert Baden-Powell, to give just a few of the famous names.[2]

What was the nature of this recourse to ancient Rome, and what function did it serve in these writings and in the culture at large? And in particular, as Lenin implies, why were Lucas and others appealing to a 'Greater Britain' in these comparisons and references to Rome? To answer these questions means to understand nineteenth-century and early twentieth-century justifications and anxieties regarding British imperialism. Invariably, the comparisons between Rome and Britain point to contemporary concerns about empire, race, decay, and decline; invariably, these concerns are obfuscated or contained in ways that reveal the ideological motivation of this precise historical comparison. These writers were purporting to provide comparisons between Rome and Britain; in fact, they were betraying in their writings the contradictions of liberal empire. It is also significant that the books by Bryce, Cromer, and Lucas – which constitute the most extensive of the comparisons – appear almost immediately after the most aggressive phase of

Britain's imperial history. As these examples suggest, not only was the comparison between Roman and British empires implicated in the development of Roman historiography; the very vision of empire articulated in these works enabled a particular form of imperialism.

In what follows, I would like to sketch the background to these comparative studies and discuss how British writers legitimised their own empire through the turn to ancient Rome. In showing the conceptual debt of the comparisons to influential writers of the mid-Victorian period such as Charles Dilke and John Seeley, I make the following claim: writers such as Bryce, Cromer, and Lucas reshape arguments about the British Empire made by mid-Victorian intellectuals and put them in service of comparisons with Rome. These writers offer critical and elaborate comparisons of the Roman and British empires. The fact that they, like many of the writers considered in this essay, had significant investments, whether academic, financial, or political, both in ancient studies and in colonial ventures tells us much about who was authorised to speak about comparative empire. My point is that the writers' arguments about the Roman Empire are inseparable from their claims about the British Empire, and in fact reveal more about the latter than the former. These writers were all establishment figures, they were immersed in Victorian imperial culture, and they also had a personal stake in British imperialism. This is, moreover, an account about the collusion between classics and empire, given that these authors derived their materials and their legitimacy from the institutionalised study of the ancient world. Not all the writers were professors of Greek or Roman history, to be sure. Nevertheless, the authors discussed most extensively in this essay were all strategically situated in relation to the structures of knowledge, power, and desire that supported the contemporary British academy. Finally, I note also the interconnectedness between classics and competing spheres of activity inside and outside the university. Despite the argument that narrow specialisation and professionalism take hold of classics in the early twentieth century, our examples indicate precisely how discourses of antiquity intersect with the worlds of politics and empire, or with concepts of race and nationhood.[3] In short, classics is still embedded in national politics and national culture at this point, and to speak authoritatively about antiquity can also be a way to make an intervention in (the history of) the present.

1

The culture of mid-Victorian colonialism and imperialism structures the comparisons between Greater Rome and Greater Britain; it mediates the comparative projects of later writers and produces the discursive space in which the subsequent comparisons take their evaluative and imaginative expression. The relevance of this mid-Victorian culture to the later comparisons is borne out, in particular, by examination of the works of the writers Charles Dilke and John Seeley. It is not just that Dilke's and Seeley's influential books shape the concerns of the comparisons between Rome and Britain or that they prefigure the very issues that were taken up later by writers such as Bryce, Cromer, and Lucas; they also inform them through their political idiom, their conceptual repertoire, and their ideological apparatus.

The phrase 'Greater Britain' itself was first used in print by Sir Charles Wentworth Dilke (1843-1911) in his book, *Greater Britain: A Record of Travel in English-Speaking Countries during 1866 and 1867*, published in 1868, and then again in the book that contained his second thoughts on the subject, *Problems of Greater Britain*, published in 1890.[4] Dilke uses the expression 'Greater Britain' to refer not just to the British Empire, but to the British Empire and America together. In *Greater Britain*, Dilke uses plentiful charm and narrative skill to describe his travels as he 'followed England round the world' through places such as the United States, Australia, and India (Dilke 1880: vii). These two were not Dilke's only books on the subject of British imperialism, and he was also the author of *The British Army* (1888), *Imperial Defence* (1891), and *The British Empire* (1899). The first book, *Greater Britain*, was an immediate success, in Britain and in America, and by 1880 the book was in its seventh edition. In a letter to Dilke, John Stuart Mill wrote, 'It is long since any book connected with practical politics has been published on which I build such high hopes of the future usefulness and distinction of the writer.'[5] The success of the book and the largely favourable reviews it received tell us much about the attitude to imperialism at the time.[6]

It is instructive to begin with Dilke's particular inflexion of whiteness and his anxieties about race, which become apparent to the reader almost immediately.[7] On the first page of his preface, Dilke remarks that he found the white British to hold the same basic values and traits even when living in different continents: 'If I remarked that climate, soil, manners of life, that mixture with other peoples had modified the blood, I saw, too, that in essentials the race was always one' (Dilke 1880: vii). Dilke's tour is a travel through regions such as America and Australia, in which white British settlers had established colonies in allegedly unpopulated spaces, and through areas such as India, in which the British were ruling over other peoples. The collective culture of the white British peoples, whether in Britain or abroad, forms something

40

that he refers to as Saxondom, and Saxondom must be upheld and defended everywhere. 'The result of our survey,' he notes, 'is such as to give us reason for the belief that race distinctions will long continue, that miscegenation will go but little towards blending races ... and that Saxondom will rise triumphant from the doubtful struggle' (Dilke 1880: 572). The British Empire, which is 'four and a half times as large as the Roman Empire at its greatest extent', provides the opportunity to the English 'of planting free institutions among the dark-skinned institutions of the world' (Dilke 1880: 572, 573). This responsibility cannot be shirked, because 'the power of English laws and English principles of government is not merely an English question – its continuation is essential to the freedom of mankind'.[8] Dilke's work was unabashedly a eulogy to Saxondom and a warning to white Britishers to take up arms against the darker forces of barbarism and chaos.

Rule over India gave special encouragement to the Victorians to think of their own empire as an entity worthy of comparison to other empires, and it is Dilke's discussion of India that takes up a substantial part of the book. Since Dilke's Saxon races constitute a minority in the region, India represents a great challenge to Saxondom, and Dilke writes extensively of the benefits that British sovereignty has already bestowed and the responsibilities that it carries. Like many Victorian writers before and after him, Dilke suggests that India should eventually be ruled by its own people, but since the natives are not yet ready for such rule or for such democracy, the British must govern them until then. Once the Indians have learned English, 'the Hindoos will soon place the government of India in native hands, and thus, gradually relieving us of an almost intolerable burthen, will civilize and set free the people of Hindostan'.[9] Until self-rule comes, Dilke says, it is the responsibility of the English in India to teach the natives the English language and to rule the country as wisely and justly as possible. Dilke is not fully blind to the excesses of the British in India, and he comments extensively on examples of British misrule in India. Nevertheless, even if British rule is not perfect, 'it may fairly be contended that the mass of the people live in more comfort and ... are less likely to starve, in English, than in native territory. No nation has at any time ever governed an alien empire more wisely or justly than we the Punjab' (Dilke 1880: 509).

Dilke cannot deny that British behaviour in India often is despotic and anti-democratic. Indeed, the despotic behaviour of British rulers in India is a point to which Dilke returns several times. 'England in the East is not the England that we know,' he writes. 'Flousy Britannia, with her anchor and ship, becomes a mysterious Oriental despotism, ruling a sixth of the human race, nominally for the natives' own good, and certainly for no one else's ...' (Dilke 1880: 550). But the British government in India is not to be dismissed on that count. 'Although despotic, our government of India is not bad, indeed, the hardest thing that can be said of it is that it is too good' (Dilke 1880: 551). By that remark, Dilke means that the natives in India do not fully understand British institutions and laws or appreciate the benevolence of British justice. Indians are corrupt, slaves to caste and prejudice, followers of uncivilised customs, and not ready for freedom. Even at the present, government cannot quite be maintained in India on democratic principles, Dilke suggests, and British rule is already democratic in a manner that the native population is unable to grasp. Furthermore, the people of India may be contrasted with the English, who clamour at home for such things as reform and the extension of the franchise. 'Just as in England the people are too democratic for the Government, in India the Government is too democratic for the people.'[10] In response to these pressures, thus, the English must necessarily maintain a democracy at home and a despotism overseas.

If there is a lurking anxiety in Dilke's book, it concerns the dissolution of the Empire and the decline of Britain's fortunes. The author often speculates on potential causes of decline and on how the British might ensure the preservation of the Empire. This is evident, for instance, in comments about native self-rule that he frequently introduces into the discussion and in his remarks about the British eventually having to quit India. In regard to colonies such as Canada, Dilke gives serious thought to the cause of separation, but he does not in the end recommend the complete independence of the colonies in his own day, just as he cannot in the end recommend the independence of India at the time of publication. But hovering over these thoughts is the worry that the day will come when Australia, Canada, India, and other territories assert their independence and break away from Britain. Such fears are, perhaps, intimated by Dilke's dismissal of the claim that 'extent of empire is power' because 'those who have read history with most care well know that at all times extent of empire has been weakness' (Dilke 1880: 397, 398). The loss of colonies such as Australia is not necessarily to be mourned because it is not certain that colonies make a country great. A smaller empire, Dilke implies, does not diminish from the greatness of Greater Britain. 'That which raises us above the provincialism of citizenship of little England is our citizenship of the greater Saxondom which includes all that is best and wisest in the world' (Dilke 1880: 398). The three long sections of Dilke's book – out of four sections altogether – that concern the Americas, Australia, and

India conclude by returning to the influence of Saxondom and Saxon institutions. The British Empire may decline and fall, Dilke says, but the continuation and dispersion of Saxon culture will be its noblest achievement. Through this racial triumphalism, Dilke is able to accommodate but not conceal his anxieties about imperial decay.

Fifteen years after the publication of Dilke's book, and just after the fierce debates about empire and imperialism that took place in the 1870s, the expression 'Greater Britain' was once again used in an influential discussion about the British Empire. Where Dilke offered a travelogue together with critical analysis, John Robert Seeley (1834-95) omitted travel narrative entirely and gave the discussion of the British Empire a historical basis. His discussion of English history in *The Expansion of England*, published in 1883, encompasses the First and Second Empires, that is, the two phases of the British Empire divided by the American Revolution.[11] In famously claiming, 'We seem, as it were, to have conquered and peopled half the world in a fit of absence of mind', Seeley was arguing not just that British imperialists had acted 'unintentionally' and 'accidentally', but that the British were forgetting the early history of their empire in America and Asia.[12] For our purposes, it is necessary to recall that Seeley's background was in classics, and that he was a professor of Latin before he became a professor of modern history. Seeley was elected a lecturer in classics at Cambridge in 1858, served as a teacher of classics at the City of London School for two years from 1861, and was then Professor of Latin at University College London until 1869, when he returned to Cambridge as Regius Professor of Modern History. *The Expansion of England* was first given as a series of lectures at Cambridge in 1881 and 1882, of which the lectures pertaining to India were intended for candidates aiming for the Indian Civil Service.[13] The spectacle of a Latin scholar giving lectures to ICS candidates is not as surprising as it initially might seem since Greek and Latin were almost indispensable for successful entry into the ICS.[14] Even the non-language entrance examinations required knowledge of the ancient world, often in conjunction with the history of the modern Empire. (Sample question: 'What lessons with regard to the principles which should be observed in the government of British India may be learned from the history of the Roman dominions under the Republic and the Empire?'[15]) Seeley was a pivotal figure in Victorian imperialism and a member of the Imperial Federation League, and it is crucial to read him in order to appreciate better the claims made through the comparisons of Rome and Britain.

Race poses as much of a problem for Seeley as it did for Dilke before him, and Seeley is unable to give his reader a definition of Greater

Britain without further qualifying his remarks in one form or another to allow for the situation in India. At various times, Seeley defines 'Greater Britain', an expression he lifts from Dilke without acknowledgement, as more or less coterminous with the British Empire. For example: 'But Greater Britain is a real enlargement of the English State; it carries across the seas not merely the English race, but the authority of the English government. We call it for want of a better word an Empire' (Seeley 1909: 43). Greater Britain may, for Seeley, consist of Canada, the West Indies, South Africa, Australia and New Zealand, and India. Yet Seeley remains uneasy with India's place in this Greater Britain, for 'this enormous Indian population does not make part of Greater Britain in the same sense as those tens of millions of Englishmen who live outside of the British Islands'. With the 'alien race and religion' of India in mind, Seeley is made to qualify his comments and say, 'When we inquire then into the Greater Britain of the future we ought to think much more of our Colonial than of our Indian Empire' (Seeley 1909: 11). In other words, think much more of white British inhabitants and their descendants in places such as Australia and Canada rather than of darker Indians in south Asia, much less the indigenous peoples of Australia or Canada. Nevertheless, Seeley cannot omit India from his discussion of imperial expansion, because of the impact India has on England, and he devotes half the book to the problem of 'another Greater Britain' (Seeley 1909: 176).

Like Dilke, Seeley comes to argue that the British are in India for meaningful reasons, not just for Britain's sake, but above all for India's. 'What is the use of it?', he asks. 'Why do we take the trouble and involve ourselves in the anxiety and responsibilities of governing two hundred millions of people in Asia?' (Seeley 1909: 184). There are many reasons for the British not to take the trouble with India: India is not bound to Britain by ties of blood, religion, or common interest; it is not situated in geographical proximity to Britain; its climate is difficult for English children to grow up in; and it is a heavy burden on foreign policy. On the other hand, the country is vast and populous, 'something like what the Roman Empire was at its greatest expansion', and it is 'an ancient civilization, with languages, religions, philosophies, and literatures of its own' (Seeley 1909: 186, 188). And the reasons for the British not to leave India are that their system of government is superior to the one they found when they conquered the country, and 'that our Government is better than any other which has existed in India since the Mussulman conquest' (Seeley 1909: 194). In fact, Seeley makes repeated statements about the inadvisability of Britain's leaving India: 'A time may conceivably come when it may be practicable to leave India to herself, but for

the present it is necessary to govern her as if we govern her for ever ...
it is impossible for the present to think of abandoning the task we have
undertaken there ... it appears wholly impossible ... a dangerous experiment ... the most inexcusable of all conceivable crimes' (Seeley 1909:
193-6). Self-rule cannot be indulged at the moment because, as Dilke
reminded his readers earlier, the natives are not capable of managing it:
'India then is of all countries that which is least capable of evolving out
of itself a stable Government' (Seeley 1909: 196). The country's ancient
glories are not in doubt, Seeley says, but they are no guarantee of what
India can achieve in the years ahead: 'India is all past and, I may almost
say, has no future' (Seeley 1909: 176).

Seeley is also troubled, though not as much as Dilke, by the contradictions of Britain's empire, that is, by Britain's fostering of democracy
and civil rights in some parts of the world and by its tyrannical and
despotic behaviour in other parts. 'How can the same nation,' Seeley
writes, 'pursue two lines of policy so radically different without bewil-
derment, be despotic in Asia and democratic in Australia, be in the East
at once the greatest Mussulman power in the world and the guardian of
the property of thousands of idol-temples, and at the same time in the
West be the foremost champion of free thought and spiritual religion,
stand out as a great military Imperialism to resist the march of Russia
in Central Asia at the same time that it fills Queensland and Manitoba
with free settlers?' (Seeley 1909: 177). Of the numerous tensions
contained in this question, the tension between democracy and despotic
imperialism is one that runs through the second half of Seeley's book.
The author often implies that British behaviour in India is extreme, but
that the Indian situation warrants such actions, actions that the British
would not tolerate at home. The reasons given for this treatment of the
natives are various: some of the factors to which Seeley refers are
India's medievalism, population, diversity, inability to progress, low
status, and the lack of nationalist sentiment among Indians. In the end,
the immense responsibility of ruling India has fallen on England, he
writes, and it is England's duty to maintain that rule in a manner that
is appropriate to the history, culture, and political situation of the
subcontinent, even if it entails the suppression of democratic principles
in favour of colonial stewardship.

The expansion of England makes Seeley explore the possibility of
imperial decline, but he is considerably less anxious about decline than
Dilke. The white British race is spread all across the colonies if not the
dependency of India, hence the union between Britain and these
colonies is not 'mechanical' or 'forced', and so the Empire is not subject
to 'that weakness which has brought down most empires' (Seeley 1909:

46). Seeley argues that the British Empire is the sole survivor of a whole series of empires that emerged during the discovery of the New World, empires such as Greater Holland, Greater Portugal, Greater Spain, and Greater France that have since gone into grave decline. Greater Britain has avoided the missteps and dangers that plagued the other empires, he writes, but it has not avoided them altogether, so the challenge for it in the present is to follow a route different from those taken by failed great powers. However, the situation in India does not mirror the situation in colonies such as Canada because, in south Asia, Britain 'advances beyond the limits of the nationality' and its rule 'becomes precarious and artificial' (Seeley 1909: 46). Thus, India may pose a threat to the long-term stability and prosperity of the British Empire. Nevertheless, even the 'Oriental Empire', as he puts it, 'is not an Empire attached to England in the same way as the Roman Empire was attached to Rome; it will not drag us down, or infect us at home with Oriental notions or methods of Government' (Seeley 1909: 304). This empire, he says, inaccurately, is not a financial drain on Britain and its destiny is not linked to Britain's own future. In general, Seeley is disinclined to accept the possibility of decay in the future of Greater Britain and argues that even the special case of India does not present any danger to the empire.

Reflecting the difference between the writers' backgrounds, Seeley develops the comparison between the Roman and British empires in more detail and more expansively than Dilke does in *Greater Britain*; in fact, Seeley at times even equates the two empires and claims that the British Empire holds the same historical importance as the Roman. He notes that in the generation before his the Roman Empire was not considered worthy of study because writers supposed that liberty did not exist in the Empire, whereas the Republic was held up for scrutiny as an example of a free state. However, now Victorians study civilisations even if they did not preserve liberty because the British have learned 'that there are many other good things in politics besides liberty; for instance there is nationality, there is civilisation'.[16] Moreover, although 'the incubus of the Empire' crushed liberty in Rome, the British Empire is far enough from India and the metropolis is so little affected by the colonial situation that Britain and British values are not going to be destroyed by empire in the same way as Rome (Seeley 1909: 245). Britain is concerned to raise India to its level, and there is no possibility of India lowering Britain or even stalling its progress. Although it was a despotism, then, the Roman Empire is held to be worthy of study, Seeley writes, because the conquerors were demonstrably superior to the conquered in respect to their civilisation. The civilising effects of the Roman Empire on Europe are remarkable, and the civilising phenomenon that was the Roman Empire is one of the most consequential features of European history. It goes without saying that, for Seeley, British rule in India is of the Roman type in so far as it also involves the rule by the superior over the inferior races. The British have brought the English language, law, peace, and order to India, and so, just as Rome was a beacon to the less advanced peoples of Gaul and Iberia, Britain brings a light to the tropics: 'It is not a glorious light shining in darkness, but a somewhat cold daylight introduced into the midst of a warm gorgeous twilight' (Seeley 1909: 244).

Dilke and Seeley were two of the most influential writers – the historian James Anthony Froude (1818-94) is perhaps a third – of the phase of empire sometimes referred to as mid-Victorian imperialism, and Seeley is considered by some scholars to be the founder of modern imperial studies. For his part, Froude had written a book on Julius Caesar, and his biography was notable chiefly for the author's approval of Caesar's overthrow of the Republic and for the parallel he drew between Caesar and Jesus Christ. [17] Froude also accepted the theory of the cycle of corruption and decay that Edward Gibbon had made famous: 'Virtue and truth produced strength, strength dominion, dominion riches, riches luxury, and luxury weakness and collapse – fatal sequence repeated so often.'[18] These writers are of interest to us here because their work is programmatic for the comparisons between the British and Roman empires that developed in the late nineteenth and early twentieth centuries. From the admittedly brief portrayal above, a significant part of the mid-Victorian imperialist claim may be summarised as follows: *the British Empire involves the rule of superior white peoples over inferior dark races, apart from places such as Canada and Australia; these dark races are incapable of ruling themselves, at least for the moment, and must therefore be ruled by Britons; such rule entails the maintenance of a despotism overseas even while Britain becomes increasingly democratic at home; however, there is a danger that the fact of overseas rule and contact with the inferior, darker races may corrupt Britain and bring about the collapse of the Empire, and this decline needs to be avoided at all cost.* With Seeley, the idea of a broader comparison between Rome and Britain is also broached, though not in any detailed or systematic fashion. Thinking in terms of intellectual genealogy, we might say that the comparisons of Greater Rome and Greater Britain follow in a direct line of descent from these writers and address precisely these issues. The comparisons were written retrospectively to re-authenticate the points that were made by figures such as Dilke and Seeley who were writing when Britain was entering its most aggressive period of imperialist expansion.

2

The comparisons of the Roman and British empires were made possible, largely though not exclusively, through the vision of a Greater Britain. The imperialist and racialised idea of Greater Britain, propagated by figures such as Dilke and Seeley, opened up a space in which the comparisons could take shape and flourish. By the second half of the nineteenth century, the concept of a Greater Britain had moved closer to the centre of national debate as a response to political and imperial pressures. To be sure, men such as Curzon would later contest the definition of Greater Britain and argue for the inclusion of India within its geographical purview, but these were internal critics of empire. By the time of Victoria's coronation as Empress of India, in 1876, the concept of Greater Britain was directly feeding into the imperialism that 'had become by general consensus a common policy in the British establishment, and the overall guiding strategy of British foreign policy' (Young 2001: 40). What the phenomenon suggests is that the Empire enabled the conditions in which the detailed comparisons between Rome and Britain were able to emerge, and, at the same time, these very comparisons also assisted British imperial interests. We might put this in other terms and say that comparisons between Rome and Britain accommodated and validated the idea of a Greater Britain, and simultaneously the British Empire offered the ideological framework within which a particular interpretation of the relationship between Rome and Britain might gain currency.

The three most sustained and elaborate comparisons of Rome and Britain are James Bryce, 'The Roman Empire and the British Empire in India' and 'The Extension of Roman and English Law throughout the World', in *Studies in History and Jurisprudence* (1901); the Earl of Cromer (Evelyn Baring), *Ancient and Modern Imperialism* (1910); and Charles Lucas, *Greater Rome and Greater Britain* (1912).[19] Bryce, Cromer, and Lucas reflect the views advocated by many among the Victorian elite after 1870 or so. Britain had embarked on an ambitious policy of imperialist expansion in this period, which lasted until about 1914, and the word 'imperialism' itself came to acquire a positive connotation that it did not have earlier, when it was associated pejoratively with the Napoleons in the continent. The early standard-bearer for the so-called new imperialism was Benjamin Disraeli, who famously signalled the importance that he was giving to an imperialist foreign policy in his Crystal Palace speech of 1872, and who was instrumental in the coronation of Victoria as Empress of India. One response to this promotion of Britain's overseas empire was the assertion of some kind of union or federation among the white settler colonies, along the lines suggested, differently in each case, by Dilke, Seeley, and Froude.[20] The other side to this assertion, of course, was the uncertainty about the place of India and the dependencies within the framework of the British Empire. Paradoxically, however, neither Dilke nor Seeley called for the British to leave India in their own day, and in fact, when Dilke returned to the question of Greater Britain in his second book on the subject, the *Problems of Greater Britain* of 1890, he appeared to have changed his mind as well about Canada, which he had earlier thought could separate from Britain; now Dilke wrote only about the perils of colonial separation. In this sense, Dilke and Seeley were only part of a larger picture of the aggressive imperialism practised by men such as Disraeli and his supporters. Disraeli's dramatic insistence on British supremacy and hegemony overseas had attracted a fair share of powerful defenders, even if they were not always in agreement with Disraeli or with each other. Thus, the three comparisons with Rome discussed below, which begin to appear in print roughly at the point of the empire's greatest territorial size, belong very firmly to the chauvinist climate that Disraeli went to great lengths to foster in late Victorian England.

These three writers, like many other Victorian imperialists, were involved with classics and government service at some point or another in their careers. In this respect, the connection of figures such as Bryce and Lucas to the Oxbridge colleges, in general, and to Oxford classics, in particular, is a point worth stressing.[21] During the nineteenth and the early twentieth centuries, many of the men who administered the British Empire in London and overseas were trained in classics at Oxford. In the years from 1888 to 1905, for instance, three successive viceroys of India came from Balliol College alone. Like many others, James Leigh Strachan-Davidson, the Master of Balliol and author of *Problems of Roman Criminal Law* (1913), campaigned hard to send his students into the Indian Civil Service and to keep Greek and Latin as central subjects in the entrance examinations. 'I have fought for the Civil Service at Oxford for the last thirty years,' he said to the Royal Commission in 1913.[22] Cambridge also sent numerous men into the Indian Civil Service, as Seeley's case indicates, though its impact on empire was arguably smaller than Oxford's.[23] Thus, the elite educational establishments, the study of Greek and Roman antiquity, and British imperialism intersect with important consequences in the period.

The life and work of Bryce is illustrative in this regard.[24] Bryce (1838-1922) secured a first class in classical moderations at Oxford in 1859, won the Gaisford prize for Greek prose in 1860, and then obtained a first class in *literae humaniores* and the Gaisford prize for Greek verse in 1861; he also won the Chancellor's Latin essay prize in 1862, and in 1863 he won the Arnold historical essay prize with an essay on the *Holy Roman Empire*, which was published as a book in 1864. He served as the Regius Professor of Civil Law at Oxford from 1870 to 1893, and was a member of Gladstone's cabinet, briefly the Chief Secretary for Ireland, and the British Ambassador to the United States from 1907 to 1913 (partly because of his influential book, *The American Commonwealth*, 1888). The two essays about the Roman Empire and the British Empire were published again as a book in 1914 for candidates to the ICS examinations (Collini, Winch, and Burrow 1983: 246).

The career of Bryce's slightly younger contemporary, Cromer (1841-1917), is so well studied that it barely requires detailed exposition in this essay. It is perhaps less well known that the man who was proconsul of Egypt also taught himself Greek and Latin as a young boy in Corfu.[25] Nor is it a coincidence that the material contained in *Ancient and Modern Imperialism* was first presented as an address to the Classical Association when Cromer served as its President in 1909-10.

As for Lucas (1853-1931), he obtained a first class in classical moderations and in *literae humaniores* at Oxford, was awarded the Chancellor's Latin essay prize, and was also placed first on the civil service examination list of 1877, when he joined the Colonial Office.[26] The author of several books about the British Empire, he ended his career as a Fellow of All Souls College, Oxford.

With this intellectual and biographical background in mind, it should perhaps not be expected that the comparative works of Bryce, Cromer, and Lucas differ radically in details or conclusions concerning empire, and, in fact, their books conform to one programme, that of legitimating the British Empire and so ensuring its preservation. What is notable is that these books are unreflective restatements of an orthodoxy rather than more innovative explorations of Roman history. They delineate a platform that ultimately serves to justify British imperialism. As we shall see, they stage a return to the mid-Victorian movement and are content to extend the claims of authors such as Dilke and Seeley on a range of topics including race and nationhood. Rather than repeat all their arguments, however, I would like to present here, in an admittedly schematic and hasty manner, the points made by Bryce, Cromer, and Lucas that follow in the tradition of mid-Victorian imperialism.

2. Greater Rome and Greater Britain

The British Empire involves the rule of superior white peoples over inferior dark races. All three writers agree that the question of race and colour is vital to the study of the British Empire; Cromer devotes the appendix to his book to the issue of inter-racial marriage, and Lucas considers race and class in a separate chapter. Bryce and Cromer argue that the Romans were able to achieve a fusion of the races and were correspondingly expert at assimilation, while Lucas claims that the Roman Empire avoided the problem of colour since it did not bring together people of different colours. However, in the modern period, all three writers state, antipathy based on colour is an undeniable and prominent feature of civilised life. 'Now to the Teutonic peoples,' Bryce remarks, 'and especially to the English and Anglo-Americans, the difference of colour means a great deal. It creates a feeling of separation, perhaps even of a slight repulsion' (Bryce 1901: 54). In India, racial antipathy is found among both the rulers and the ruled, with the additional complication of caste barriers among the latter, and so from a combination of pride, caste bias, and racial prejudice, the Indian may also look down on the white Briton. Nevertheless, Bryce, Cromer, and Lucas observe that since, in many parts of the British Empire including in Egypt and India, a superior white race is ruling over an inferior darker race, and since a people at a higher level of civilisation are ruling over a people at a lower level of civilisation, there must necessarily be a separation between the rulers and the ruled, and it is absolutely impossible to conceive of a fusion between the races.

The darker races are incapable of ruling themselves, and must therefore be ruled by Britons. The ancient Romans in their provinces were in some respects more corrupt than the British are in theirs, according to Bryce, Cromer, and Lucas, but the Romans nevertheless managed to rule over other peoples and brought civilisation and peace to them. The Gaulish druids would have continued to practise human sacrifice, for instance, and it was only Roman law and resolve that squashed the custom. Similarly, the natives of places such as India are, with some exceptions, backward and stuck in the past, members of an inferior civilisation, observers of barbaric practices such as sati (which is comparable to the druids' rites), susceptible to bribery and corruption, and are therefore not able to govern themselves.[27] There was once a civilisation in India, but this fact does not by itself indicate that it is suited for self-rule. In these circumstances, self-rule for India is out of the question. 'The idea is not only absurd; it is not only impracticable,' Cromer observes. 'I would go farther, and say that to entertain it would be a crime against civilization, and especially against the voiceless millions in India whose interests are committed to our charge' (Cromer

1910: 123). Indeed, many natives actually look to the British for justice and prefer British rule to rule by local aristocratic families and maharajas. While they find it advantageous for India to be ruled by the British, however, the three writers also submit that Britain needs to encourage greater participation of the natives in the government of India, so as to give the natives some say in the rule of their country.

Such rule entails the maintenance of a despotism overseas and a democracy at home. 'The government of India by the English resembles that of her provinces by Rome in being thoroughly despotic' (Bryce 1901: 25). The despotism of Rome during the Empire is not in doubt, the writers state, but the despotism of the British in their Empire is justified and benevolent, and milder than the Roman. Moreover, where Rome was ruled by an emperor even within Rome itself, Britain maintains this despotism while it governs its own country on democratic principles. But this discrepancy in the British Empire is unavoidable, since democracy is well established in Britain whereas it is completely alien to India, the Indians themselves are unfit for democratic institutions, and, in addition, democracy is not even desired by many Indians other than those educated in European values and ideas. Indians are also submissive by nature, and they do not care who rules them so long as their rulers let them continue with their native religions and customs. Further, as Lucas notes, there are parts of the British Empire where there is a great deal of autonomy and self-rule, and these are the self-governing dominions of Canada and Australia, where whites are settled in large numbers (Lucas 1912, ch. 9). By this reasoning, it may be said that while the Roman Empire was uniformly despotic and undivided, the British Empire has actively fostered liberty in some of its far-flung provinces and given natives some say in local government in others; and that the larger it has become, the more liberty there is to be found in it.

The fact of overseas rule and contact with the inferior races may corrupt Britain and bring about the collapse of empire. Ever since Gibbon, the spectre of imperial decline and fall haunted British writers, and Bryce, Cromer, and Lucas are no exceptions in the anxiety they evince concerning the end of empire, though this anxiety takes various forms in their works. The writers say they are confident that the decline of the British Empire is not a possibility on the near horizon, but the very fact that the subject is raised points to an unease on their part. Cromer is least direct in confronting the question of decline; on the other hand, he observes that nations grow large and small, and argues vehemently against India's separation from Britain (Cromer 1910: 127). For Lucas, the question of decline is subsumed under a chapter entitled 'The British Instinct and the Law of National Life' and is answered essentially along racial lines (Lucas 1912, ch. 10). In an argument reminiscent of Dilke, he touches again on the non-fusion of the races and explicitly appeals to the white British and white settlers in Canada, South Africa, Australia, and elsewhere to serve the cause of empire and to preserve the rule of Britain overseas. Bryce cannot conclude the discussion in his first essay 'without reverting once more to the Roman Empire, and asking whether the events which caused, and the circumstances which accompanied, its dissolution throw any light on the probable fate of British dominion in the East' (Bryce 1901: 68). According to Bryce, the Roman Empire died through violence and internal causes such as inefficiency, corruption, lack of manpower, and a general decline of physical and intellectual vitality, but Britain is not suffering from the same weaknesses at the moment, and so it is not subject to the same dangers as Rome was. The one thing that Britain should be wary of is the natives' reuniting and threatening to drive out the British, though this too is not likely to happen in the near future. The anxiety about the decline of empire, then, takes various forms in Bryce, Cromer, and Lucas.

Against these legitimating views of empire, it is a matter of pivotal significance to recall that not all those who invoked ancient Rome did so solely or largely for the purpose of supporting British rule overseas. None of these critics offered comparative evaluations of Rome and Britain on the same scale as Bryce, Cromer, and Lucas, but they did contradict or repudiate the claims made by strong-minded imperialists. What this phenomenon suggests is that in this period Rome appealed most, and most extensively, to those who justified the British Empire rather than to those who fought against its excesses or wished to end it altogether. One might have explained this by the fact that most of the men who ruled the British Empire in London and overseas, from 1870 to 1914, were trained in classics, if it were not the case that men who studied classics, such as Gilbert Murray, the Regius Professor of Greek at Oxford, also opposed aggressive imperialism and took the Liberal view on empire (Wilson 1987). In this connection, however, it can be suggested that the Greek example of democracy and of colonial autonomy proved more attractive than the Roman Empire to critics and opponents of the new imperialism.[28] In a book entitled *Greater Greece and Greater Britain* (1886), for example, Edward Freeman criticised Seeley's notion of the Anglo-Saxon imperial federation and argued that the Greek model meant real autonomy for the colonies. In this scenario, the '*true* Expander of England' was none other than George Washington.[29]

Another critic of the new imperialism was Disraeli's prime ministerial rival, William Gladstone, who always opposed British imperialist expansion even when he was unable to prevent it. Gladstone, like Dilke or Seeley in this respect, supported the notion of an Anglo-Saxon empire based on the Greek model of mother-city and colony, but he also believed that Britain, having already conquered India, ought to remain in it for moral and civilising reasons. As early as 1855, he declared that the British had much to learn from the Greek model of colonisation, for 'no country known to us appears so fully to have realised or to have given such remarkable effect to that idea' (Gladstone 1999a: 369). By the time of his essay 'England's Mission' of 1878, he is quoting Horace and attacking Disraeli for entering London as if he were a general in a Roman triumph. In the same essay, he denies the inferiority of the Indian mind or of India's civilisation and compares Britain's rule over India to Rome's rule over Greece; but he also adds that Britain's current policy toward India needs to be re-examined and to be brought more into line with Britain's own economic, moral, and political interests (Gladstone 1999b). For a politician such as Gladstone, then, ancient Rome can be used to restrain the extreme imperialism of the Conservative Party and to oppose expansion.

'Is it not just possible,' Richard Cobden asked, in 1860, 'that we may become corrupted at home by the reaction of arbitrary political maxims in the East upon our domestic politics, just as Greece and Rome were demoralized by their contact with Asia?'[30] The answer came from John Atkinson Hobson, in 1902: 'Not merely is the reaction possible, it is inevitable.'[31] At the time of the jingoism of the Boer War of 1899-1902, Hobson mounted one of the first combined economic and ethical British critiques of imperialism in his study, *Imperialism*, which influenced many anti-imperialists including, among others, Lenin in the essay quoted above. Hobson found the Roman Empire to be analogous to the British Empire, but turned this into a reason to disband the British imperialist system: 'This is the largest, plainest instance history presents of the social parasitic process by which a moneyed interest within the State, usurping the reins of government, makes for imperial expansion in order to fasten economic suckers into foreign bodies so as to drain them of their wealth in order to support domestic luxury,' he wrote in the last chapter of his book. 'The new Imperialism differs in no vital point from this old example.'[32] Hobson's book was first published in 1902, but his earlier writings were also used by other opponents of empire. Not least among these critics were three men educated in classics at Oxford, namely Gilbert Murray, Francis W. Hirst, and John L. Hammond, who jointly wrote the book *Liberalism and the Empire*

(1900). This fiercely anti-imperialist work takes as its point of departure a word of caution from Book 3 of Thucydides, and adduces Roman
slavery as a reason not to practise imperialism.[33] In a glance back at
Dilke and Seeley, moreover, the writers argue that 'the greatness of
Greater Britain' is not compatible with despotism, militarism, and
financial exploitation (Hirst, Murray, and Hammond 1998: xvi). While
Bryce, Cromer, and Lucas were restating claims based on ancient and
modern evidence to hold on to the British Empire, then, writers such as
Hobson and Murray, themselves informed about the ancient world,
were preparing at the very same time detailed reasons to dissolve the
Empire.

No British critic of empire could match M.K. Gandhi in successful
opposition to British rule in India, and Gandhi intervenes in this debate
in a manner consistent with his political philosophy in general. By this
time, he had read Justinian in Latin, while studying in the Inns of
Court in London, and also come to an appreciation of Plato's *Apology*.
In *Hind Swaraj* ('Indian Home Rule') of 1909, which is written in the
manner of a Platonic dialogue, he explains what civilisation is and so,
indirectly, responds to the British accusation that India is at a lower
level of civilisation than the British:

> I believe that the civilisation India has evolved is not to be beaten in the
> world. Nothing can equal the seeds sown by our ancestors. Rome went,
> Greece shared the same fate, the might of the Pharaohs was broken,
> Japan has become westernised, of China nothing can be said, but India is
> still, somehow or other, sound at the foundation. The people of Europe
> learn their lessons from the writings of the men of Greece or Rome, which
> exist no longer in their former glory. In trying to learn from them, the
> Europeans imagine that they will avoid the mistakes of Greece and Rome.
> Such is their pitiable condition. In the midst of all this, India remains
> immovable, and that is her glory.
>
> Gandhi 1997: 66

In its excess of national self-pride, the passage is typical of Gandhi's life
and work. But here the author also brings in the issue of decay, and
turns it against other civilisations of Europe, Africa, and Asia. India's
immobility contrasts with the quality of other cultures, which by reason
of their very pliancy are either fallen or in a deplorable condition.
Another Indian writer, Bhudev Mukhopadhyay (1827-94), who wrote
textbooks in Bengali on the histories of Greece and Rome, had adopted
a more sympathetic attitude to the British. He believed that the British
rule of India could be understood better through historical comparison
with other empires such as the Roman. But even though he predicted a

long rule without imperial decline for the British in India, Bhudev was ultimately quite confident, on the basis of his wide studies, about the superiority of Hindu, and especially Brahmin, values and customs (Raychaudhuri 1988: 64, 85). In different ways, thus, Bhudev and Gandhi indicate that the subjects of British rule in India understood the special status enjoyed by the classical civilisations in British culture, but were themselves not therefore ready to acknowledge the superiority of the imperial culture.[34]

3

What made Victorian writers turn to Rome when writing about the British Empire? At one level, it is not surprising to hear that comparisons with the Roman Empire played a role in Victorian books that dealt with British imperial themes, especially given the contemporary status of classics; indeed, it would have been surprising to learn that the Roman Empire had *not* been prominent in discussions about the British Empire. At another level, the seeming naturalness of the comparison with Rome itself calls out for scrutiny, and can be contextualised here in a little more detail. The phenomenon of the comparisons between the Roman and British empires is linked to larger and interconnected forces such as class, education, elitism, national identity, and the symbolic capital of Greek and Latin, in addition to the status of classics. The comparisons have implications that ramify widely in the worlds of culture, politics, and society, and ramify more widely than the texts might seem to convey at a first reading. It would be possible, given enough space and time, to enlarge on the analysis presented here and to show precisely how the comparative works by Bryce, Cromer, Lucas, and others related to these socio-political factors, and to understand how they sustained them, produced them, or were produced by them in turn. For the moment, however, it will be sufficient to note that these comparisons should be situated within a complex and evolving context in which imperialism, British identity, and the reception of classical antiquity were related. 'Comparisons between the two empires were in fact always rather forced,' writes P.A. Brunt: 'there were more points of contrast than of likeness'.[35] We may say that this discussion has not merely been a case of finding material, in texts from the late Victorian period, that we would now consider historically inaccurate – or racist, or ethnocentric, or condescending, though it remains important to analyse the mechanics of these attitudes. It is, also, to understand the location of these texts and to give them a hermeneutic and political depth that can be reconstructed from contemporary Victorian discourses and practices. Again, Francis G. Hutchins was largely correct in stating that 'the study of the Comparative Empire had always been a favourite pursuit of the classically educated servants of British India. For centuries classical analogies had come naturally to the lips of Englishmen discussing any subject; the subject of empire was no different and in fact lent itself more easily to classical analogy than did many other things' (Hutchins 1967: 214). But the word 'naturally' in this context, as Hutchins implies, conceals a great deal about the relationship between culture and power, just as does the suggestion that empire opened up 'more easily' to analogy with the classical world. In fact, an immense pressure had to be generated by social, cultural, and political forces to render natural and immediate the resort to ancient Rome by Englishmen in connection with the British Empire. This particular feeling of naturalness on the part of Englishmen was historically conditioned, constituted, and constructed by a complex interplay of such things as class, education, race, and the nation.

Consider a major study of ancient history by a British author in the nineteenth century that pointed definitively to the benefits of the Roman world empire, namely, Charles Merivale's *A History of the Romans under the Empire* (1850-64), a work that ranged roughly from the late Republic up to the era with which Gibbon's history began.[36] Appropriately for a defender of imperial statesmen, Merivale was educated first at Haileybury College, the college of the East India Company, and then at Cambridge. The brother of the Under Secretary of State for Colonies, Merivale 'admired the Roman Empire for its peace, its sound administration, and the general security of its citizens and subjects' (Turner 1993: 249). In the third volume of his history, Merivale provided the basis for a defence of Augustus' principate and the policies on which it was established. He justified the Augustan empire by referring to the wide-scale benefits that it conferred on the mass of citizens across the territories, including 'the extension of rights, the protection of property, and the multiplication of enjoyments and expansion of the natural affections' (Merivale, vol. 3: 555). In the same spirit, late Victorian British writers found congenial an implication of Theodor Mommsen's work, which was translated into English and made available to British readers already in the 1860s, that Augustus, rather than being the absolute commander of empire, shared power with the Senate.[37] By 1910, when the British Empire had claimed vast territories in Asia and Africa, and the maintenance of a global empire was firmly on the agenda, Augustus' stewardship and administrative efficiency came to look increasingly appealing to various scholars, not least to H.F. Pelham in the notorious eleventh edition of the

Encyclopaedia Britannica. Pelham described Augustus, who became more prominent in Victorian thought at the end of the nineteenth century after the fall of the French Second Empire, as 'one of the world's great men, a statesman who conceived and carried through a scheme of political reconstruction which kept the empire together, and secured peace and tranquillity and preserved civilization for more than two centuries'.[38]

A particular turn to the Augustan 'court poet' Vergil reminds us as well of the globalist and universalist charge of the comparisons between Rome and Britain. 'Advocates of the British Empire,' one scholar writes, 'began to thrill to Virgil's celebration of Imperial Rome bounding her Empire with the earth (*Aeneid* 6.781f.)' (Vance 1997: 141). Seeley himself likened Aeneas to Abraham, and suggested that Aeneas was a pioneering man of national destiny, while, some years later, Bryce called Vergil 'the national poet of empire' and Cromer referred to him as 'an enthusiastic imperialist'.[39] Throughout the nineteenth century, in fact, Anchises' advice to Aeneas in Book 6 of the *Aeneid* had echoed in the speeches and writings of establishment figures such as John Henry Newman, Lord John Russell, and Sir Robert Peel. But no less important to the late Victorian political programme was the infinitudinal frame given to the theme of imperial mission and national destiny by Jupiter when he prophesied to Venus, in Book 1, 'For them I set no limits in space and time; I give them empire [*imperium*] without end' (*Aeneid* 1.278-9). As if in anticipation of Gibbon's history of the decline and fall, Jupiter defers into eternity the end of empire and indicates that the date of its fall lies outside of time and hence outside of history. 'With this definition of empire,' Duncan F. Kennedy notes, 'an event such as the sack of Rome by Alaric in 410 AD marks not the demise of empire, but opens up the discursive opportunity to speak of Rome as a historical episode within the continually and ever-receding horizon of empire' (Kennedy 1999: 26). In that sense, Rome functioned as a figure, a figure of empire and for empire, and it lent itself to use by those who wished to transfer *imperium* to themselves and who claimed the authority to speak for empire in their own time. Of course, *translatio imperii* was just what lay at the heart of the comparison between the Roman and British empires, and was its driving engine in many respects. Surely, one of the points of the comparisons was that the 'authentic' imperial experience of the ancient Romans was now available to British administrators, intellectuals, and politicians. But underlying the *translatio imperii* at work in Jupiter's declaration was the promise of a dominion unbounded in space as well as time – a greater and greater Britain – and it was the sense of an expanding, global empire that appealed to British imperialists at the turn of the century.

Among other reasons, the sheer extent and territorial scale of their multiethnic, multiracial world empire, which was far larger than the Belgian, French, and Spanish empires, caused British imperialists to turn for comparison to the Roman polity rather than, say, the Assyrian, Persian, Athenian, or Macedonian empires. These latter empires were brought up by writers for discussion on occasion, but the comparisons were generally brief or made in passing. Robert Young notes that 'the great original of empire in the nineteenth century was always the Roman, which enabled people to identify with a concept of the benign spread of civilization over benighted barbarian tribes' (Young 2001: 33). As noted above, Athens' ancient history was often considered as a means to understand the dilemma, once presented by Thucydides, of how a state could maintain a democracy at home and an empire overseas.[40] But Athens' empire was insignificant in size and duration in comparison to the Roman and the British, and so it was also the Roman Empire that the British ruling classes increasingly placed alongside their own. In addition to scale, however, there were other factors, too, that brought the Roman analogy to British writers. For one thing, the Roman Empire was admired 'as a providential vehicle for the spread of Christianity' by historians in the second half of the nineteenth century, and the proselytising opportunities of empire remained important, though not necessarily central, to imperialist ambitions.[41] For another, there was the rivalry with the Holy Roman Empire and the revival of its emperor, in 1871, in the figure of William I, King of Prussia, at the end of the Franco-Prussian War. When the Queen was assuming the title 'Empress of India', she was responding in part to pressures from other European royal courts with imperial interests. The imperial title Kaiser-i-Hind, which was promoted in India, was based on the understanding by the Viceroy, Lord Lytton, that the title Kaiser, familiar from earlier Indian texts, was 'not hackneyed or monopolized by any Crown since the Roman Caesars'. At an Imperial Assemblage that was held in Delhi to mark the Queen's accession to the title, the Viceroy presented the gathered Indian rulers 'large silk standards, 5 ft by 5 ft, in the Roman style' (Cohn 1983: 201, 203).

It was also in the period of Victoria's reign, as Javed Majeed has shown in a related context, that the very *method* of comparative enquiry was deeply and inextricably entangled in British imperialist practices and discourses.[42] The phenomenon of imperial comparativism cannot be understood apart from British colonialism and imperialism in the second half of the nineteenth century and in the early twentieth century. Indeed, while the 'Comparative Method' was a stimulating mode of investigation for Victorian intellectuals, it was an approach that found its most gifted practitioners in colonial and imperialist circumstances. As far back as the late eighteenth century, Sir William Jones had promulgated his view about linguistic comparativism when he made his path-breaking claims concerning the similarities between Greek, Latin, Sanskrit, Persian, and other languages. The example of Jones, then a judge in Calcutta, shows that English intellectuals and administrators were approaching the cultural history of India from a comparativist point of view.[43] It is no accident that the Comparative Method reached its heights in the second half of the nineteenth century at a time when the British Empire was also reaching its greatest point of expansion and was entering its aggressive Victorian phase. From this perspective, Friedrich Max Mueller, the comparative philologist, and Sir James Frazer, the comparative anthropologist, are two very different representatives of one and the same episode in Victorian intellectual life. Another influential exponent of the Comparative Method was Sir Henry Maine, the author of *Ancient Law*, first published in 1861, and *Village-Communities in the East and West*, published in 1871 (Maine 1883 and 1871). Maine lived in India from 1862 to 1869, and his works were intensely comparative, both in the use of evidence and in the attempt to lay the groundwork for the study of shared Aryan cultures, ideas, and values. Maine's writings, which had a huge impact in their day, typify how comparativism sustained British work on India, especially in relation to such fields as law, history, and culture. Significantly, the figures who directly or indirectly extended and built upon Maine's work were John Seeley, Edward Freeman, and James Bryce, each of whom at different times also produced notable statements about ancient and modern imperialism.

The careers of these men, lastly, draw our attention to a Victorian matrix that brought together the academic practice of classics and the use of antiquity by intellectuals outside of the academic world. Not all the figures considered in this essay were professional scholars of antiquity or even writers who earned their living mainly from the study and teaching of antiquity. In this sense, therefore, it is not accurate to say that the writings on empire quoted here can rightly be understood as the work of classicists or of a group that identified as such. As described above, however, most if not all of them had backgrounds in classics and were in contact with academic discourses about antiquity, as students, as professors, or in some other capacity – Cromer, for instance, served as the President of the Classical Association, but did not have an Oxbridge career worth the mention; on the other hand, Seeley served as a professor of Latin for some years, while Bryce, also a professor, and Lucas, a Fellow of All Souls, came from the tradition of Oxford 'Greats'. At any rate, the discipline of classics became professionalised only gradually, and not very systematically, over the course of the long nineteenth century, and Victorians seemed to go in and out of academic positions in Greek and Latin with some fluidity. But what is significant about the phenomenon is that, in the Victorian period, the institutionalised study of antiquity authorised and participated in a national culture in which it was possible, and even legitimate, to establish a specific view of the relationship between the Roman and British empires. The most elaborate explorations of this relationship, while often alert to the problems inherent to the comparison, endorsed the British Empire both on its own terms and in contrast to the Roman. To grasp the worldliness of Victorian scholarship is to understand why some contemporary writers 'naturally' wished to forge a dynamic connection between Greater Rome and Greater Britain.

Notes

I am very grateful to Barbara Goff for providing the initial impetus for this essay. Thomas Habinek and Josiah Ober offered critical readings of an earlier draft. Versions of the paper were also presented at the University of Chicago, the University of Michigan, and the University of North Carolina at Chapel Hill. I am thankful to the audience on each occasion for valuable discussion. My deepest thanks go to Dr Goff and to Miriam Leonard for helpful comments and criticism.

1. Lucas 1912; Cromer 1910; Bryce 1901.
2. Betts 1971; Freeman 1996; Hingley 2000: 25-7. For a survey of Victorian attitudes to ancient Rome, see also Vance 1997.
3. See Stray 1998 and Goldhill 2002, ch. 4.
4. Dilke 1880 and 1890. For a discussion of Dilke's work in the context of mid-Victorian imperialism, see Bodelsen 1968: 60-75; for the life, see Nicholls 1995. The term 'Greater Britain' may be the translation of 'Britannia Major', used famously by John Major in his Latin history of 1521; see Major 1892. The expression spawned a range of books and essays about the British Empire that drew on the term for title and theme: both Barker 1910 and Jose 1913 contain brief discussions of ancient and modern empires; Ogg 1902 and Cross 1914 were written mainly for American audiences; Mosley 1932 is a fascist's account of Britain. See also the disparate materials in Colomb 1880, Clifford 1899, Wynne 1901, Kirkman 1909, and Hughes 1919. For a discussion of 'Greater Britain' in British imperial history, see Thompson 2002, ch. 1; for its relationship to the imperial legacy of the American revolution, see Gould 1999; for a discussion of the usefulness of the term, see Armitage 1999.
5. Quoted in Bodelsen 1968: 71.

6. See Bodelsen 1968: 71.

7. There is an important subtext running throughout this essay concerning race and the interaction between British racial discourses about India and ancient Rome. This is a challenging topic, and in need of further discussion, but it can begin to be approached through such studies as Ballhatchet 1980, Trautmann 1997, and Mandler 2000.

8. Dilke 1880: 573. The elisions or slippages among and between 'Saxon', British, and English identities is typical of Dilke and many other writers of the period.

9. Dilke 1880: 549; cf. 468.

10. Dilke 1880: 440. The word 'democratic' in Dilke's book needs to be read in its Victorian context; it was much disputed, and had different connotations from the contemporary modern term.

11. Seeley 1909. For discussions of Seeley's work, see the introduction to Seeley 1971 by John Gross; Burroughs 1973; Greenlee 1976; and Wormell 1980. For Seeley's use of the concept 'Greater Britain', see Deudney 2001. I have not seen Luigi Loreto, *Guerra e liberta nella Repubblica romana: John R. Seeley e le radici intellettuali della Roman revolution di Ronald Syme* (Rome: L'Erma di Bretschneider, 1999).

12. Seeley 1909: 8, 179. It is worth noting that some modern scholars have also characterised Rome's acquisition of empire as accidental or unintentional. See also Harrison in this volume.

13. Wormell 1980: 94; for Seeley's lectures on Roman imperialism and other subjects, see also Seeley 1870.

14. On the role of classics in the ICS examinations, see n. 23, below.

15. *Regulations and Examinations for Open Competition for the Civil Service of India*, question from 1893, quoted in Collini, Winch, and Burrow 1983: 356.

16. Seeley 1909: 238. Seeley's concept of liberty should be taken in its Victorian context, and as conditioned by contemporary concerns over class, nation, and race. See also Holland 1901.

17. Froude 1879; see Turner 1993: 252-4.

18. J.A. Froude, *Short Studies on Great Subjects*, 4 vols (London, 1898), vol. 2: 30, quoted in Collini, Winch, and Burrow 1983: 190. In his *Oceana* (1886), Froude wrote: 'Horace had seen in Rome what we are now witnessing in England – fields deserted, the people crowding into the cities. He noted the growing degeneracy. He foretold the inevitable consequences.' On the use of Horace in imperialist Britain, see Gaisser 1994. Froude's work had followed the publication, in 1884, of a *History of the Decline and Fall of the British Empire* by Edwarda Gibbon (sic). At about the same time as Froude, Elliott Evans Mills published, anonymously, a book on the decline and fall of the British Empire, ostensibly set for schools in Japan in 2005: see Mills 1905.

19. See also the briefer treatment in Cramb 1900.

20. It is worth noting that Seeley, Froude, and Bryce were supporters of the Imperial Federation League, which was founded in 1884 by W.E. Forster; the league broke up in 1893 after disagreements among the members.

21. Symonds 1991 and 2000; Murray 2000.

22. To which he added: 'and not always successfully'. See Mackail 1925a: 81.

23. 'Between 1892 and 1914 Oxford obtained 48.2 per cent of the places, Cambridge 29.5 per cent. In due course this pattern was reflected at the top. In 1938, the last normal year of British Rule before the Second World War and

Independence, of the eight provincial Governors who were members of the I.C.S., six were Oxford men, all of whom had read Greats and taken their degrees between 1897 and 1910: of the remaining three Governors, who were appointed from outside the Service, two were Oxford men' (Symonds 1991: 191). For the central place of Greek and Latin in the ICS examinations, see Majeed 1999: 91-8, and Tietze Larson 1999: 197-207.

24. The source for Bryce is the *Dictionary of National Biography*.

25. Marlowe 1970: 20. For the impact of British classics on Cromer's rule in Egypt, see Reid 2002, ch. 4.

26. *Dictionary of National Biography*; for Seeley's influence on Lucas, see Greenlee 1976. Lucas' book *Introduction to a Historical Geography of the Colonies* (1887), was revised by Hugh Edward Egerton and published under the title *The Origin and Growth of Greater Britain* in 1924.

27. Many British writers compare the British suppression of sati to the Roman suppression of druids' sacrifices: 'Augustus contented himself with abolishing certain practices [among the Gaulish Druids] like that of human sacrifice – just as the English government in India, though in a general way its attitude towards the native religions has been one of impartial tolerance, has abolished Suttee and Juggernaut – and with setting up a rival religion which was as distinctively Roman as its predecessor had been Gaulish' (Arnold 1906: 92-3).

28. See Jenkyns 1980, Turner 1981, and Clarke 1989.

29. Freeman 1886; Wormell 1980: 169.

30. Quoted in Knorr 1944: 359.

31. This section of the book concludes: 'Could the incomes expended in the Home Counties and other large districts of Southern Britain be traced to their sources, it would be found that they were in large measure wrung from the enforced toil of vast multitudes of black, brown, or yellow natives, by arts not differing essentially from those which supported in idleness and luxury imperial Rome' (Hobson 1965: 151). The basic study of Hobson and imperialism is Cain 2002.

32. Hobson 1965: 367. In 1880, F. Seebohm had also warned that imperialism in Britain might lead to a collapse in the Roman manner; see 'Socialism and Imperialism', in Cain 1999, 303-4.

33. Cf. Robertson 1899. Thucydides 3.82: 'The cause of the whole catastrophe was empire pursued for covetousness and ambition.'

34. For Egyptian uses of the Graeco-Roman past in the same period, see Reid 2002: 163-71.

35. Brunt 1990: 111; cf. Miles 1990. Of course, it should be said that few Britons suggested the empire of ancient Rome was exactly and wholly analogous to that of Britain.

36. For a survey of Victorian histories of ancient Rome, see Turner 1993, ch. 9.

37. Hingley 2000: 114. For the English translation of the *History of Rome*, see Mommsen 1862-75; the German edition of the history was published in 1854-6. Mommsen's *Provinces of the Roman Empire* (German edn, 1885) was first translated into English in 1886 (the translation was revised by Francis Haverfield in 1909). On British and German historiography in the Victorian period, see Stuchtey and Wende 2000.

38. H.F. Pelham, *Encyclopaedia Britannica*, 11th edn, s.v. 'Augustus'.

39. Seeley 1909: 135; Bryce 1901: 66; Cromer 1910: 14.

40. This question was urgently debated in the Victorian period: see e.g. Holland 1901, with discussion in Taylor 1991. The most forceful statement of the issue comes from Disraeli: 'I know [the citizens of London] will not be beguiled into believing that in maintaining their Empire they may forfeit their liberties. One of the greatest of Romans, when asked what were his politics, replied, *Imperium et Libertas*. That would not make a bad programme for a British Ministry. It is one from which Her Majesty's advisers do not shrink' (Benjamin Disraeli, in November 1879, quoted in Vance: 230-1).

41. The phrase comes from Turner 1993: 249.

42. See Majeed 1999; with Collini, Winch, and Burrow 1983, ch. 7.

43. See Trautman 1997.

3

'We Speak Latin in Trinidad':
Uses of Classics in Caribbean Literature

Emily Greenwood

> Among my contemporaries was Grantley Adams, who is now a very distin-
> guished citizen. When I was talking to him a few years ago, he told me
> that before he left Harrison College he had read Homer, Hesiod,
> Euripides, Sophocles and Aristophanes; he could read Greek almost as
> well as he could read English. That is the way he was educated, and later
> he went to an English University and studied law.
>
> James 1996: 164[1]

The reception of classics in the Caribbean is a relatively unexplored
subject; insofar as classicists have studied this subject, they have
tended to focus on Derek Walcott's *Omeros* and his stage version of
the *Odyssey*.[2] A dominant theme in the existing literature is the
apparent incongruity of classics in the context of the Caribbean,
where the discipline would seem to be on the wrong side of the racial,
imperial, and political oppositions that have divided the region historically. Hence scholars have pointed to the complex tensions that
Homeric allusions engender in Walcott's oeuvre.[3] However, classicists
are increasingly insistent that the Homeric epics, for example, are
themselves counter-cultural and 'errant' texts, and that 'reading
backwards' from Walcott to Homer is not the subversive enterprise
that it might at first seem.[4] This last strategy of reading has lead to
the intriguing phenomenon of classicists *writing back*, in the manner
of postcolonial theory, to defend the discipline of classics against accu-
sations of inveterate cultural chauvinism, and to assert that the
'classics' of Greek and Roman literature are 'classics' precisely
because they cannot be limited by the restrictions of place and time.[5]
In what follows I argue that Walcott's readings of Homer and other
classical authors need to be understood in a Caribbean context, as
part of a tradition of using classics creatively according to regional
and national needs.

Political independence and independent readings

In his autobiography, *Inward Hunger*, Eric Williams, the first Prime Minister of the independent nation of Trinidad and Tobago, devotes a substantial proportion of the narrative to the theme of education, describing both the process of his own privileged education, and the process of educating the Trinidadian masses for self-government.[6] Williams assigns a prominent role to classics in both processes. Key pedagogical stages in Williams' career are punctuated by felicitous encounters with Latin. Thus, in the third chapter of *Inward Hunger*, which is titled 'The Education of a Young Colonial', Williams recalls the occasion of his introduction to Latin as an eleven-year-old, on his first day at Queen's Royal College (1969: 32):

> We were given our textbooks, and requested to learn for the next after-noon a few tenses of *amo*. Within a short period at home that night I had learned not only all the tenses of *amo*, but of *moneo*, *rego* and *audio*, that is to say, all the conjugations.

Williams' enthusiasm for Latin persisted, and in 1931 he won the one 'Island Scholarship', which enabled a Trinidadian student to attend the University of Oxford. In the same chapter, Williams recounts the experience of his first Latin class at Oxford, in which he proved his mettle by outstripping his contemporaries in a Latin translation. As narrated by Williams this is no neutral tale of schoolboy rivalry; an exercise in literal translation becomes an expression of the colonial scholar *writing back* and outwitting the colonisers with his command of Latin[7] – an 'imperial' language which is here claimed and possessed by a Trinidadian on the underside of the British Empire (1969: 34).[8]

> In our first class in Latin, the lecturer, an ascetic, irascible man, gave us, as a test of our ability, a long passage, about forty lines, of Latin unprepared translation; he told us that, as we almost certainly lacked the ability to complete the passage in the forty or so minutes at our disposal, we should do only the first twenty lines. The passage from Ovid, I believe, was of School Certificate standard, and child's play as far as I was concerned. I finished the entire passage in twenty minutes, turned in my paper, and walked out of the class.

The episode is framed by a confrontation between Williams and one of his colleagues, 'a tall English chap with a long nose and an air the quintessence of superciliousness', who questioned his ability to speak English, let alone translate Latin. When the latter expresses bafflement at Williams' superlative performance in the Latin translation, Williams retorts, 'You see, we speak Latin in Trinidad' (this alludes to the Englishman's remark, upon overhearing Williams speaking to someone, 'Oh, you do speak English in Trinidad, do you?').[9] Williams' interpretation of this incident as a loaded cultural encounter between coloniser and colonised, accords with a motif in Caribbean literature where the struggle for political and cultural autonomy is contested through the classics.[10]

In the passage quoted above, Williams' dismissal of the Latin translation exercise at Oxford as 'child's play' rates the level of Latin at the metropolitan university as backward in relation to that taught in the best schools in Trinidad. In evoking the metaphor of childhood, Williams inverts imperial prejudices about the people of the West Indies, whose apparent lack of history and culture had been characterised as a state of childishness by prominent English scholars. In *Froudacity* the Trinidadian autodidact and schoolmaster, J.J. Thomas, quotes an example of this prejudicial motif at work in the racist pseudo-historical sketch of the West Indies published by J.A. Froude, Professor of Modern History at Oxford, in 1888.[11] On page 145, Thomas quotes Froude for the view that:

> The Negroes of the West Indies *are children, and not yet disobedient children* ... If you enforce self-government upon them when they are not asking for it, you may wilfully drive them back into the condition of their ancestors, from which the slave-trade was the beginning of their emancipation.

It is notable that Froude's argument against West Indian self-government enlists a symbol from ancient Greek epic – the bow of Ulysses (Odysseus) – to support his claims about the cultural superiority of the English over their colonial subjects in the West Indies. As C.L.R. James observes in 'The West Indian Intellectual' – an article that forms the introduction to *Froudacity* in the 1969 reprint,

> The sub-title, *The Bow of Ulysses*, could be taken as a reminder of the failure of the rivals for the hand of Penelope to satisfy her demands that any suitor should be able to bend the formidable bow of her absent husband, Ulysses. The blacks were thus unsubtly labelled as seeking a self-government which they could not exercise. At any rate the subtitle would remind the reader of the great reputation for classical scholarship of Mr. Froude, a most distinguished scholar.[12]

Thomas' argument in *Froudacity* exposes the irrational prejudices on which Froude's work is based, and musters the odd classical allusion against Froude. Hence on page 92, Thomas borrows the word 'kepha-lalgeia' (which he translates as 'brain-dizziness') from Xenophon to describe the witlessness of the English officials sent out to govern Trinidad.[13] On page 143 he refers to the 'auri sacra fames' of the slave dealers, and at page 162 he employs a mixed Greek analogy, referring to the English colonisers as '... Eumolpids who would fain impose a not-to-be-questioned yoke on us poor helots of Ethiopia'.

While the reception of European colonial scholarship has been decid-edly hostile (cf. C.L.R. James at n. 34 below), Caribbean authors of the generation(s) of Thomas, James, Williams, Walcott, and Césaire see classics as a discipline which can be redeemed, albeit tainted by associ-ation with European colonial scholarship. This open-mindedness about classics manifests itself in two strategies of reading. The first strategy (exemplified by the quotations from Thomas above) represents the Caribbean intellectual as an independent reader of the classics, in oppo-sition to the readings that are promoted by the colonisers. The second strategy involves appropriation – casting Greece in the image of the Caribbean, as a region that is on the 'frontiers' of Europe.[14]

Continuing in the tradition of Thomas, the strategy of staking an independent claim to the classics is also evident in Aimé Césaire's *Discourse on Colonialism* (1955). Césaire quotes the writer Jules Romains with great scorn, noting that in the expanded second edition of Romains' novel *Salsette Discovers America* (1950) the latter writes:

> I will not even censure our Negroes and Negresses for chewing gum. I will only note ... that this movement has the effect of emphasizing the jaws, and that the associations which come to mind evoke the equatorial forest rather than the procession of the Panathenaea. ... The black race has not yet produced, will never produce, an Einstein, a Stravinsky, a Gershwin.

Césaire rejoins (1972: 30-1):

> One idiotic comparison for another: since the prophet of the *Revue des Deux Mondes* and other places invites us to draw parallels between 'widely separated' things, may I be permitted, Negro that I am, to think (no one being master of his free associations) that his voice has less in common with the rustling of the oak of Dodona – or even the vibrations of the cauldron – than with the braying of a Missouri ass.

Césaire's rejoinder puts Romains squarely in his place with a counter-reading whereby Romains' attitude shows that he is no intelligent reader of classics. Césaire himself was educated at the prestigious Lycée Victor Schoelcher in Martinique, and then subsequently at the Lycée

3. 'We Speak Latin in Trinidad'

Louis le Grand and the École Normale Supérieure in Paris (the latter from 1935-9). Gregson Davis, who has written an excellent study of Césaire, argues that his classical education informed the term 'négritude' which Césaire coined to articulate the conscious identity of being a Negro with a past and a sense of pride in this identity:

> The form of the new lexeme marvellously embodies what we have been calling the tension between assimilationist and counter-assimiliationist worldviews. On the one hand, the final syllable of negritude is formed by analogy with Latin-derived abstract nouns ending in the suffix -*tudo*; on the other, the syllable nègr-, though ultimately derived from the Latin *niger* ('black', in a value-neutral sense) had come close to acquiring in French, the semantic cargo of a racial slur. Thus the very form of the word is redolent both of its author's classroom instruction in Greek and Latin and of his subversive resistance to the process of unexamined cultural assimilation.[15]

That Latin had a hand in the architecture of négritude is an argument that crops up elsewhere, to buttress arguments for teaching Latin in St Lucian schools.[16] Hunter Francois, a St Lucian intellectual who was Minister of Education in St Lucia in the late 1960s, argued that four years of Latin should be compulsory in the secondary schools of St Lucia. On Tuesday 20 June 1978 an article by Francois appeared in the *Voice of St Lucia*, bearing the title 'Latin in Schools Should be Compulsory':[17]

> I now propose in writing what I have so tirelessly proposed in conversation: – THAT THE STUDY OF LATIN SHOULD BE COMPULSORY FOR THE FIRST FOUR YEARS OF EVERY SENIOR SECONDARY SCHOOL; and I further propose that it be included in Teachers' Training Courses and extended to Junior Secondary Schools as well.[18]

Francois proceeds to quote extensively from the text of a lecture delivered by Leopold Sedar Senghor, the then President of the Republic of Senegal, in Rome on 28 March 1973 under the auspices of the Institute of Roman Studies:

> Please allow me, therefore, as a statesman, but also as a professor who once taught the classical languages, to put before you some of my ideas, some of the ideas we Senegalese have about the value of these languages in shaping the human personality, in this age which delights in describing itself as the "Technological" age.
>   I feel all the more free to do so today ... because I belong to the small group of black students who in the 30s launched the movement of

69

Negritude in the Latin quarter of Paris. And, since then, that movement has stood up against all the onslaughts of the materialistic ideologies I shall mention in a moment ... Well, then, in the heyday of our enthusiasm ... we never poured vituperation on Latin. We refrained from doing so, because we had all studied it and many of us had studied Greek as well ...

Do not suppose that it is rash for an African to sing the praises of Latin and the Humanities in general. A large number of Africans who achieved brilliance in an age generally described as the 'classical' age, made an important contribution to the building-up of European civilization in this Mediterranean basin which was its matrix. One need only recall the names of the Egyptians Philo, Plotinus and Origen who wrote in Greek, and of the Berbers such as Tertullian, Cyprian and Augustine who wrote in Latin, and a host of others. Need I recall the fact that among their civilizing agents, the ancients numbered the Egyptians, and that from Homer to Strabo, it was their writers who showered the greatest praises on the 'Thiopians', in other words, the Negroes? And today, we know, thanks to the research done by black university graduates, among others, that in Athens and Rome there were more Negroes than now, living there as full citizens.[19]

There are many reasons why the study of classics may not be considered 'politic' in the contemporary Caribbean.[20] These reasons are alluded to by the writers whose works I discuss: that it is irrelevant and that the study of classics can only serve to buttress the mythology of European civilisations which have exploited the region in a very uncivilised manner. Since the dominant discourses of the colonial powers in the Caribbean claimed the inheritance of Greek and Roman civilisation to legitimate their status as slave-owners and colonial powers, there is a reaction that distances itself from Greek civilisation which becomes tainted by association – a sort of receptacle for European cultural arrogance and barbarism.

The compact between modern colonialism and Greek and Roman antiquity is derided in a passage in Frantz Fanon's *The Wretched of the Earth* where he describes how, as part of the 'white-washing' process, colonised intellectuals have had instilled in them deference for Greece and Rome as the cradle for Western civilisation ('the Graeco-Latin pedestal') (1990: 36):

The colonialist bourgeoisie, in its narcissistic dialogue, expounded by the members of its universities, had in fact deeply implanted in the minds of the colonized intellectual that the essential qualities remain eternal in spite of all the blunders men may make: the essential qualities of the West, of course. The native intellectual accepted the cogency of these ideas, and deep down in his brain you could always find a vigilant sentinel ready to defend the Graeco-Latin pedestal.

3. 'We Speak Latin in Trinidad'

Educational syllabuses in the Caribbean are still vexed by the question of the colonial legacy. Although secondary schools in the Anglophone Caribbean no longer prepare students for exams set by the Cambridge Examining Board, many text-books on West Indian history are still written in Britain and exported to the Caribbean (by the publishing house Macmillan, in particular). As well as the problematic content of the educational syllabus, there is also a strong association between education and literacy in English or French (the 'colonial' or 'metropolitan' language), to the disadvantage of Creole / Patois oraliture. Consequently, West Indian literature abounds with reference to schooling and there are numerous classroom scenes and motifs, such as Wordsworth's 'Daffodils', which have come to symbolise the misfit between the subject-matter of Great English literature and the Caribbean context to which it was exported.[21] Often classics is marginal to this debate, but it is cited as an extreme example of trying to override local cultures. I give one example here, taken from *School Days*, an account of his childhood education in Francophone Martinique by the novelist Patrick Chamoiseau.

Chamoiseau recounts the anonymous teacher's attempt to teach his class the alphabet, which flounders on the difference between French and Creole words. He pulls out a pineapple, a native fruit (*ananas* in French), from his bag, to designate the letter 'a', but the children call it by its Creole name, which begins with a 'Z': *zananas*. Chamoiseau describes the teacher's response as that of a Hercules, confronted with the task of civilising the wild (1998: 60):

> The teacher gulped. His face was contorted with anguish. His eyes became glittering stones. Zounds! ... However do you expect to travel along the path to wisdom with a language like that! His indignation was absolute
>
> ...
>
> Then he seemed to take refuge upon a distant shore, where he wondered just how deeply bogged down in ignorance we were. His outstretched arms invoked the massive cleansing required for the salvation of our fold: *Before these Augean stables, even Hercules would quail!*
>
> Through lesson after lesson, Hercules laboured mightily to drag examples of a few elementary sounds from his herd.

Stupid historicism

In several published interviews, Walcott has decried the 'stupid historicism' that consigns what comes after chronologically, or historically, to inferior cultural status. In the case of his own so-called 'epic' poem,

Omeros, Walcott has complained that critics explain *Omeros* in terms of Homer:

> ... the kind of thing that many reviewers and critics saw in *Omeros*: a reinvention of the *Odyssey*, but this time in the Caribbean. I mean, what would be the point of doing that? What this implies is that geologically, geographically, the Caribbean is secondary to the Aegean. What this does immediately is to humiliate the landscape and say to the Caribbean Sea, 'You must think of yourself as a second-rate Aegean, or, on a good day, you can look like the Mediterranean.' The *stupid historicism* of thinking that way leads some people to say that I also, as the author of *Omeros*, am trying to make it via Homer.[22]

This complaint originates in Walcott's broader credo that one cannot judge literature in temporal terms, and that 'the idea of art has no tense apart from the present'.[23] Walcott argues that to approach art in terms of chronology is to patronise certain cultures, particularly those of the 'New World' – a term which itself bespeaks European cultural arrogance.[24] In an interview with Shaun McCarthy in October 1990, Walcott complains about the tendency of critics to judge poetry chronologically. He argues that whenever something new appears, in a particular work from overseas (seen from the perspective of Europe), critics compare it to pre-existing works that are already familiar to them and thereby harness the novelty of this unfamiliar work by saying 'it's like x, or like y': 'The critic will say you see we did it before and now you are learning how to do it.' Critical responses that see Walcott's poetry as 'an imitation of Homer' risk being accused of the patronising stance of the former colonial powers who saw themselves as exporting culture to the West Indies. In the essay 'The Muse of History', Walcott supplants imperialism with the idea of language as an empire over which any great poet of any time and place holds sway: 'It is the language which is the empire, and great poets are not its vassals, but its princes. We continue to categorize these poets by the wrong process; that is, by history.'[25] There are no inequalities involved in the empire of language at the level of great writers – they write as contemporaries, across the spaces created by geography and history.

Walcott's aesthetic, which wrests literature away from the clutches of history, is an altogether more radical argument than the claim that all peoples, at all times and in all places, have a stake in the past.[26] This argument is used elsewhere in Caribbean literature, for example by Frantz Fanon, who sees the condition of blackness as being the slave of the past, but who insists by virtue of his shared humanity that 'the Peloponnesian War is as much mine as the invention of the compass'.[27]

Walcott's position is complex: at one level he endorses the need for a 'national literature' in the Caribbean.[28] But the way in which he creates a space for Caribbean literature is by arguing for the simultaneity of time in art / literature, whereby artists, poets, and novelists can travel in any direction and all directions are neutral.[29] While this logic side-steps the colonialist hierarchy of history and traditional literary genealogies, it leads to the anti-national and anti-imperial position that privileges the order of art over political regimes. This stance enables Walcott to lend his poetic voice to the region, but also to raise his voice against the region as a critical outsider by virtue of his status as poet.

It is notable that when Walcott takes issue with internal Caribbean politics, whether in St Lucia or Trinidad, he allies himself with ancient Greek and Roman poets – Ovid in particular. The clearest instance of Walcott using a conversation with a Roman poet to distance himself from the politics of the present is in the poem 'The Hotel Normandie Pool', in which Walcott converses with an apparition of Ovid.[30] The voice of Walcott invokes the Roman poet ('Turn to us, Ovid') as a fellow exile, complaining that:

> Our emerald sands
> Are stained with sewage from each tin-shacked Rome;
> Corruption, censorship, and arrogance
> Make exile seem a happier thought than home.
>
> *Collected Poems*, 442

In turn, Ovid articulates the tensions that Walcott feels between European culture (symbolised by 'Romans') and his native Caribbean culture (symbolised by 'the slaves') and identifies this tension with the politics of his own career, only to assert that 'art obeys its own order':

> 'Romans' – he smiled – 'will mock your slavish rhyme,
> the slaves your love of Roman structures, when,
> from Metamorphoses to Tristia,
> art obeys its own order.'
>
> *Collected Poems*, 444

Relativity of empires

Another conceptual move that maps Greece onto the Caribbean in Caribbean literature is the claim that the process of civilisation is cyclical.[31] When seen from this perspective, the examples of the finite grandeur of ancient Greece and Rome console the Caribbean by putting British, French, and Spanish imperialism in their place and, what is more, suggesting the possibility that the nations of the Caribbean will enjoy their share of dominance. Marcus Garvey, the Jamaican intellectual who was the architect of pan-African nationalism, frequently articulated this possibility in his writings and speeches, drawing solace from the great Egyptian civilisation of the past and claiming its legacy for all black people:

> I make no apology for prophesying that there will be a turning point in the history of the West Indies. ... This may be regarded as a dream, but I would point my critical friends to history and its lessons. Would Caesar have believed that the country he was invading in 55 BC would be the seat of the greatest Empire of the World? Had it been suggested to him would he not have laughed at it as a huge joke? Yet it has come true.[32]

Garvey's treatment of history is inventive – unashamedly so. He writes about Black History in the knowledge that many contemporary white scholars saw this as a contradiction in terms (cf. 'The History of the Negro' in Garvey 1967). Faced with 'history as prejudice' Garvey defines the task of educated black men of his day as being to manufacture history in their turn. This regional attitude to history is expressed by C.L.R. James in a lecture on 'The Artist in the Caribbean' (originally delivered at the University of the West Indies in Jamaica in 1959):

> Perhaps the most important thing I have to say this evening is that if the threads of a tradition can be discovered among us and made into a whole, if we are to be shocked into recognition of what we are, and what we are not, with the power that this will bring, it is the great artist who will do it. He may by fiction or drama set our minds at rest on the problem which intrigues so many of them: what is Africa to us? *He may be a great historian. (His history might be denounced by professional historians and justly. It would not matter. It would have served the national need: look at the illusions most of these European nations have had of themselves.)*[33]

In the above passage James does not reject history as a discipline, but he rejects its usefulness for the task of fashioning a coherent cultural and national identity for the region. This distaste for academic subtleties is typical of James' approach to the past: although his writings are steeped in *both* 'classical' allusions, *and* references to the classics of Western literature, James is careful to distinguish between the 'profound discoveries of Western civilization' (good) and 'European colonialist scholarship' (bad).[34] Although C.L.R. James wrote about the thorough schooling in classics that he received at Queen's Royal,[35] he insisted that his profound understanding of classics was self-taught.[36]

3. 'We Speak Latin in Trinidad'

Many of James' analogies with ancient Greece stem from his own, idiosyncratic conception of ancient Greece and from his belief that there is a natural affinity between the ancient Greeks and the peoples of the Caribbean.

> In the course of duty and for my own information I have read the classics of educational theory and taken an interest in systems of education. Each suited its time, but I have a permanent affinity with only one, the ancient Greek. When I read that the Greeks educated their young people on poetry, gymnastics and music, I feel that I know what that means, and I constantly read (and profit by) the writings of most learned professors of Greek culture, who I am sure don't know what they are talking about.[37]

It is the notion of a natural affinity between the contemporary Caribbean and ancient Greece that enables C.L.R. James to bypass 'European colonialist scholarship', as epitomised by J.A. Froude (1888), for example. *Beyond a Boundary*, the book from which the above quotation was taken, was written before Trinidad gained independence. Rather than symbolising a remote apex of Western culture, James' ancient Greece is a model for what the Caribbean might become, in the spheres of literature and politics. At the same time, James' understanding of the Caribbean region and its particular history and sociology informs his interpretation of ancient Greek institutions.

The process of cross-fertilisation whereby ancient Greece is cast in a Caribbean image is most evident in James' study of the role of cricket as a means of West Indian national expression. For James, cricket is a drama and it fulfils a comparable function within West Indian society to that fulfilled by drama (tragedy and comedy) in Athenian society.[38] Although James read the ancient Greek tragedians – particularly Aeschylus – avidly, he does not depict them as hallowed authors.[39] Rather, in James' view, the relevance of Greek tragedy for the Caribbean lies in the sociopoetics of Athenian drama: in the crowd and their participation. Whereas Plato derided what he dubbed the *theatrokratia* (the rule of the theatre audience) in the *Laws*, James embraces the world of the spectators as the key to understanding ancient Athenian drama.[40]

In the pre-independence history of the game of cricket that James chronicles in *Beyond a Boundary,* the *agôn* between the batsmen and the bowler was constitutive of social and racial tensions. James identifies this symbolic confrontation at the wicket with 'the central action that characterizes all good drama from the days of the Greeks to our own: two individuals are pitted against each other in a conflict that is strictly personal but no less strictly representative of a social group'. It is beyond a doubt that the *agônes* of Athenian drama were 'representative of a social group'; although how the one-on-one rivalry of the batsmen and the bowler would map onto the complex matrix of contending positions depicted in any one tragedy is less clear. But to begin to scrutinise the details of the analogy is to miss the point and to misconstrue James' purpose and his perception of the kind of history that needs to be told of ancient Greece in a Caribbean context (to meet 'the national need').

In fact, like Walcott, James detects cultural influence in both directions. Thus, in the following quotation, James begins by evoking the institution of Athenian drama to make a point about cricket as a cultural fixture. Athenian drama is the cultural reference point. However, having set up the comparison, James then proposes, daringly, that Caribbean cricket can elucidate the question of the origin of Greek drama:

> Once every year for four days the tens of thousands of Athenian citizens sat in the open air on the stone seats at the side of the Acropolis and from sunrise to sunset watched the plays of the competing dramatists. All that we have to correspond is a Test match. The manner in which the drama arrived will tell us something valuable about Test matches *and (for the moment let us whisper it) the way Test matches arrived may start a trail into that vexed question: the origin of Greek drama.*[41]

Many of the references to ancient Greece in *Beyond a Boundary* are figurative: when the cricketer George John was dropped from some of the matches in the Trinidadian side's 1923 tour, and sat, sulking in a remote corner of the pavilion, James describes him as 'gloomily resentful, like Achilles in his tent' (1994: 75). When Shannon – one of the foremost rivals of James' own club, Maple – beat Maple by only one wicket in an epic game, James comments that 'you would have thought that they were the last of the Three Hundred at Thermopylae' (1994: 56). It is notable that the only instance in which James points to the incongruity of 'classics' in the Caribbean is when he narrates how the cricketer George John surprised him with his uncharacteristically philosophical attitude to a dropped catch in the slips. James comments, 'It was as if he had quoted a line of Virgil at me. He must have sensed my surprise' (1994: 77). This passage seems to accord with the view that in Trinidadian society of this time, Latin was the mark of an elite cultural education (cf. Williams' boast 'we speak Latin in Trinidad'). Although ancient Greece and ancient

Greek had a greater rarity value than ancient Rome and Latin in the twentieth-century Caribbean, in James' works Greece is not perceived to be as alienating as ancient Rome; perhaps the inaccessibility of Greek in relation to Latin meant that Greek did not enter the cultural equation in the way that Latin did.[42] Just as James claimed that his particular inheritance equipped him to understand aspects of education in ancient Greece that professional scholars did not comprehend, he suggests that the ancient Greeks would have understood Caribbean issues. In the course of his narrative of the Trinidadian cricketer, Telemaque, who was omitted from the 1923 tour on (suspected) grounds of race and colour (Telemaque was a dark black ship-front worker), James describes how his fellow workers and the people in his neighbourhood wept public tears at the injustice of this exclusion: 'No wonder men and women stood around and wept. Plato and Pythagoras, Socrates and Demosthenes would have understood that these public tears expressed no private grief' (1994: 70).

The Athens of the Caribbean

When Eric Williams entered politics in Trinidad, he embarked upon a demagogic campaign to educate the Trinidadian masses in politics and Caribbean nationalism. To this end he set up an adult education programme in September 1954. This educational programme consisted of a series of lectures centred on the Trinidad Public Library in Port of Spain; among the lectures that Williams delivered in November 1954 was a polemical lecture on 'Some Misconceptions of Aristotle's Philosophy of History', in which he attacked the arguments put forward by a local educator and Benedictine monk, the Reverend Dom Basil Matthews, for the view that religion should have a hand in education.[43] The classical subject was not an anomaly; one of Williams' pedagogical aims was to educate his audiences about the democratic tradition in Western civilisation and this theme gave rise to frequent references to ancient Athenian politics and culture.[44]

When Williams finally parted ways with the Caribbean Commission in June 1955, he announced his plan to form a political party by giving a lecture in Woodford Square – an open square in the Port of Spain – to an estimated audience of 10,000 people.[45] This square became the venue for frequent lectures / political speeches, and Williams referred to this square as the 'University of Woodford Square', drawing parallels between this open-air auditorium and ancient Athenian institutions in which the *dêmos* was schooled in the ways of politics:

The University of Woodford Square has for the past 12 years been a centre of free university education for the masses, of political analysis and of training in self-government for parallels of which we must go back to the city state of ancient Athens. The lectures have been university dishes served with political sauce.[46]

Speaking on 'Party Politics' in Woodford Square on 13 September 1955, Williams ended his lecture with a quotation from Pericles' funeral oration (Thucydides 2.35-46), promising that his party – the People's National Movement – would hold up to the electorate 'the ideal of the ancient democracy of Athens'. After recounting the occasion of this lecture in his autobiography, Williams recalls that when Harold Macmillan visited Trinidad and heard about the institution of the 'University of Woodford Square', he described Trinidad and Tobago as 'the Athens of the Caribbean'.[47]

We have seen above how C.L.R. James frequently likens aspects of ancient Athenian cultural life to the Caribbean in *Beyond a Boundary*. Elsewhere, James adduces demographic arguments to suggest that Trinidad (or any other Anglophone Caribbean island, for that matter) is a potential 'Athens in the Caribbean'. In a lecture first delivered in 1959 at Mona in Jamaica, James argues that the size of the ancient Greek polis (which he gives as 50,000 citizens) demonstrates that art thrives in relatively small communities like the Caribbean islands (1977: 186-7):

> Is everything historical, the whole history of art against us in the Caribbean? I don't think so. You will have noticed the references I make to Greece, where the political form was the city state, to Florence, Rome, to Toledo. These were cities in which it was possible for the impact of the artist to be felt by a substantial number of the population. This world in little concentrated his own impressions and theirs. I believe that this was the environment which created more men of genius in a Greek or Florentine city of 50,000 citizens than in modern societies of 150 million. … our situation in the Caribbean is very similar. Trinidad and Barbados are already very close in their demographic structure to the cities of ancient Greece or the Italian towns of the middle ages.[48]

To prove that this is no idle analogy, James proceeds to identify a Caribbean artist who is good enough for the ancient Greeks. One example he gives is the Calypso artist, Sparrow, of whom James claims: 'I believe Shakespeare would have listened very carefully to him and Aristophanes would have given him a job in his company' (1977: 188).[49] In the prose works of C.L.R. James and Derek Walcott, Greece is held up as a cultural paradigm for how to overcome a geographical situation, which might otherwise lead to a region becoming a cultural backwater, through art. Writing about 'Society and the Artist' in the Jamaican journal *Public Opinion* in 1957, Walcott remarked: 'Without them [*sc.* artists] Greece would have been a Tourist Resort, and these islands will be beautiful but dumb.'[50]

Walcott, writer of classics

Walcott's encounter with Homer in *Omeros* has a long history: not only is *Omeros* the apex of an ongoing experiment in Walcott's poetics, but, as we have seen, it also belongs within a broader Caribbean intellectual tradition of using Ancient Greece as a cultural reference point. If we approach the Odyssean motifs in Walcott's oeuvre in light of this tradition, it is possible to sense the influence of *Froudacity* in Walcott's approach to the myth of Odysseus. In Thomas' work, more important than the explicit Greek and Latin references[51] is the overarching paradigm of Froude as a latter-day Ulysses whose travels symbolise an ill-conceived exercise in racist ethnography:[52]

> Like the ancient hero, one of whose warlike equipments furnishes the complementary title of the book, the author of *The English in the West Indies*; or, *The Bow of Ulysses, sallied forth from his home to study, if not cities, at least men (especially black men)*, and their manners in the British Antilles.[53]

Thomas' character sketch of Froude as an ill-informed and myopic Ulysses is recalled by Walcott's poem, 'Prelude', in which Walcott refers to the islands of the Caribbean as:

> Found only
> In tourist booklets, behind ardent binoculars;
> Found in the blue reflection of eyes
> That have known cities and think us here happy.[54]

We can detect a reference to the opening lines of the *Odyssey* in these lines,[55] but this reference is mediated through the Froude-Ulysses motif in *Froudacity*. In the Francophone Caribbean, Aimé Césaire's *Cahier d'un Retour au Pays Natal* offers a Caribbean *nostos*, which combines the notion of the journey away from the metropolis, with ideas of literary departure, and distance from Western civilisation.[56] Hence, in 'Prelude', the classical allusion to Homer's *Odyssey* alludes, simultaneously, to local re-readings of the Homeric epics.[57] Or, to put it another way, the Homeric epics already have a distinctive tradition of reception in the Caribbean prior to Walcott's *Omeros*.

In a poem entitled 'Homecoming: Anse la Raye' (dedicated to his childhood friend, Garth St Omer) Walcott reflects on the two of them in school 'like solemn Afro Greeks eager for grades', learning about 'Helen and the shades of borrowed ancestors' (*CP*: 127).[58] There are other instances of Walcott playing with the inherent shock value of such juxtapositions as 'Afro Greeks'. In part four of the volume *Another Life* ('The Estranging Sea'), Walcott addresses his St Lucian friend, the painter Dunstan St Omer:

> But, ah Gregorias,
> I christened you with that name because
> it echoes the blest thunders of the surf,
> because you painted our first, primitive frescoes,
> because it sounds explosive,
> a black Greek's!
>
> *Collected Poems*, 293-4

We are given a vision of what the young Walcott learnt and taught himself as an Afro-Greek in the poem 'The Divided Child'. Walcott's inventiveness in this poem, written in 1973, already looks forward to the passage in *Omeros* (book 7, chapter 56: iii) where Walcott tells the apparition of Homer, that: 'master, I was the freshest of all your readers'.[59] In the earlier poem the young Walcott enacts magic lantern shows, apparently parodying classroom lessons, prompted by a didactic voice: 'Boy! Who was Ajax?' Walcott's imagination translates Homer into his world by christening the characters of his local community: Ajax is a horse, the blind albino Darnely is the Homeric bard, but, as if to show how the label 'Greek' has lent itself to all sorts of things, the 'Greekest' figure in this community is the transvestite who embodies the Victorian notion of Greek love:

> Gaga,
> The town's transvestite, housemaid's darling,
> is window-shopping, swirling his plastic bag,
> before his house-boy's trip to Barbados,
> *most Greek of all*, the love that hath no name, ...

It is only through such feats of adaptation that Homer 'fits' into the world of St Lucia. In chapter 5 of the same poem, we are given an insight into a schoolroom where the 'boy' of Walcott's childhood is being tested on the Latin motto of St Lucia: *statio haud malefida carinis* (Vergil's tag) (*CP*: 172).[60] Prompted about the position of Castries in the hierarchy of the best harbours in the world, the schoolboy replies, on cue:

> 'Sah, Castries ees a coaling station and
> der twenty-seventh best harba in der worl'!
> In eet the entire Breetesh Navy can be heeden!'
> 'What is the motto of St. Lucia, boy?'
> '*Statio haud malefida carinis.*'
> 'Sir!'
> 'Sir'
> 'And what does that mean?'
> 'Sir, a safe anchorage for sheeps!'

As well as alienating the teacher from the reader, this exchange also alienates the poet who switches into phonetic spellings in order to imitate the speech pattern or accents of the student – albeit that the schoolboy is probably the young Walcott – and who is hence forced into the position of outsider.[61] From a postcolonial perspective, the poem offers an indictment of education as sponsored by colonial powers whereby the pride and glory of the island of St Lucia is its ability to receive the entire British navy in its foremost harbour. Walcott's stance is ambivalent (if not trivalent, or polyvalent). There is disapproval for this kind of pedagogy, but also collusion from a poet who takes pride in his knowledge of Latin. One thinks of the poem 'The Hotel Normandie Pool', in which Walcott stages a conversation with the ghost of Ovid. Addressing Ovid in Latin, Walcott refers, nostalgically, to 'the lovely Latin lost in all our schools' (cf. above).

Walcott's experience of Latin in the classroom, from the perspective of both teacher and student, is explored in the poem 'A Latin Primer' (Walcott 1988: 21-4) – as a schoolboy Walcott learnt Latin at St Mary's College and then stayed on to teach Latin and Art as a Junior Master.[62] Walcott the schoolboy picks from distant literatures to adorn his education, but at the same time, resents aspects of learning Latin. The image of 'the bronze dusk of imperial palms / [curling] their fronds into questions / over Latin exams' encapsulates the awkward legacy of Latin and, in the following stanza, the strokes of scansion become like strokes of the lash: 'darkening discipline'. However, the backlash – the gesture of skipping a pebble into the sea in rage – imitates the rhythms that he has been learning in scansion, suggesting an association often made in Walcott's poetry that there is a natural or geographical parallelism between ancient Greece and Rome and the physical environment of St

Lucia, which he, the New World Poet, like Adam, is naming and inventing for the first time.[63] The poem then shifts to the perspective of teacher and Walcott drilling Latin verbs into his students:

> I taught Love's basic Latin:
> *Amo, amas, amat.*
>
> The discipline I preached
> made me a hypocrite;
> their lithe black bodies, beached,
> would die in dialect;

Walcott speaks of 'neither world being theirs'. In the end, the tension between the two cultures is expressed by the image of a Frigate bird: *Fregata magnificens* in Latin, *ciseau-la-mer* (sea-scissors) in St Lucian patois. This exercise in translation whereby St Lucian patois has a word for Latin terms echoes the strategy of viewing the Caribbean as analogous to, contemporary to, and parallel to ancient Greece. Not because Walcott ignores the historical context of Homer, but because he conceives of the Caribbean, like Homer's Greece, as its own beginning – exempt from the trajectories of history that the West recognises.

We can subdivide this parallelism into two different categories. The first category is that of *historical parallelism*. Whereas European colonisers were tempted to see the Caribbean as the polar opposite of ancient Greece ('new' as opposed to 'old' world), Walcott puts the two side by side, so that the two regions of the world become mutually suggestive. Walcott has a way of collapsing the centuries between the Caribbean and Greece, resulting in a Greece in the present tense, before the 'past' of history set in.

In poem 43 of the Collection *Midsummer*, entitled *Tropic Zone*, Walcott sees the Caribbean and Greece as analogous, denying the constraints of time imposed by imperialism, which would keep the Caribbean and ancient Greece separate. This is back to the idea of 'Afro Greeks' (a phrase which is pregnant with controversy in light of Martin Bernal's *Black Athena*). Walcott often uses the metaphor of the 'shallows' of the Caribbean sea to evoke its lack of official history, in contrast to the depths of ancient Greece; but then proceeds to undercut this antithesis by levelling Greece with the Caribbean, pointing to the seedier and more garish aspects of ancient Greek society:

> Only the *shallows* of this inland ocean mutter
> lines from another sea, which this one resembles –
> myths of analogous islands of olive and myrtle,

the dream of the drowsing Gulf. Although her temples,
white blocks against green, are hotels, and her stoas
shopping malls, in time they will make good ruins;
...
Genius will come to contradict history,
and that's there in their brown bodies, in the olives of eyes,
as when the pimps of demotic Athens threaded the chaos
of Asia, and girls from the stick villages, henna-whores,
were the hetaerae.

Collected Poems, 500

From the shallows of this sea comes the 'raw' material for Walcott's poetic oeuvre. Thus in the 'The Villa Restaurant', Walcott envisages ancient marble busts telling him: 'Your sea has its own *Iliads*, / *Noli me tangere*.'[64]

Another aspect of the parallelism is *geographical parallelism*, in which the archipelagoes of modern Greece and the Caribbean are brought into comparison; sometimes the effect of this comparison is dissonance, when a superficial geographical likeness proves misleading. Thus in the poem 'Gros-Ilet', Walcott addresses the drifting soul of Elpenor, telling him not to settle in the Caribbean, much that it might resemble Greece, his home:

Elpenor,
...
keep moving, there is nothing here for you.
There are different candles here and customs here, the dead
are different. Different shells guard their graves.
There are distinctions beyond the paradise
of our horizon. *This is not the grape-purple Aegean.*
There is no wine here, no cheese, the almonds are green,
the sea-grapes bitter, the language is that of slaves.[65]

This play with the geographical parallelism picks up on a habit of the early European cartographers who sometimes did see the Caribbean archipelago as a potential mirror image of Greece, naming Andros in the Bahamas after Andros in Greece because it has the same size, shape and orientation as the Greek island. Walcott describes such Hellenocentric cartography in *The Bounty*, but insists that the symmetry is mutual: 'in maps the Caribbean dreams / of the Aegean, and the Aegean of reversible seas'.[66]

In the poem 'White Magic' this insistence on distance is explained in part as a counter-reaction to the cultural chauvinism that invests in Greek mythology, while rejecting Caribbean myths as 'ignorance':

> these fables of the black and the poor
> marbled by moonlight, will grow white and richer.
> Our myths are ignorance, theirs are literature.[67]

But in other instances the geographical parallel encourages solidarity. As a result of the patronising attitude fostered by European imperialism, according to which the cultures of the Caribbean could only ever be poor copies of colonial paradigms, the Caribbean is in a position to console modern Greece on its secondariness to ancient Greece and its struggle to achieve an independent cultural identity, as opposed to being treated like a poor copy of an ancient Greek paradigm. In several interviews, Walcott has explained his interest in modern Greece (in spite of not having visited Greece) as due to the fact that the Greeks are like 'the niggers of the Mediterranean'.

There have been some searching critical discussions of the dialogue between Walcott and a Greek woman called Antigone (*Omeros* book 1, chapter 2: iii) which leads to him giving his epic a modern Greek title.[68] In Walcott's stage version of the *Odyssey*, he evokes the junta of the Colonels in Greece to symbolise the desolation of what life under the Cyclops or under the suitors might look like [act 1, scene 8]. In the poem 'From this Far',[69] a Greek tanker on the ocean prompts Walcott to think of the modern Greek poets Cavafy and Seferis and their complex relationship with the ancient Greek past. In Walcott's imagination the ship becomes a cultural vehicle, with 'a cargo of marble heads; / from Orpheus to Onassis'. Walcott alludes to Seferis' poetry in which buried marble statues and ruins symbolise the underlying layers of Greek culture in all its different historical guises, protruding through the surface, always being dug up and interfering with the present:[70]

> in the soil of our islands, no gods are buried.
> They were shipped to us, Seferis,
> dead on arrival.
>
> *Collected Poems*, 414

The reference to Seferis' poetry becomes more specific as the poem proceeds: in section 3, Walcott writes, 'I remember you holding a heavy marble head'. This line refers to the third poem in Seferis' sequence *Mythistorêma* (written Dec. 1933 – Dec. 1934), which begins: 'I woke with this marble head in my hands' (translation from Keeley and Sherrard 1995: 5). In Seferis' poem the marble head is a dead weight. This allusion recurs in *Omeros*, where the figure of Omeros / Homer is a marble bust.[71] Although Walcott disclaims the cultural inheritance of

Greece in the poem 'From this Far' ('I stayed with my own.'), the fact that the poem entails a complex web of allusion to Greek literature from Homer to Seferis immediately undermines this claim. In fact, the claim itself could even be seen as a version of the ancient Greek and Roman literary trope of *recusatio*.[72]

While Walcott has made a point of not knowing Greek and not having read all of Homer, his poetry puts his classical education into many different, heterogeneous and non-obvious uses: speaking to Homer as a contemporary, through modern Greece. As I have argued, there are very good reasons why Walcott resists attempts to categorise *Omeros* as 'Homeric' which relate to a more general unease about the role of criticism and critics in mediating the position of postcolonial or commonwealth literature in the canon of world literature. In response to a question posed by Nancy Schoenberger about the 'epic' proportions of his poem 'The Schooner Flight', Walcott replied:

> The only epical thing in 'The Schooner Flight' is the width of the sea, for which I'm not responsible. It's not my intention to have a hero who takes on battles, who becomes an emblematic figure. The fact is, critics are looking for a repetition of the past; one wants a sort of *Iliad* in blackface. Writers won't do that, what's new about a classic is that is stays new.
>
> Interview with Nancy Schoenberger (1983), in Baer ed. 1996: 92

The remark that 'What's new about a classic is that it stays new,' explains how Walcott is able to conceive of many of his poems as parallel to or contemporary to Homer. What better way to promote your own status as a classic than to insist on simultaneity among works of great literature and to work with an alternative theory of the relationships between past and present that dominate the discipline of classics as we know it?

> and my own prayer is to write
> lines as mindless as the ocean's of linear time,
> since time is the first province of Caesar's jurisdiction.[73]

Notes

Italics in quotations are my own.

1. Grantley Adams was the first premier of Barbados (1954-8), which was then a self-governing colony, and was subsequently the Prime Minister of the West Indies Federation. He received his Hellenocentric education at Harrison College in Barbados, and in 1918 he won the Barbados scholarship to Oxford, where he began his undergraduate career in 1919.

2. Walcott 1990 and 1993, respectively.

3. Cf. Taplin 1990; Cartledge 1993; Davis 1997; and Hardwick 2000 (the latter also discusses Walcott's responses to Homer as a two-way intercultural exchange).

4. On 'reading backwards' cf. Dougherty 1997; on alterity and opposition to dominant cultures as aspects of ancient Greek and Roman epic, cf. Farrell 1997 (especially 251-2). Farrell's reading finds confirmation in the work of the Martinican intellectual, Edouard Glissant: 'However, and this is an immense paradox, the great founding books of communities, the Old Testament, the *Iliad*, the *Odyssey*, the *Chansons de Geste*, the Icelandic Sagas, the *Aeneid*, or the African epics, were all books about exile and often about errantry. This epic literature is amazingly prophetic. It tells of the community, but, through relating the community's apparent failure or in any case its being surpassed, it tells of errantry as a temptation (the desire to go against the root), and, frequently, actually experienced' (Glissant 1997: 15).

5. On 'writing back' cf. n. 7 below.

6. Williams 1969. Williams was Prime Minister of Trinidad and Tobago from 1962-81.

7. The phrase 'the empire writes back' – which became a slogan for subaltern or postcolonial studies – originated in the title of an article by Salman Rushdie: 'The Empire Writes Back with a Vengeance', *The Times*, 3 July 1982: 8. Cf. Ashcroft, Griffiths, and Tiffin 1989.

8. Williams was at Oxford from 1932-9 (his DPhil was conferred in December 1938, for the doctoral dissertation 'The Economic Aspect of the Abolition of the West Indian Slave Trade and Slavery'); Trinidad gained independence on 31 August 1962.

9. Williams 1969: 34-5.

10. Cf. the allusion to Caesar (ibid. 43): 'I had come, seen and conquered – at Oxford! What next?'. On the equation between mastery of classics and political mastery in Trinidadian politics in the first half of the twentieth century, cf. nn. 42-4 below.

11. *The English in the West Indies. The Bow of Ulysses*. The full title of J.J. Thomas' work, which was published the following year in 1889, is *Froudacity. West Indian Fables Explained*.

12. James in Thomas 1969: 25.

13. The reference is to Xenophon's *Anabasis* 2.3.15, where Xenophon uses the adjective 'kephalalgês' to describe a variety of dates that taste pleasant, but cause headaches.

14. The Caribbean can be said to be 'on the frontiers' of Europe by virtue of the imperial relationship whereby Caribbean colonies were perceived to be peripheral to European metropolises. Cf. Birbalsingh 1996: ix.

15. Davis 1997a: 12.

16. Cf. Nettleford 1992: 88-9, who argues that it is precisely the continuity of European ideas and Latinate language that has made it possible for the French to assimilate Césaire as a 'French' poet, as opposed to a Martinican / Caribbean poet.

17. I was first made aware of the existence of this article by King 2000: 65 (with n. 23, p. 636).

18. Francois 1978: 5. Francois wrote this article in support of a letter by Luther Gajadhar on 'The Value of Latin' that had appeared in the *Voice of St*

Lucia on 9 March 1978: 2. Gajadhar's letter had argued that Latin is instrumental for mastering the terminology used in professions such as law or medicine, not to mention the Romance languages. He had also advocated the mental discipline to be derived from studying Latin: 'Then too, the mental discipline and linguistic refinement achieved in translating Latin is seldom achieved with the possible exception of Greek. It has been said that a Latin sentence is like a Roman column on the march all under the undisputed leadership of a main verb.'

19. ibid. (the omissions are present in Francois' article). The alleged prevalence of Negroes in ancient Athens and Rome and their status as 'full citizens' is inventive, but meaningful in light of the process of (re)possessing the Graeco-Roman past for Africans and their descendants, from Marcus Garvey to Martin Bernal. For further discussion of the triangular dialogue between the Caribbean, Africa, and Graeco-Roman antiquity, see E. Greenwood 2004. For a brief discussion of Garvey, cf. below.

20. On the sociology of classics as a discipline vis-à-vis racial politics, cf. Haley 1989 (for a black American perspective).

21. Cf. the reference to Wordsworth's 'Daffodils' in Jamaica Kincaid's novel *Lucy* (1990: 17-18), quoted in Donnell and Welsh eds 1996: 491-2. Cf. also ibid. 4-5 on the texts promoted by school syllabuses in British colonies in the Caribbean.

22. Walcott 1997: 232. From a talk entitled 'Reflections on *Omeros*' which was originally delivered at Duke University in the spring of 1995.

23. Walcott 1996: 23.

24. On the patronising influence of chronology, cf. Walcott 1997: 241. Walcott has written about the tyranny of history in the New World in 'The Muse of History' (Walcott 1998: 36-64).

25. Walcott 1998: 51.

26. For the latter argument, cf. Mary Lefkowitz's review of *Omeros*: 'Mr Walcott's epic is a timely reminder that the past is not the property of those who first created it: it always matters to all of us, no matter who we are or where we were born' (Lefkowitz 1990: 35).

27. Cf. 'The Fact of Blackness' in *Black Skin, White Masks*: 'The Negro, however sincere, is the slave of the past. None the less I am a man, and in this sense the Peloponnesian War is as much mine as the invention of the compass' (quoted in Ashcroft, Griffiths, and Tiffin eds 1995: 326).

28. For a definition of 'national literature' by a Caribbean intellectual, cf. Glissant 1989: 99: 'I define national literature as the urge for each group to assert itself: that is, the need not to disappear from the world scene and on the contrary to share in its diversification'. Cf. King 2000: 42 who imputes to Walcott 'the nationalist task of avoiding the European prejudices that nothing of value really existed in the New World'.

29. Cf. Walcott in Baer ed. 1997: 158: 'Therefore, the strength of the sea gives you an idea of time that makes history absurd. ... and by history I mean a direction that is progressive and linear. With the sea you can travel the horizon in any direction, you can go from left to right or from right to left' (interviewed by J.P. White). On the reversibility of the Homeric references in Walcott, Cf. Dougherty 1997, especially 336, 339, and 355-6. Dougherty has exemplified this idea of 'reading backwards' by taking Walcott as her point of departure for her recent work on Homer (cf. ch. 1 of Dougherty 2001).

30. 'The Hotel Normandie Pool' was first published in the volume *The Fortunate Traveller* (1981).

31. Walcott 1997b: 75.

32. Garvey 1977: 165-6; cf. also ibid. 64. Compare Thomas 1969: 180: 'We see that in the past different races have successively come to the front, as prominent actors on the world's stage. The years of civilized development have dawned in turn on many sections of the human family, and the Anglo-Saxons, who now enjoy pre-eminence, got their turn only after Egypt, Assyria, Babylon, Greece, Rome and others had successively held the palm of supremacy.'

33. James 1977: 189.

34. Cf. James 1980: 179: 'And here let me, in advance, correct a misunderstanding very prevalent today. I denounce European colonialist scholarship. But I respect the learning and the profound discoveries of Western civilization.'

35. Cf. James 1994: 28: 'I spent eight years in its [sc. Queen's Royal College] classrooms. I studied Latin with Virgil, Caesar and Horace, and wrote Latin verses. I studied Greek with Euripides and Thucydides.'

36. Cf. ibid. 33: 'All this had nothing to do with my education in school. ... what was even more tragic was that boys who after six years had acquired a remarkable competence in Latin and Greek treated them ever afterwards as dead languages. All that did not encourage me to change my ways.'

37. James 1994: 32-3.

38. Cf. Lazarus 1999: 149.

39. Cf. ibid. 157: 'Aeschylus, Sophocles and Euripides were not culture.' James views these tragedians as popular entertainers.

40. On the notion of an organic relationship between ancient Greece and the contemporary Caribbean, cf. *Omeros* book 7, chapter 59: iii: 'All that Greek manure under the green bananas.' This line is read as an expression of the tension between the 'cultural enrichment' offered by classical culture, and the incongruity of Greek influences in the Caribbean landscape, given the Greek associations of empire and slavery. Cf. Hardwick 2000: 99, from whom I have taken the phrase 'cultural enrichment'.

41. ibid. 158.

42. Admittedly the cultural associations of Latin and Greek were more complicated than the simple dichotomy that I have sketched here. If Eric Williams and his peers 'spoke Latin in Trinidad', it was the scholars of Barbados who claimed real cultural prestige through their mastery of Greek – cf. the example of Grantley Adams quoted above. Speaking of his schooling in St Lucia, Derek Walcott has often commented that while he got to learn Latin, his contemporaries in Barbados learnt Latin *and* Greek (Walcott interviewed by Rowell in Baer ed. 1996: 125). Cf. Cudjoe 1993: 42, on the sociology of language in pre-independence Trinidad: 'Because most members of the bourgeois class aspired to "speak properly" it was not unusual for a person who wanted to be perceived as being educated to spice his language with as many Latin quotations as possible to show his distinctive difference from the ordinary masses.'

43. Delivered at the Trinidad Public Library on 17 November 1954. A summary of this lecture was published in the *Trinidad Guardian*, 18 November 1954 (p. 10). The 'Aristotle' debate originated during the question time that followed a lecture given by Williams at the Port of Spain Public Library on 'Some World Famous Theories and Developments Relevant to West Indian

3. 'We Speak Latin in Trinidad'

Conditions'. In question time Dom Basil Matthews had challenged Williams' citation of Aristotle to illustrate the argument that state education should be secular. Subsequently Matthews gave a lecture, again at the Public Library, on 9 November 1954 on the topic 'Aristotle, Education and State Control' [summary in the *Trinidad Guardian*, 11 November 1954 (p. 12)]. It was this lecture that provoked Williams' lecture on 'Some Misconceptions of Aristotle's Philosophy of Education'. Cf. Williams 1969: 113-14.

44. Cf. Cudjoe 1993: 49-50, on the same debate. Cudjoe explains the political significance of the debate as follows: 'Williams' victory in this oratorical contest (for contest it was) and the demonstration of his mastery of the language and subject matter of the master philosopher signified an important moment in the launching of Williams' public career. Because of his mastery over the classics, in the public's eye, Williams assumed the role of the prodigal son in possession of the full power of the master's language.' Cudjoe (cf. especially 51) traces a shift in Williams' political development, in which Williams increasingly downplayed Latin and the emphasis on elite education in favour of greater respect for Trinidadian patois and the culture of the masses. Oxaal 1968: 104-5 also offers a commentary on the 'Aristotle' debate. The 'Aristotle' debate between Williams and Matthews, and Williams' duplicitous appropriations of Aristotelian philosophy in particular, merit a separate study.

45. Williams 1969: 131.

46. ibid. 133.

47. ibid. 135-6.

48. Compare Walcott on the prejudice that the tropics aren't supposed to produce anything: 'It's a sort of Graham Greenish fantasy about the tropics that was perpetuated. But Greece is a hot country, and you've got to ask: What has Greece produced?' (interviewed by David Montenegro, in Baer ed. 1996: 138). Here the example of Greece's cultural exports functions as an enabling comparison for the Caribbean.

49. For another parallel between Caribbean humour and the Old Comedy of ancient Greece, cf. Walcott in Baer ed. 1996: 84: 'I keep my vulgarity healthy by living in a 'backward' but hearty place, the Caribbean. There laughter is loud and ringing, weeping is wailing, everything is at the pitch it must have been with the early Greeks. Primal, even provincial tragedy, bawdy, vulgar, even cliché humor. Suppose Aristophanes had had good taste?'

50. In Hamner ed. 1997: 17.

51. Cf. above.

52. Cf. Dougherty 2001, for an account of Homer's *Odyssey* that focuses on its 'ethnographic imagination'. Cf. also Hartog 1996, for the Ulysses figure as a proto-ethnographer.

53. Thomas 1969: 63. My italics.

54. 'Prelude' was first published in the collection *Poems in a Green Night. Poems 1948-1960* (1962).

55. Cf. *Odyssey* 1.3 (my trans.): 'he saw the cities of many men and he learnt their ways of thinking'.

56. The first version of the *Cahier d'un Retour au Pays Natal* appeared in the Paris periodical *Volontés*, number 20, August 1939; it was first published in book form in 1947 (New York: Brentano's), and a definitive edition was published in 1956 (Paris: Présence Africaine). In a lecture on 'The Artist in the Caribbean' delivered in 1959 (referred to above), C.L.R. James described the

Cahier as 'the desperate cry of a Europeanised West Indian poet for reintegration with his own people' (James 1977: 189).

57. By 'local' I do not mean to imply 'provincial'. Walcott prefaces the poem 'Air' with a quotation from Froude 1888, which expresses Froude's view that 'There are no people there [*sc.* in the West Indies] in the true sense of the word, with a character and purpose of their own'. 'Air' was first published in the collection *The Gulf* (1970).

58. Here and henceforth *CP* refers to Walcott's *Collected Poems* (Walcott, 1992).

59. Walcott 1990: 283.

60. It is notable that Walcott points to the Vergilian origin of St Lucia's motto. The phrase '*statio male fida carinis*' occurs at *Aeneid* 2.23, in reference to the island of Tenedos, nearby Troy. In his narrative of Troy's fall, Aeneas tells how the Greeks launched their insidious assault on Troy from Tenedos and adds, in an aside, that this island was once prosperous when Priam was alive, but is 'now just a bay and an untrustworthy mooring place for ships' (*nunc tantum sinus et statio male fida carinis*). Hence the St Lucian motto interpolates the negation '*haud*' into the original Vergilian line to imply that the colony is safe and dependable vis-à-vis its colonial overlords. However, the Vergilian intertext suggests tensions between the St Lucians and the British imperial power.

61. The alienating Latin motto of St Lucia, drilled into schoolboys, is echoed in the Latin phrase 'victor ludorum' which is inscribed on the crowns in the Village Olympiad described in *Omeros* book 1, chapter 5: iii.

62. For the biographical context of 'A Latin Primer', cf. King 2000: 54-5. Walcott was a junior master at St Mary's from 1948-50. From 1950-3 he did a B.A. in liberal arts (including Latin) at the University of the West Indies in Jamaica, and stayed on for a D.Ed. (1953-4). He subsequently taught Latin and English as Assistant Master at Grenada Boys' Secondary School, St George for four months, before returning to teach at St Mary's in St Lucia. In 1955 Walcott took up a position teaching English, Latin, and French at Jamaica College, Kingston.

63. Cf. 'The Antilles: Fragments of Epic Memory', p. 79): 'A boy with weak knees skims a flat stone across the flat water of an Aegean inlet, and that ordinary action with the scything elbow contains the skipping lines of the *Iliad* and the *Odyssey* ... '. Compare *The Bounty*: 'All of these waves crepitate from the culture of Ovid, / its sibilants and consonants; a universal metre / piles up these signatures like inscriptions of seaweed' (Walcott 1997a: 11).

64. Walcott 1988: 26.

65. Walcott 1998: 34-5.

66. Walcott 1997a: 62.

67. Walcott 1998: 39.

68. Cf. Farrell 1997: 264 with n. 45.

69. Originally published in *The Fortunate Traveller* (1981). *Collected Poems*: 414-17.

70. Cf. Padel 1985: 92: 'Throughout Seferis' work 'statues' are an increasingly packed and serious shorthand sign for the apparently inert remnants of the past in the present. The past is in pieces, incarcerated in museums, yet pursues you with mysterious life of its own.'

71. Cf. *Omeros* book 1, ch. 2: iii, and book 7, ch. 56: i.

72. The trope of *recusatio* is associated primarily with Roman poetry, but it is no less a trope in Greek literature, ranging from the disavowal of Homeric epic in funeral orations (cf. e.g. Demosthenes *Funeral Oration*, 9-11 and Thucydides 2.41.4), to the Alexandrian poet Callimachus.

73. 'Tropic Zone', part i: Walcott 1992: 497.

4

The British Empire and the Neo-Latin Tradition:
The Case of Francis Williams

John Gilmore

The eighteenth-century Jamaican writer Francis Williams is a figure of considerable interest for two main reasons. In the first place, he appears to be the earliest black writer from the British Americas, and indeed the earliest black writer from anywhere in the English-speaking Atlantic world. His career predates that of better known figures like Phillis Wheatley (1753-84) from North America, or Black British writers like Olaudah Equiano (*c.* 1745-97) or Ignatius Sancho (1729-80).[1] Secondly, Williams was known mainly as a writer of Latin verses, something which made him an important symbolic figure for writers on both sides of the great debate about slavery in the late eighteenth and early nineteenth centuries. For defenders of white racial superiority such as the Scottish philosopher David Hume or the Jamaican historian Edward Long, it was essential to belittle Williams' intellectual accomplishments, while for anti-slavery writers like the Scottish clergyman James Ramsay or the French priest and politician Henri Grégoire, Williams was a major exhibit in their campaign to persuade Europeans of the humanity and equality of black people.[2]

In the past three decades, Williams has attracted the attention of many modern writers in the fields of Caribbean, Black British and African American history and literature, who have given him at least a passing mention, and sometimes more extended discussion. Recent examples include Thomas W. Krise, who finds space for Williams in his anthology *Caribbeana*, and Vincent Carretta, who puts Williams into an appendix of his Penguin Classics edition of the *Complete Writings* of Phillis Wheatley. All of these writers depend heavily, however, directly or indirectly, on the account of Williams given by Edward Long in his *History of Jamaica* (1774). With the exception of a recent study by Carretta ('Who was Francis Williams?'), which uses a much wider range of biographical sources, all of them appear to accept at face value Long's statements about the facts of Williams' life, and nearly all of them, whilst recognising the prejudice evident in Long's account, rely uncrit-

92

ically on the translation which Long provides of the Latin poem which Williams addressed to George Haldane, Governor of Jamaica, on his arrival in the island in 1759, and which remains the only work definitely ascribable to Williams which has survived (see Appendix).

I do not intend here to discuss Long's view of Williams, except in passing, or the tendentious nature of his translation of Williams' poem, which I have dealt with elsewhere (Gilmore 1998). Nor will I discuss the wider issue of Williams as a symbolic representative of black racial capacity. What I would like to do in the space available is to try to present some sort of context for the poem itself, and to look at what it is saying.

Francis Williams was born in Jamaica towards the end of the seventeenth century – his baptism was recorded there in 1697 – and he died there in 1762 (St Catherine Copy Register No. 1, pp. 40, 332). He was the third son of John and Dorothy Williams, who were free black people. This was an extremely unusual status in Jamaica, or indeed the entire Caribbean, at the time, when most black people were enslaved and Caribbean societies existed for the purpose of producing slave-grown sugar for export to Europe – exports which helped to create the wealth which led to the Industrial Revolution and Britain's commercial and military supremacy in the eighteenth and nineteenth centuries. It is also clear that Williams and his family were rich – again, highly unusual even for free black people in that time and place – and that, even if they were at times on the receiving end of prejudice and bigotry, they could also call on the help and influence of powerful acquaintances among the white oligarchy of Jamaica. Francis Williams received at least some of his education in Britain – he himself says in his poem 'Insula me genuit, celebres aluere *Britanni*' (l. 43), and he was admitted as a member of Lincoln's Inn in 1721. However, he had returned to Jamaica by late 1724 and he would appear to have spent the greater part of his life there.[3]

Edward Long suggested that Williams' poem was a 'rare phenomenon' – he meant because it came from the pen of a black writer. Modern writers on Williams have tended to view the poem in the same way, for somewhat different reasons, simply because they have been unable to locate any sort of context for it. For example, Locksley Lindo, a twentieth-century Jamaican classical scholar, says that:

> Williams' ode, interesting as it is, suffers from its isolation, and can be placed only with the greatest difficulty in the history of Caribbean Literature. There is no evidence to show what, if any, indigenous material existed from which it could draw, nor is there any evidence of contempo-

rary or immediately subsequent literary activity on which it could exert some influence.

Lindo 1970: 79

Now that Latin is no longer widely taught, there is a tendency to think that it is rather odd for anybody to be writing Latin poetry, and particularly odd for anybody from the Caribbean to be doing so. It might be possible to draw interesting parallels between Williams and Latin writers from the classical or immediately post-classical period of African origin such as Terence, Lactantius or Augustine, or with a figure like the sixteenth-century black Spanish Neo-Latin poet Johannes Latinus (Spratlin 1938). However, the most useful cultural context for Williams is almost certainly that of his own time, in which the study of the Greek and Roman classics in general and the composition of Latin verse in particular enjoyed considerable prominence.

At least one nineteenth-century writer of Barbadian origin wrote verses in classical Greek which his British contemporaries thought worthy of preservation, but he would seem to have been something of an exception. Although not one, but two Barbadian churches boasted seventeenth-century fonts with palindromic inscriptions in Greek, when in 1835 the Bishop of Barbados wanted to include Greek quotations in a locally printed charge, there was apparently no Greek type available, and the quotations had to be supplied in manuscript.[4]

Latin, on the other hand, has been more prominent in Caribbean history and literature since the days when some of the earliest works describing the Caribbean for a European reading public, such as one of Columbus' letters and the *Decades* of Peter Martyr, were first published in Latin. Material ranges from the Jesuit Andrew White's rather elegant Latin prose of a *Relatio Itineris in Marilandiam* in 1633, which includes some of the earliest description of the recently established English settlement in Barbados, to the appalling dog-Latin of a begging letter addressed to the Lieutenant-Governor of Jamaica in the mid-eighteenth century by a penniless Italian stranded on the island.[5]

One type of source material which offers something more than anecdotal evidence about the use of Latin is that offered by epitaphs and monumental inscriptions. A survey of published collections of such material for the British Caribbean suggests a proportion of Latin to English perhaps not very far removed from that to be found on monumental inscriptions in England in the eighteenth century.[6] While we recognise that this is somewhat slender evidence, it suggests that although Latin in the Caribbean was used only by an elite for special purposes, this was perhaps no more the case than it was in England. If

94

a Latin epitaph was intended as a status symbol, it probably did not need to be understood in its entirety (or at all) by the relatives of the deceased, or by more than a small proportion of the general public, in order to achieve the desired effect. However, one does wonder just who was supposed to be impressed by the Latin inscription set up 1797 over the door of the slave hospital at Orange Valley in Trelawney, Jamaica (Wright 1966: 262). Nevertheless, it is clear that at least in the larger Caribbean colonies in the seventeenth and eighteenth centuries there would always have been enough people like Robert Hooper, the Attorney General of Barbados who died in 1700, and who was described on his monument as *'Vir haud vulgariter eruditus et egregio Ingenii acumine ornatissimus'* (Oliver ed. 1915: 12) to provide a readership for such inscriptions, and to feel that one of the distinguishing marks of such a 'man uncommonly learned and greatly distinguished by an exceptional sharpness of intellect' was a good command of Latin. Edward Long's father, Samuel Long, might feel that 'Plain English wrote in an easy manner is more agreeable to the reader than high flights and forced conceits, larded with scraps of Latin and Greek without any coherence' and Edward Long himself felt that 'Scholarship' (i.e. classical scholarship) was more important from the point of view of prestige than of practical use: 'if it be of any real value, it must arise from the Honour of getting Rank'. In spite of this, and in spite of his having bridled at the schoolboy task of turning most of a book of the *Iliad* into Latin hexameters, Edward Long made sure that his sons got a conventional classical education: we find him praising his son Edward Beeston Long (born in Jamaica) for his efforts at Latin verse composition and for 'a very elegant and affectionate Epistle written in Classical latin, such as Pliny, ought not to have been shamed of', as well as supervising a younger son's blundering efforts to construe Ovid (Howard ed. 1925 vol. I: 102, 125, 141, 150, 154-5, 160).

A blunter expression of Samuel Long's doubts was given by a character in J.W. Orderson's *Creoleana*, a novel set in the Barbados of the 1790s. When the father of John Goldacre, the young hero, expresses the wish that he had spent more money on his son's education, his wife demands: 'And what's the good of all that grammar, Latin ... and outlandish gibberish they make such a fuss about? It won't buy the hair of a nigger, nor an acre of land ....' But young Goldacre is painfully aware that money is not enough to fit him for the hand of the heroine, and when he is free of his parents' immediate supervision, he sets out to get a proper education, which includes securing himself 'the able assistance of Mr. Cater, a man of unimpeachable morals, and of great classical attainment'.[7]

Mr. Cater was to be found in Bridgetown. As early as 1676 there were teachers of Latin in Barbados (Bridenbaugh and Bridenbaugh 1972: 396-7), and while the history of education in the Caribbean is a story of fluctuating fortunes, until the middle of the twentieth century the 'education of a young colonial' in the region meant, for the privileged few, the same sort of classical training which was long regarded in Britain as providing the best which Western civilisation had to offer. Sometimes, at least, the Caribbean was able to offer this kind of education to a standard at least equal to that which prevailed in the 'Mother Country' – as Eric Williams (the later Prime Minister of Trinidad and Tobago) found at Oxford in the 1930s, when his performance in an unseen translation from Ovid enabled him to put down 'a tall English chap with a long nose and an air the quintessence of superciliousness' with the retort, 'You see, we speak Latin in Trinidad.'[8] But while a few still-surviving Caribbean schools date back to the eighteenth century, and in that period it was sometimes possible for upper-class youths to be tutored by the local clergyman, it was often (elsewhere as well as in Jamaica), as Long put it (2002 [1774]: vol. II, 246-7):

> ... the custom for every father here, who has acquired a little property, to send his children, of whatever complexion, to Britain, for education. They go like a bale of dry goods, consigned to some factor, who places them at the school where he himself was bred, or any other that his inclination leads him to prefer.

A glance at the pedigrees and genealogical histories compiled by antiquarians of a previous generation[9] shows that many sons of planter families were sent to some of the best-known schools in England, and that many went on to university. The Creole who went to Edinburgh had most probably decided on a career in medicine – one bibliographer notes twelve medical dissertations in Latin published at Edinburgh in the second half of the eighteenth century by Barbadians alone.[10] Those who went to Oxford or Cambridge – still, until 1828, the only universities in England and Wales – found themselves in academic communities in which (whatever their failings in terms of narrowness of curriculum and lack of research in the modern sense) classical scholarship was treated with respect, and the ability to write Latin verses was regarded as the mark of an educated gentleman.

In England, the eighteenth century was perhaps the modern period when the composition of original Latin verses was most highly prized as an intellectual activity. In the words of Leicester Bradner's wide-ranging survey of Anglo-Latin poetry (1940: 226):

4. The British Empire and the Neo-Latin Tradition

> The eighteenth century represents the height of classical culture in England. Education in the great public schools consisted of a wide acquaintance with Greek and Latin writers and a smattering of mathematics. ... The ability to write Latin verse was implicitly accepted by most educators as one of the signs that a boy was proceeding satisfactorily in his work. The result was to spread this ability over the literate part of the population to a greater degree than ever before or since. At the same time the quality of the output – at least that part of it which got into print – improved considerably.

Well-known figures in English literature, such as Addison, Gray and Johnson, wrote Latin poetry as a matter of course. It was still possible for a man like Vincent Bourne to acquire a considerable reputation for his poetry in Latin alone – because he did not also write English poetry, he is now generally forgotten. Numerous anthologies and collections of Latin verse by modern writers were published in Britain, and some of this material has been the focus of scholarly attention in recent years.[11]

Latin verse was considered particularly suitable for commemorating great events, or for tributes to monarchs and other distinguished personages. One of the major outlets for Latin verse was the anthologies published by the two universities in honour of such occasions as a royal visit (or, more rarely, a visit by the nobleman who was the university's chancellor), a notable victory, the death of one sovereign and the accession of a new one, or a birth or marriage in the royal family. As Bradner comments, 'Such collections gave many members of the university an opportunity to appear in print, no matter how small their poetical ability, and they were therefore popular in academic circles' (1940: 99).

It is therefore not surprising that these anthologies include a few Latin poems by Caribbean writers, though they seem to have been generally ignored by students of Caribbean literature.[12] We find a figure well-known in Barbadian history, Christopher Codrington, expressing his devotion to William III in 1690.[13] In 1713 two Barbadians appear in an Oxford anthology in honour of the Peace of Utrecht: one of them, John Maynard, has a poem on the Asiento, which offers, in elegant hexameters, an apology for the slave trade as rescuing its fortunate victims from a barbarous Africa given to cannibalism and human sacrifice, while the other Barbadian, John Alleyn, contributed a poem on the South Sea Trade, which was reprinted in a general anthology of Latin verse in 1717.[14] Another Barbadian, this time a Cambridge man called James Edward Colleton, published a poem on the death of George I (1727),[15] and an Antiguan, John Gilbert, sang the praises of the Duke of Newcastle, Chancellor of the

97

University, when he visited Cambridge in 1755 to lay the foundation stone of the new university library.[16]

These poems cannot be dismissed as the work of men whose only connection with the Caribbean is the accident of birth. If the later career of Maynard is obscure, and Colleton seems to have spent most of the rest of his life in Britain, where he became a member of the Westminster parliament, Codrington, Alleyn and Gilbert all returned to the Caribbean. Other Caribbean pupils of the English universities and public schools must have produced similar poems which either have not survived or remain undiscovered. It may be generally true where poems of this sort – more or less written to order for particular occasions – are concerned, that, to quote Bradner again (*Musae Anglicanae*, p. 100), 'No matter how competent the handling of the Latin verse may be from the technical point of view, the lack of any genuine inspiration on the part of the writers usually prevented them from contributing anything of permanent value.' Nevertheless, these poems by Caribbean writers are both of interest in themselves, and valuable for the light they shed on Francis Williams.

Some of them suggest both originality and a sense of Caribbean identity on the part of the authors.[17] The opening line of Codrington's short poem offers 'Indian laurels' to William III; he then goes on to point out that his father is fighting for the King's cause in the Caribbean, and that he himself hopes soon to be following his father's example, sword in hand, instead of merely praising the King in song.[18] In the midst of much that is conventional, Colleton asserts that, following the death of George I, his successor George II will be worthy to guard 'the golden Indies, treasury of Europe, chambers of shining wealth'.[19] Particularly interesting is Alleyn's poem, *Commercium ad Mare Australe*, 'The South Sea Trade'.

Alleyn praises Robert Harley, the leading English politician of the day, and the British sovereign, Queen Anne, in fulsome terms, while gloating over the defeat of Britain's enemies. Harley is congratulated for having brought about a peace which opened up the Spanish American colonies to British trade. A large part of the poem is taken up with a fantastical description of the arrival of British ships on the coast of Chile, where the British sailors are met by the 'Southern natives', who are Amerindians, not Spanish colonists – in spite of being a 'savage race', the natives are more than friendly; they sing the praises of Queen Anne, and hasten to load the ships with gold and silver. Alleyn then continues his celebration of the advantages which the treaty has brought to British trade with a description of the Thames receiving the wealth of the Indies. So far this is the sort of thing which was written, in one form or another, by many Englishmen of the period. But in the conclusion of his poem Alleyn reminds his listeners or readers that he is not an Englishman at all, but a Barbadian:

> Tu quoque luxurians nativo Nectare Tellus,
> Chara mihi Patria, exultes; Tu debita jungas
> Gaudia; Te posthac supremo in limite Regni
> Non distare querar; non terminus Ultimus ANNÆ
> Sceptri eris: *Angliacum* nunc ipsum respicis *Austrum*,
> Teque Orbis mediam video, Imperiique *Britanni*.

For Alleyn, the third generation of his family to have been born in Barbados, his *patria*, his Fatherland, is not England, but Barbados. Alleyn's loyalty to the rule of Queen Anne, to the British Empire, is combined with an intense local patriotism, and his praise of Harley and the treaty he has brought about leads up to an assertion that it is no longer the metropolis, but the Caribbean colony which is at the centre of the Empire. Superficially this is stated in geographical terms, but Alleyn's description of Barbados points out its economic importance: It is a land abounding in its native nectar, the cane juice from which was obtained the sugar which was a source of wealth to England as well as Barbados. Implicit is the suggestion that the Peace of Utrecht will bring England increased profit from the sugar industry as well as from the possibility of Chilean gold.

When we look at Francis Williams' poem to Governor Haldane side by side with these other Latin poems by Caribbean writers and the anthologies of which they formed part, the poem addressed to Haldane begins to seem less unusual. It is not just that Williams was, as Long put it, 'fond of this species of composition in Latin, and usually addressed one to every new governor', though we may note the assumption that every new governor at least ought to have been able to appreciate such a tribute. Wherever he learnt to compose Latin verses (something which remains uncertain), Williams is writing in a well-established genre, and he shows his awareness not only of Latin poets of the classical period, but also of modern Latin writing by the way in which he suggests that Buchanan would have been better qualified to sing Haldane's praises. Long criticised Williams for comparing Buchanan to Vergil, but it is a most adroit piece of flattery on Williams' part, for Haldane, like Buchanan, was a Scot, and the achievements of George Buchanan (1506-82) as a Latin poet were a matter of national pride well into the eighteenth century.[20] The black Jamaican and the sons of white Creoles are writing in the same genre: Long complained that Williams' 'strain of superlative panegyric' was 'scarcely allowable even to a poet', but the work of the other poets shows that Williams is doing no more than what is characteristic of this type of poem at the period, and is, indeed, to be found in earlier examples in English, such as Aphra Behn's 'pindarick' on the Duke of Albemarle's voyage to Jamaica (1687), or the anonymous 1718 ode on Governor Lawes' arrival in the island (the earliest known example of Jamaican printing).[21] If John Gilbert hails the Duke of Newcastle as a Maecenas, the poem immediately before his in the same anthology (by an Englishman, Edward Tew) goes a step further and compares the Duke to Apollo. When we read Codrington saying that the Caribbean wants to weave her laurel wreaths into the 'sacred hair' of William III ('sacris texere serta comis'), or Colleton referring to the recently expired George I as 'Divus' as though he were a deified Roman emperor, it will not seem to us quite as much a matter for criticism as it did to Long that Williams should call Haldane 'the Cæsar of the West' – nor will we be terribly surprised to find a later colonial governor, who was a member of a prominent Creole family from the Leewards, calling himself 'Imperator & Gubernator Insularum Charib[æarum]' on a Latin inscription erected in Antigua in 1780.[22] Echoes of Vergil, Horace and Juvenal in Alleyn suggest the bias inherent in Long's criticism of Williams for using the same sort of echoes – criticism intended to suggest that the black poet was little better than a plagiarist, even though the recycling of phrases from classical authors was a widespread and accepted feature of modern Latin poetry. Alleyn's praise of Barbados can be paralleled by Williams' defence of his status as a black poet in a white world. The other poems make that of Williams look rather less of a 'rare phenomenon' – it is written within a set of established conventions, something which Long did his best to disguise in his attempts to put down Williams. This, I feel, makes it easier to appreciate Williams' position: he is unusual because he is black, not because he is a Caribbean poet writing in Latin.

To turn now, albeit briefly, to the poem itself. It begins by suggesting that, with Haldane's arrival, Jamaica will once more enjoy peace and the rule of law after a period of upheaval – very probably, as Long suggested, a reference to the turbulent politics of the island under a previous governor, Admiral Knowles. Haldane is praised as a soldier who has distinguished himself in battle against the French, the traditional enemy of Britain in the Caribbean, as elsewhere. He is the victor of Guadeloupe. He is twice referred to as *Optimus*. His native Scotland rejoices in his *genius* – perhaps here in the sense of intellectual distinction. Buchanan, that *decus patriæ* of the *patria* he and Haldane shared, would compare him to Achilles, and there is no doubt Haldane and other readers are intended to take it that the comparison would be a fitting one. He is the Cæsar of the West, and Jamaica will not perish while his paternal care continues (l. 44). No doubt with this in mind, earlier in the poem (l. 16) he is promised what Long termed 'somewhat more than antediluvian longevity' though it turned out that 'the poet proved a false prophet, for Mr. Haldane did not survive the delivery of this address many months'. While Long endeavoured to suggest the contrary, this 'adulation' – however excessive it may seem to modern readers – is quite normal for the period. So too are Williams' expressions of conventional modesty: Buchanan would have done a better job of praising Haldane; eloquence wilts under a tropical sun.

But there are other aspects of the poem which suggest more than simple sycophancy. Not only the *populus*, but also the *plebecula*, of Jamaica are aware of the fact that their yoke has been lifted (l. 7), and here for once I think we must follow Long's translation, which suggests that the *populus* referred to the masters, and *plebecula* to the slaves. Not many masters would have agreed that slaves had any interest in – or right to be interested in – the politics of Jamaica, in such burning questions of the day as the great controversy of Governor Knowles' administration, whether the island's capital should be Kingston or Spanish Town. In a slave colony, there are some rather curious resonances involved in referring to Governor Haldane, the King's representative, as *servus*, even *Optimus ... servus* (l. 13). And just as Christopher Codrington used his praise of William III as an excuse to blow his own trumpet, so Williams makes it clear that his expressions of conventional modesty are indeed purely conventional, something which riled Long considerably. Williams does indeed say that Minerva forbids an Ethiop to sing the battles of great leaders (ll. 21-2). Yes, Buchanan would be more suited to the task. However, for a writer of Latin verses to admit that he was not as good as Buchanan is far from suggesting he was a hopeless scribbler – many would have agreed with the suggestion that Buchanan was little, if at all, inferior to Vergil (l. 26). In lines 29-38 Williams explicitly defends his right to be a black poet and to address such an exalted personage as Haldane: *non cute, corde valet* – his words derive their worth from his sincerity, and the colour of his skin should not be taken as detracting from this. I believe this is also the suggestion of lines 37-8, with their opposition of *candida* and *nigra* deliberately calling attention to itself. *Candidus* can mean not only 'white' but also 'sincere'; *corpus* can refer not only to a physical body, but also to the substance of an argument. Williams' couplet can thus mean more than the literal 'Go to greet him [i.e.

Governor Haldane], nor let it be a cause of shame to you that you have a white body in a black skin' – it carries the suggestion that, whatever the prejudiced might be led to assume from his appearance, the poet is inwardly sincere. Writing in eighteenth-century Jamaica, in a society where the habitual abuse of blacks by whites included the stereotype that, as Long put it (*History of Jamaica*: II, 407), 'They are excellent dissemblers', Williams can perhaps be seen here as making a positive assertion of black dignity. He insists, contrary to the whole tenor of Jamaican slave society which was based on concepts of white superiority, that God has given the same soul to all, that *virtus* and *prudentia* have nothing to do with colour, that there is no colour in an honest mind, *nullus in arte color,* which we can perhaps translate as 'no distinction of race in artistic capacity'. Indeed, he goes on (ll. 39-42) to praise his own accomplishments in no uncertain manner; while Long dismissed this as unseemly boasting, we should remember that for Williams, maintaining his own dignity as a black man and a black poet in a white-dominated world would have been a constant struggle.

Finally, we may look at one other aspect of what Williams says about his identity. It seems to be a matter of pride to him that he was nour-ished by the *celebres Britanni*, the authority of the British King is unquestionably accepted and the defeat of Britain's French enemies treated as matter for congratulation. However, loyalty to the British Empire is combined with a more local patriotism, which is perhaps more intense. While the *patria* of Buchanan and Haldane is Scotland, the *patriæ ... amor* which distinguishes Williams is more ambiguous. *Patria* here could be the British Empire as a whole, but I think it is more likely to refer to the island which gave birth to Williams, and which in l. 43, with its echo of the famous epitaph of Vergil, he contrasts with the *Britanni*. He concludes the poem by expressing the hope that *terra, Deique locus* will continue to see Haldane ruling *Florentes populos.* These are clearly the peoples of Jamaica, and the *terra* in the last line, as it is in l. 4, is Jamaica itself. But what is the *Dei ... locus*? It probably is opposed to *terra*, so that *terra, Deique locus* is, as Long translates it, 'earth and heaven'. It is tempting, however, to see the *terra* as *being* the *Dei ... locus*, in anticipation of the twentieth-century Jamaican play on words: 'Jamaica, Jah mek yuh'.

Appendix

Text of Francis Williams' poem addressed to George Haldane, Governor of Jamaica, 1759:

4. The British Empire and the Neo-Latin Tradition

Integerrimo et Fortissimo
Viro
GEORGIO HALDANO, Armigero,
Insulæ *Jamaicensis* Gubernatori;
Cui, omnes morum, virtutumque dotes bellicarum,
In cumulum accesserunt,
CARMEN.

DENIQUE venturum fatis volventibus annum
    Cuncta per extensum læta videnda diem,
Excussis adsunt curis, sub imagine clarâ
    Felices populi, terraque lege virens.
Te duce, quæ fuerant malesuadâ mente peracta   5
    Irrita, conspectu non reditura tuo.
Ergo omnis populus, nec non plebecula cernet
    Hæsurum collo te relegasse jugum,
Et mala, quæ diris quondam cruciatibus, insons
    Insula passa fuit; condoluisset onus   10
Ni victrix tua Marte manus prius inclyta, nostris
    Sponte ruinosis rebus adesse velit.
Optimus es servus *Regi* servire *Britanno*,
    Dum gaudet genio *Scotica* terra tuo:
Optimus herôum populi fulcire ruinam;   15
    Insula dum superest ipse superstes eris.
Victorem agnoscet te *Guadaloupa*, suorum
    Despicet meritò diruta castra ducum.
Aurea vexillis flebit jactantibus *Iris*,
    Cumque suis populis, oppida victa gemet.   20
Crede, meum non est, vir *Marti* chare! *Minerva*
    Denegat *Æthiopi* bella sonare ducum.
Concilio, caneret te *Buchananus* et armis,
    Carmine *Peleidæ* scriberet ille parem.
Ille poeta, decus patriæ, tua facta referre   25
    Dignior, altisono vixque *Marone* minor.
Flammiferos agitante suos sub sole jugales
    Vivimus; eloquium deficit omne focis.
Hoc demum accipias, multâ fuligine fusum
    Ore sonaturo; non cute, corde valet.   30
Pollenti stabilita manu, (Deus almus, eandem
    Omnigenis animam, nil prohibente dedit)
Ipsa coloris egens virtus, prudentia; honesto
    Nullus inest animo, nullus in arte color.
Cur timeas, quamvis, dubitesve, nigerrima celsam   35
    Cæsaris occidui, scandere Musa domum?
Vade salutatum, nec sit tibi causa pudoris,
    Candida quod nigrâ corpore pelle geris!

Integritas morum Maurum magis ornat, et ardor
  Ingenii, et docto dulcis in ore décor;   40
Hunc, magè cor sapiens, patriæ virtutis amorque,
  Eximit è sociis, conspicuumque facit.
Insula me genuit, celebres aluere *Britanni*,
  Insula te salvo non dolitura patre!
Hoc precor; o nullo videant te fine, regentem   45
  Florentes populos, terra, Deique locus!

FRANCISCUS WILLIAMS

Text from Edward Long, *History of Jamaica* (London, 1774): II, 478-81. I have not followed the eighteenth-century practice of leaving a space before certain punctuation marks, but spelling and punctuation are otherwise as given in Long. The accents are as in the text, and in accordance with the normal usage of the period, as is the italicisation of proper names. I have not, however, followed Long's italicisation of some other words and phrases to which he drew attention in order to comment on them unfavourably.

l. 8, *relegasse* Long suggests this is an error for *relevasse*.

Notes

1. See the editions of their works by Vincent Carretta (listed in the Bibliography).

2. Hume's dismissal (which is quoted by Long) of the capacities of black people in general, and of Francis Williams in particular, appeared as a footnote to his essay 'Of National Characters'. The essay was first published in the 1748 edition of Hume's *Essays Moral and Political*, but this particular note was not added until the version of the essay which appeared in Hume's *Essays and Treatises on Several Subjects* (4 vols, London and Edinburgh, 1753-4). See Green and Grose eds 1964: III, 252. The text of the essay is perhaps more accessible in Copley and Edgar eds 1993: 113-25, with this note at 360).

Edward Long discusses Williams in 2002 (1774): II, 475-85). Williams' poem, 'Integerrimo et Fortissimo Viro Georgio Haldano ... Carmen', is given at 479-81, with Long's translation at 481-3. The text of the poem is reproduced as an appendix to the present discussion. Ramsay (1784: 238-9) and Grégoire (1991 [1808]: 235-45) offer early responses to Long.

3. I owe the detail about Lincoln's Inn to Vincent Carretta (personal communication). See also Carretta 2003 for further biographical information. I am currently working on a full-length study of Francis Williams, based on material in archives and libraries in Jamaica and the United Kingdom.

4. Poems of Edward Elder in Haig-Brown ed., 1870: 29, 31, 356-7; Reece and Clark-Hunt ed. n.d.: 25; Gilmore 1979: 50-65, especially 61.

4. The British Empire and the Neo-Latin Tradition

On Elder, see *Dictionary of National Biography*, and Gilmore 1987: 16-18. The Greek palindrome is printed in Aspinall 1914: 100.

5. See White 1995 (1633) and review by the present writer; also, undated letter, Jacobus [?Giacomo] Giani, to Henry Moore (Lieutenant-Governor of Jamaica, 1756-62), in Howard ed. 1925: I, 160-1. Moore was married to one of Edward Long's sisters – 1925: I, 120, 185, 186.

6. Based on analysis of Wright 1966; Oliver ed. 1915 and 1927; and Ravenshaw 1878. In spite of the pseudo-archaic title, this last is a fairly serious piece of antiquarian scholarship.

7. Orderson 2002: 34, 50 (= 1842: 22, 49). Orderson was an old man when he published the novel, and was describing late eighteenth-century Barbados from personal experience.

8. See the chapter on 'Education of a young colonial' in Williams 1969, especially 34-5, and Greenwood in this volume.

9. A very large part of Oliver 1894-9 consists of accounts of planter families, and similar material for the British Caribbean as a whole fills much of *Caribbeana*, a periodical he edited. Brandow 1983 brings together many articles of this type.

10. Handler 1971: 39, 43, 45, 46, 57, 58. Handler 1991: 12 notes another Latin medical dissertation by a Barbadian, published at Leiden in 1751.

11. See, for example, Binns ed. 1974 which includes a chapter by Mark Storey on 'The Latin Poetry of Vincent Bourne', Baldwin 1995 and Money 1998. IJsewijn 1990 provides a comprehensive survey of modern literature in Latin, including (295) a brief mention of Francis Williams.

12. Brathwaite 1979 and 1979a provide comprehensive surveys of material published in English in the pre-emancipation period for the territories covered, but do not include works in Latin.

13. In *Academiæ Oxoniensis Gratulatio* (unpaginated). See Harlow 1990 (1928) for biographical details. This poem is not included in Harlow's 'Appendix B: Literary Remains and References' (221-41), which does print an English ode Codrington published in a similar anthology in 1688 in commemoration of the birth of James II's son, later the Old Pretender.

14. Maynard and Alleyn's poems in *Academiæ Oxoniensis Comitia* (unpaginated). Alleyn's poem was reprinted in *Musarum Anglicanarum Analecta* ... Vol. III, pp. 28-31 (NB this volume was an unauthorised addition to an earlier collection of the same name by a different publisher). Maynard is identified as the son of Samuel Maynard of Barbados in Foster ed. 1887-92: III, 995. Alleyn (or Alleyne) is specifically identified in both editions of his poem as 'Reynoldi Alleyn de Barbadoes Arm. fil.' ('son of Reynold Alleyn of Barbados, gentleman') and full biographical details about John Alleyn[e] (1695-1730) and his family may be found in a series of articles by Louise R. Allen originally published in the *Journal of the Barbados Museum and Historical Society* and collected in Brandow 1983.

15. In *Academiæ Cantabrigiensis Luctus* (unpaginated). Biographical details on Colleton, including his birth in Barbados, in Venn and Venn 1922-7: I, 371.

16. In *Carmina ad ... Ducem de Newcastle inscripta*. John Gilbert was the son of Nathaniel Gilbert of Antigua, and born there – biographical details in Venn 1940-54: III, 46. One of John Gilbert's brothers was another Nathaniel Gilbert, who was Speaker of the House of Assembly of Antigua (1763-9) and responsible for the introduction of Methodism into the island; see information on the family in Oliver 1894-9: 12-15.

17. It could be argued that this is true even of the three-line fragment we have of a Cambridge composition in Latin verse by Edward Beeston Long, who left Jamaica at the age of five – even if it owes more to imagination than experience, it is a description of a hurricane (Howard ed. 1925: I, 141).

18. For the 'Indian laurels' ('Suscipe & hæc, *Gulielme*, suas habet *India Lauros*'), compare Addison's poem, 'Pax Gulielmi Auspiciis Europæ Reddita, 1697', where he says of Codrington, 'India progenuit' ('India gave you birth'). From classical times, Latin poets frequently used singular for plural, and vice versa, to accommodate the demands of metre, and 'India' is thus equivalent to 'the Indies'. On Addison's friendship with Codrington, see Harlow.

19. ' ... ecquis qui ... / ... flavos muniat Indos, / Thesaurum Europæ, nitidæque cubilia gazæ? / Dignus adest, dignus Sceptrum qui sumat ab illo ... '

20. For an introduction to Buchanan as a poet, see Ford 1982, which includes an edition (text, translation and commentary) of Buchanan's *Miscellaneorum Liber* by Philip J. Ford and W.S. Watt.

21. Todd ed. 1992: I, 222-5; McMurtrie 1942, which includes a facsimile of the 1718 second edition of 'A Pindarique Ode on the Arrival of his Excellency Sir Nicholas Lawes, Governor of Jamaica, &c.' (no copy of the first edition is known to exist).

22. Oliver ed. 1927: 4. 'Imperator' could of course mean 'general' or 'ruler' as well as 'emperor', but the word has clearly been chosen for its grandiloquence. The governor was William Mathew Burt; for the family, see Oliver 1894-9: I, 87-91 and III, 414; and *Caribbeana* V (1919): 89-96, 315-16.

5

Refiguring Classical Texts: Aspects of the Postcolonial Condition

Lorna Hardwick

This paper looks at the relationships between modern refiguration of ancient texts and the development of new literatures and performance traditions in postcolonial contexts. It uses a practice based approach which then becomes the basis for suggesting revisions to some of the conventional assumptions about Western domination in the performance histories of Greek drama and in the tradition of epic poetry. I shall include material which demonstrates the capacity of classical plays to emerge from imperial 'domestication' and to function as counter-texts, not only in the theatre of newly liberated nations but also within colonising societies. Refiguration of classical drama can be an important means of escape from colonisation of the mind for colonisers as well as for the colonised. I shall argue that, although each postcolonial history is different, nevertheless, analysis of rewriting of classical texts in colonised and colonising societies shows that there is a pattern of features that suggest a distinctive role for classical material in provoking awareness and transformation of cultural identities.

The argument draws on research on the impact of classical referents in modern drama and poetry which has been undertaken as part of the Research Project on the Reception of Classical Texts at the Open University. It is based on analysis of examples taken from the database of well over 700 recent productions of Greek drama (published at http://www2.open.ac.uk/ClassicalStudies/GreekPlays) and also relates to work which is currently being developed on the migration of Greek images, metaphors and formal conventions into modern poetry and drama.[1] The database of plays includes performances in the original language, in close translation and in free translation, adaptations and versions. It will be obvious that this spectrum takes the term 'classical referents' to the limit and includes new works. I have argued elsewhere that the term 'translation' now includes a wide range of relationships to the original, including the non-verbal languages involved in translation to the stage.[2] My main emphasis here will be towards the creative end of this spectrum and the analysis of formal, contextual and discursive relationships and correspondences between ancient and modern.

It used to be claimed as a truism that looking at the subsequent reception and development of classical material told us something about the receiving society or culture but nothing about the ancient. I have always found this a strange claim, particularly since (paradoxically) it was most likely to be made by critics or academics who claimed that their interpretation of ancient texts or analyses of ancient history was closely revealing of the 'original' and in no way conditioned by the subjective or social filters they brought from their experiences in their own modern worlds. Of course this is not to deny that reception, whether in antiquity or subsequently, does indeed suggest a good deal about the receiving writer and society. My point is simply that the energy may flow in both directions and when it does the resulting synergy sparks new work. Responding to a modern work prompts us to return to the ancient, asking new questions, revisiting cherished assumptions and discovering in it layers which have been hidden or marginalised. [3]

The term 'postcolonial' when applied to literatures and theatres might be thought to carry the implication that the literatures under discussion emerged fully only after the end of colonisation. Colonisation, however, is not something that begins and ends in finite terms. Colonisation and decolonisation are related processes, and literature, drama and thought may already be running counter to the prevailing situation when colonial domination is still a physical fact. Equally, aspects of colonisation may still be part of the artistic and political context after independence is established. It is a feature of the relationship between classical and other literatures that classical texts and referents can play a part on either side of this divide, being viewed as either repressive or liberating. In the latter case they may have an interventionist role in creating and intensifying awareness of repression and as a result of this awareness they may be adapted and developed to create new aesthetic forms and discourses, thus resisting and outflanking those cultural forms and pressures which were associated with imperialist ideologies.

The force of colonialism as a constraint on mind and thought has been an area of continuing debate. Critics such as Ngugi Wa Thiong'o have attacked imperialism as a destroyer of culture, an inducer of shame for names, systems of belief, language, lore, art, dance, song, sculpture, colour. Since all these are important aspects of ancient culture and in particular of theatre performance, they provide a significant index for analysis of the relationship between ancient poetry and drama and postcolonial writing. It has also been argued that the term

108

'postcolonial' actually perpetuates cultural colonialism by implying that new literatures are shaped only or mainly by colonisation.[4] Furthermore, critics have pointed out how the historical specificity of colonial experiences and the diversity of the resulting discourses have combined to create shifting constructions of (for example) race, gender, Englishness.[5] Re-alignment of such constructed concepts also has implications for shifts in construction of the 'classical' in postcolonial (and postcolonialist) situations.

In the context of modern postcolonial writings the effects of re-examination of the ancient texts and the ways in which they have been mediated and appropriated are two-fold:

First, the history of the reception of the text reveals the extent to which ancient texts and cultures have now been de-centred from what used to be thought of as their dominant Western, cultural, social and political associations. This has happened also within the cultures of the colonising powers.[6] Secondly, the ancient text is liberated for reinterpretation and is distanced from at least some of the effects of its association with (for example) imperial hegemonies.

From this, I wish to argue that ancient literature and culture has not only been a catalyst for new work but has also itself undergone a quasi postcolonial experience in being released from oppressive constraints and exploitation and freed to assume new identities which are not limited by the dictates, values and material culture of colonialist appropriators. Classical languages and literature had a dual potential because of their role in colonial education and in that of the governing classes and also because, more recently, ancient cultural artefacts underwent a diaspora of their own as they became progressively detached from the colonising classes who had appropriated and transformed classical culture but who gradually ceased to have a use for it. This shift has been expressed in the changing status of ancient works – from establishment icons to figures for challenge and intervention in cultural and political processes and eventually to diaspora texts taking on new directions and identities. This process has been further energised by interaction with other traditions (some of which already had important strands derived from ancient Mediterranean culture or comparable mythologies and power struggles as well as strong theatrical traditions within their own histories).[7] This hybridity in reception and refiguration has provoked sharp debates about cultural 'ownership' and suggests that new models of interpretation and contextualisation must emerge.

However, the changes in the status of ancient texts do not necessarily follow a chronological progression. I am not proposing a Whig theory of Reception. The relationship between classical and postcolonial literatures is itself pluralist and this is an important element in the denial of monolithic generalisations about either. Furthermore, account must be taken of the different histories of colonisation. As Seamus Heaney has put it, 'in current postcolonial conditions ... the more people realise that their language and their culture are historically amassed possessions, the better' (*Sunday Times*, 26 July 1998).

Classical texts are still studied as establishment icons by some influential researchers of nineteenth-century British culture.[8] However, the use of these icons was ambivalent. It is clear that in the nineteenth century itself progressive writers and political activists used classical works, referents and discourse to gain admittance to political circles and to influence others (and sometimes to undermine dominant assumptions). Examples range from Chartist poets through leading figures in the movements for women's education and suffrage to the designers of Trade Union Banners while Karl Marx's writing was informed by his knowledge of antiquity and is peppered with classical allusions.[9] Greek drama has also played an important part in popular culture, for instance on the nineteenth-century burlesque stage where it provided a forum for reformist debate.[10]

Even in the imperial heyday of the British Empire, therefore, the potential of classical texts to subvert from within was well developed. Closely related to this subversive role is the potential of the texts and the readings they prompted to carry a double perspective. By double perspective I mean that in addition to their capacity for provoking debate and communicating radical ideas classical plays also carried with them associations of cultural authority. This sometimes allowed them to be staged even in repressive societies while in barely censored or liberal societies they slipped past the 'censors' of entrenched assumptions and collective amnesia. Despite their apparently 'safe' distance from modern events, careful translation, imaginative staging and audience response actually fostered critique of modern politics and society. Thus there might be a fluid dividing line between 'domestication' of a modern production of a classical play and its emergence as a counter-text.

The role of classical texts as a basis for critique and intervention has been important in twentieth-century Europe and in Africa as a part of resistance against various kinds of colonial domination and tyranny.[11] Some plays, such as Sophocles' *Antigone*, have been particularly important in this respect – though it is salutary to remember also that the play was performed no fewer than 150 times between 1939 and 1944 in Nazi Germany as part of an attempt to preserve Western culture in the face of threats from the so-called barbarian East.[12] In the broader aspects of postcolonial criticism, the notion of double perspectives has been developed to create the concept of double consciousness. This refers to the ways in which writers and theatre practitioners who have received an elite colonial education both share in and resist colonial traditions and mentalities. Iconic examples of interventionist drama which draws on double consciousness include Athol Fugard's *The Island* which dramatises elements of the *Antigone* as a play within a play and draws on an actual prison performance memorably referred to in Nelson Mandela's Memoirs.[13] In Irish theatre, Brian Friel's *Translations* reclaimed classical literature from imperialist appropriation and returned it to the Irish for use as a basis for asserting their own identity as well as for building a common basis for communication with the British, while Seamus Heaney's *The Cure at Troy* developed a version of Sophocles' *Philoctetes* which examined the healing process in fractured communities.[14]

Tony Harrison's *Phaedra Britannica* (staged in 1975 by the National Theatre Company and directed by John Dexter) is an example of an anti-colonial version of a classical play created within a colonising society. Harrison's play was based on the Hippolytus/Phaedra story as mediated by Racine, but set in the Durbar Hall of the Governor's residency in British India a few years before the Indian Revolt. The Governor's son, the Hippolytus figure, was represented as Anglo-Indian. The Phaedra role of Memsahib, the Governor's wife, taken by Diana Rigg, explored the racist undertones of the play. The Messenger Speech, a convention of Greek tragedy which is of special importance in the *Hippolytus,* Euripides' seminal play on the theme, was delivered in the Harrison play by the tutor Burleigh. It adapted the Hippolytus figure's last drive with his chariot and horses and situated it within the clash of Indian and British cultures:

> The jungle trees
> first lent a little to a light stray breeze ...
> The forest begins heaving like the sea ...
> An old woman told the sepoys it was Siva
> in his avatar of monster.[15]

Everyone else flees but Thomas challenges the monster and wounds it. Then the horses panic:

> The sepoys say that maddened Siva sank
> a sharpened trident into each scorched flank.
> ... I saw him with my own eyes, sir, saw him towed
> by the stallions he'd tamed himself and rode
> in the cool of the morning, saw your son
> dragged by the ponies he'd played polo on.[16]

Harrison retains the Poseidon connection by alluding to the trident (with its ironic resonances of Britannia) but substitutes for the nautical image of the helmsman (present in Euripides, Seneca and Racine) the almost satirical representation of the skills of the imperial polo-player, with the associated value-system focalised by the tutor-Messenger. Like Racine, Harrison follows the gruesome images of the wounds developed by Seneca and makes the Messenger break down in tears as he recalls them. The final irony is that the fatal polo-playing skills are an example of imperial appropriation from India.

Another key point related to the fluidity of the boundary between the domesticated and the counter-text is that interventionist drama (and poetry) is frequently characterised by re-appropriation (as the tussles over the *Antigones* show). Even the supposedly iconoclastic director Peter Sellars claimed that 'A classic is a house we're still living in'. This comment was made in 1993 in respect of his work as director of a modern dramatisation of Aeschylus' *Persians*. At first hearing, the metaphor of the house and the changes made by successive occupants has some resonance. The texts become a home where poets and drama-tists can renegotiate their lives – Derek Walcott and Ted Hughes immediately spring to mind. And of course, the notion of home has been increasingly problematised by post-modern and postcolonial critics in the context of the imagery of 'pathfinding, struggle and survival, epiphany and vision, duality of time past and present', as Edward Baugh put it.[17]

In the event, Sellars' classical house proved a straitjacket. In the aftermath of the Gulf War of 1991, Aeschylus' play was seen as the inspiration for a version that identified the army of the defeated Xerxes with that of Iraq. The play, adapted by Robert Auletta and directed by Sellars, was performed as part of the 1993 Edinburgh Festival at the Royal Lyceum Theatre Edinburgh, and attracted largely hostile reviews. However, some reviewers used the contrast with the Auletta version to uncover the daring of Aeschylus' achievement:

> Imagine Aeschylus in modern Britain: a poet and soldier back from the liberation of Europe in 1945 or from the Falklands expedition in 1982 and writing a play to celebrate British victory but instead of an easy triumphalism, going for a much harder option. He sets his play in the Nazi High Command or the Presidential palace in Buenos Aires ... the characters are stricken but dignified, giants in defeat ... to write such a play you would have to have a political maturity and a human and artistic magnanimity which the modern world does not possess.
>
> J. Peter, *The Times, Features Section*, 8 August 1993

One might speculate on how a modern version might have been received which depended less on the correspondences between victory and defeat and more on Aeschylean reflections on the folly of mounting a military expedition to a territory outside the apparent limits of a state's power, logistics and legitimate involvement. In such an example, the weeping would presumably have been amongst the women of Washington and London, widows of the defeated in the Gulf War. In my view Sellars' production displayed the limits of 'liberal interventionism' in that it failed to recognise or overcome its assumptions about the dominance of the correspondence between Greek and modern Western victories. This failure represented a colossal lack either of insight or of nerve.

Focus on the struggle for re-appropriation may in some instances lead to the examination of classical texts as diaspora texts. Diaspora texts have been imaged by Derek Walcott as broken shards of past cultures – African and Asian fragments. In a similar way classical culture was appropriated and then cast aside by the Old World and is now washed up on a Caribbean shore to play its part in the remaking of poetry, a process which Walcott sees as 'one of excavation and of self-discovery'.[18] These relationships with the past, whether African or classical, are necessarily fractured. The way in which they are brought together is crucial. Walcott regards simple mimicry as an early symptom of powerlessness in the face of the competing alternatives of violent rejection of the cultures of the past; of conservative assimilation of what is most useful in the dominant culture (whether in politics, art, language, philosophy or way of life); or of a cunning metamorphosis which sets in train the invention of new artistic possibilities (and perhaps political concepts).[19] Walcott has given a radical extension to this proposition by emphasising that the metamorphosis extends not only to the culture of the colonisers but also to the previous 'histories' and traditions of the colonised, aspects of their identity which exist in 'memory' but are not fully recoverable. In this perspective, mimicry can be part of the process of beginning anew, 'the painful, new, laborious uttering that comes out of belief, not out of doubt'. For Walcott, creativity cannot come out of revenge nor out of a nostalgic focus on 'Roots' or the past of memory, or on the afflictions and wounds of the colonial and immediately postcolonial condition.[20]

Nevertheless, there is an influential body of opinion which does not want to recognise that classical texts are not irreversibly locked into the cultures that have appropriated them. For example, Herbert Golder rejected non-European classical theatre as a source of enrichment and insight in productions of Greek drama and castigated Mnouchkine's *Les*

Atrides as 'Nipponising' Western culture.[21] Such attitudes may encode a particular perspective on the 'classical tradition', which is seen as a vehicle for passing on essentials and not as part of a dialogic process of reception and refiguration.[22]

In drama as well as epic there have been some interesting recent examples of the use of classical texts as a focus for the exploration of cultural and aesthetic identity in a manner which is neither simply interventionist nor anti-colonialist or colonialist in conception. Particularly important is the development of a 'new tradition' of classical theatre in Scotland. In 2000 a grant from the National Lottery enabled three of Scotland's leading playwrights to be commissioned to create new versions for present-day Scotland of three Greek tragedies. The grant also funded theatre babel to assemble a large company to rehearse over an extended period. The plays were performed in sequence and, with the title *Greeks,* as a triple bill in the Old Fruitmarket, Glasgow. They were: *Oedipus* (David Greig), *Electra* (Tom McGrath) and *Medea* (Liz Lochhead). David Greig's *Oedipus*, directed by Graham McLaren, was a highly politicised version of the play. The Indian dress and religious ritual distanced political change from modern time and place, yet there was contemporary impact in the theme of the handover of power and the resulting exposure of corruption and civic disease. This was brought out in the language of the play and especially in the rivalry between Oedipus and Creon. The design suggested that the sun was setting over a colonised city. Yet this never became a 'closed' reading; both usurper and liberator spoke in Scots accents and idiom and the identification of Oedipus and Creon with each role fluctuated throughout the play. Greig emphasised in the Programme Notes the tension he felt in 'being true to the foreign-ness of the original work and trying to "translate" it into dramatic and linguistic idioms which might speak more comfortably to your own audience'. He rewrote substantial parts of the play, shortened it and translated 'freely'. He said, 'It is not Sophocles' work but nor is it entirely mine. It belongs neither to Greek culture nor to Scots. It is neither truly old nor truly new. It is a hybrid, a mongrel creation. But mongrelisation is, of course, the secret of survival in a species.'

Thus the production resisted any temptation towards crude contemporisation. The setting and focus reminded anyone who was so tempted that Scots, too, were leaders in the organisation of the British Empire and thus the play resisted facile labelling of post-devolution Scotland as emerging from colonial rule. Yet both histories, of the Raj, of devolution, were there, underlying the Theban quest for assured identity and the common theme of struggle for the transfer of power.

5. Refiguring Classical Texts

There are other important features of current Scottish work on classical plays. Two contrasting examples are firstly the role of Greek drama in TAG (Theatre Around Glasgow) which works with young people to develop civic awareness and involvement and in 2000 toured an *Antigone*, and secondly Edwin Morgan's translation of Racine in a *Phaedra* in modern Scots (Glaswegian idiom). This was staged by the Royal Lyceum Company in Edinburgh in April 2000, directed by Kenny Ireland and stunningly designed by Isla Shaw. Morgan sticks quite closely to Racine's version in his translation. The directness and economy of the language are striking. Morgan, however, resisted giving the play a Scottish setting: 'I thought I'd rather do it the other way: keep the characters as they are – that is ancient Greeks – and keep the place – Ancient Greece', but the use of the Scots language was important to him – 'The very idea of being able to write about anything in Scots has always struck me as very important, because otherwise the danger is that Scotland ends up defining itself in parochial terms, whereas if a Scots translation can work with the best [French] classical tragedy there is, surely that proves something' (Interview with Sue Wilson, *The Independent*, 12 April 2000). The use of the Scots language also represented an implicit challenge to the culturally colonialist dominance of French and English as the languages of translation of classical drama. This example of migration (Euripides, Seneca, Racine, Morgan) suggests that one implication of exploring the classical diaspora is that new kinds of philological research will need to be developed. One approach would be to map the convergences and divergences in the semantic fields of key elements in the plays on the Hippolytus/Phaedra theme by (for example) Euripides, Seneca, Racine, Harrison, Hughes and Morgan. The ancient languages may rarely be spoken but creatively their energy is very much alive.

Although each postcolonial (and postcolonialist) history is different, examination of their refigurations of classical texts does point towards some broad conclusions:

(1) An important strand of modern reception of classical works is one of interaction between displaced and dynamic traditions, both ancient and modern, and that in this context the potential of the classical texts for 'double perspectives' is crucial.

(2) Classical culture has played a shaping role in interventionist theatre, resisting imperial/colonial domination, whether in Ireland, Eastern Europe or Africa, and in a plurality of colonial histories.

(3) New creative work drawing on and refiguring classical texts has become an important element in enabling postcolonial literatures and

theatres to move on from the theatre of Affliction and an obsession with Roots (whether of cultural identity or past sufferings), both of which can be a restrictive and destructive force.

(4) New narratives and explorations of classical material are constructing a new *koine*, which includes exploration of commonalities (including aesthetic and formal aspects as well as commonalities of suffering and of engagement with the problems of the transfer of power) as well as of polarities and otherness. A creative hybridity results. This is a post-Saïdan aesthetic, which assumes an understanding of the interconnected narratives of race, gender and class, and yet self-reflexively avoids reductionist meanings.

These factors suggest that the recent and current situation of classical texts meets the three-fold process of political engagement laid down by cultural critics in respect of diaspora communities:

(i) self-emancipation from slavery (i.e. resistance to appropriation)

(ii) achievement of civic participation (in new contexts of identity and debate)

(iii) creation of an autonomous space in which to develop politically and culturally

Precisely because classical texts have been displaced from their perceived centrality in Western culture, they have become part of a diaspora – migratory, open for interaction, yet enabling an awareness of their own tradition in the ancient world, which is increasingly understood as involving a multi-valent political discourse.[23] This is an exciting process. It is also threatening to long-cherished assumptions about the nature of 'the classical' – which is why those who are afraid of it persist in a patriarchal 'colonialism' in their models of Reception.

Notes

This is a slightly expanded version of a paper given at the Classics and Colonialism Conference held at the Institute of Classical Studies in May 2001. I would like to thank the organiser, Dr Barbara Goff, and the participants for their constructive comments.

1. The research website includes information about the processes of performance creation, the roles of translators, directors and designers as well as critical essays on the primary sources and reception methodology.

2. Hardwick 2000, ch. 1, 2004, 2005.

3. Hardwick 1992.

4. See Ngugi Wa Thiong'o 1986 and 1993. The origins and application of the

concept 'postcolonial' are discussed in Walder 1998, ch. 1, especially 1-6. For discussion of the resistance of writers to the imposition by critics of terms like 'postcolonial' see Walder 1998, ch. 1, 8. Various kinds of neo-imperialism are discussed in Gilbert and Tomkins 1996, ch. 6. Performance aspects are also discussed in Gainor ed. 1995, and Crow and Banfield 1996.

5. For discussion of the work of Stuart Hall in relation to this issue, including the implications of residual colonialism on the dominant culture, see Childs and Williams 1997: 75.

6. See for example, Stray 1998, especially part 3 'From Discipline to Dis-Establishment', 1902-60.

7. This process has been notable in the Caribbean and in Africa: see Budelmann and Greenwood in this volume and Hardwick 2004.

8. See in particular Clarke 1989; Jenkyns 1980; and Turner 1981.

9. See further Hardwick 2000a and 2000b.

10. For discussion see Hall 1997 and Macintosh 2000.

11. See Stéhliková 2001; Hardwick 2000, ch. 4; Macintosh 2001; and Wetmore 2002.

12. Flashar 1991. Another gloss on double perspectives.

13. Mandela 1995: 541.

14. For discussion of the Irish dimension of issues of translation and cultural politics associated with classical texts see Hardwick 2000, ch. 5.

15. Harrison 1986: 120.

16. Harrison 1986: 121.

17. Baugh 1978: 37ff.

18. Walcott 1993.

19. Walcott 1974, especially 5.

20. See, for example, 1973, 19.11 and 1974a, passim. Walcott's rejection of the Postcolonial Poetics of Affliction is discussed by J. Ramazani 1997 and, in the context of the *katabasis* in *Omeros* book 3 by Hardwick 2000, ch. 6.

21. Golder 1996.

22. See Hardwick 2001 and 2003, ch. 1.

23. For a recent analysis see Goldhill 2000.

Greek Tragedies in West African Adaptations

Felix Budelmann

Not so many years ago African adaptations of Greek tragedy would have been a most obscure subject for a classicist to write about. But since then, as a result of the ever-increasing academic interest in postcolonialism on the one hand, and in the reception of Greek tragedy on the other, a number of discussions have been published, not only by experts in African, and more generally postcolonial literatures,[1] but also by classicists.[2] This essay continues their work, focusing in more detail on a narrower, though still large and varied, geographical area: *West* Africa. Much more work, including work within Africa itself, will be necessary in the future to gain a more complete and nuanced picture. Moreover, I should state clearly that, as a classicist, I have only an incomplete knowledge of African literatures and cultures. Therefore, inevitably, much of what I say can itself only be a starting-point for more. However, I believe that such a start is well worth making, as the plays in question hold considerable interest for classicists.

On the facing page is a list, quite possibly incomplete, of relevant plays. There are eight in total – not a large number in relation to either the total output of West African dramatists or the total number of adaptations of Greek tragedies in Europe or America, but large enough to show that ancient Greek tragedy has caught the imagination of a range of West African writers over the years.[3]

As this is a long essay, it will be useful to provide a schematic summary of the argument upfront. A short **section 1** briefly sets the West African adaptations of Greek tragedies in their contexts. **Section 2**, the longest part of the paper, asks in what ways Greek tragedy has been attractive to West African dramatists: how and, as far as such a question may be answered, why have they used Greek tragedy as a basis for some of their plays? I begin, in **2a**, by summarising the well-known argument that the plays in question use the high-profile canonical European genre of Greek tragedy for 'canonical counter-discourse' against the former colonisers. Two plays, *The Bacchae of Euripides* and *Tegonni*, serve as illustrations of such counter-discourse: they very

Author	Title	1st performance	1st published[4]	Source text
J.P. Clark Bekederemo	*Song Of A Goat*	1960 '1960 Masks', Mbari Club, Ibadan, Nigeria	1964 Oxford: OUP	*Agamemnon*
Kamau Brathwaite	*Odale's Choice*	1962 Mfantsiman Secondary School, Saltpond, Ghana	1967 London and Ibadan: Evans	*Antigone*
Efua Sutherland	*Edufa*	1967 'Drama Studio' Accra, Ghana	1967 London: Longman	*Alcestis*
Ola Rotimi	*The Gods Are Not To Blame*	1968 Ori Olokun Acting Company, Ife Festival of the Arts, Nigeria	1971 Oxford: OUP	*Oedipus Rex*
Wole Soyinka	*The Bacchae of Euripides: A Communion Rite*	1973 National Theatre, London, UK	1973 London: Methuen	*Bacchae*
Jacqueline Leloup	*Guiedo*	1983 Youndé University Theatre, Cameroon	1986 Youndé: Editions CLE	*Oedipus Rex*
Femi Osofisan	*Tegonni: An African Antigone*	1994 Emory University, Atlanta, USA	1999 Ibadan: Fenix	*Antigone*
Femi Osofisan	*The Trojan Women or The Women of Owu*	2004 Collective Artistes, Chipping Norton Theatre, UK	Not known	*Troades*

obviously protest against European imperialism. The rest of section 2 accepts the notion of counter-discourse, but shows that counter-discourse should not be understood purely in the sense of protest against the former colonisers. In **2b**, I discuss all plays briefly to show that such protest is by no means the only mode in which Greek tragedy is adapted in West Africa. Following on from this, I suggest that Greek tragedy, far from being a symbol of imperialism, has at times served as a model for thinking about theatre in West Africa (**2c**), and that the importance of myth in Greek tragedy (**2d**) and the similarities between Greek and African theatre (**2e**) have allowed West African playwrights to dissociate Greek tragedy from other European literature and appropriate it as theirs. In sum, I argue that West African adaptations of Greek tragedies can indeed be seen as part of the postcolonial discourse of emancipation from the former colonisers, but that Greek tragedy plays a complicated role in this discourse. I end by calling for more detailed and more comprehensive study of these adaptations to do justice to their richness, both political and otherwise.

Finally, in a shorter **section 3**, the perspective shifts to European and American readers and spectators who bring an interest and expertise in Greek tragedy rather than West African drama to the plays under discussion. I suggest that the similarities between African and Greek theatre allow these readers and spectators (presumably including most classicists) to use the plays to engage creatively with some of the more problematic elements of Greek tragedy, such as ritual, choruses or masks. However, there are obvious limits to such engagement, and the essay ends with a brief discussion of some of these limits.

(1) Contexts

First, then, contexts. One thing to note straightaway is that adaptation is not the only genre in which West African literature engages with Greek tragedy. In fact, adaptations, West African and otherwise, are distinguished by no clear criteria from free translations or plays vaguely alluding to Greek tragedies. Thus, as we shall see, plays like Efua Sutherland's *Edufa* or, especially, John Pepper Clark's *Song Of A Goat* might arguably not deserve inclusion in the list printed above since they do not follow the ancient plays closely enough. Alternatively, along with *Edufa* and *Song Of A Goat*, several other West African plays could be discussed which share various compositional features of Greek tragedy, without imitating a particular ancient play: Soyinka's *The Strong Breed* or *The Road*, for instance, or Clark's *The Masquerade*. Going further, one might justifiably call a novel like the most famous of all African novels, Chinua Achebe's *The World Falls Apart*, tragic for the economy of its plot and for its focus on the chain of events that bring down the dominant character; and poetry by poets such as, again, Soyinka, Christopher Okigbo or (in French) Léopold Sédar Senghor repeatedly use classical references. In short, this paper concentrates on plays which appear to use particular Greek tragedies as a source text. Behind this subject, there is a wider subject worth studying: Greek tragedy in West African literature. Playwrights' adaptations, the subject of this essay, should be seen as an aspect of this larger context.

Returning to the list of adaptations, two things to note without any study of the plays is the large amount of work from the 1960s and early 1970s (*Song Of A Goat, Odale's Choice, Edufa, The Gods Are Not To Blame, The Bacchae of Euripides*), and the large proportion of Nigerian writers (Clark, Rotimi, Soyinka, Osofisan), with a significant overlap between the two categories. (Another striking observation, which I am unable to take any further, is the apparent dominance of English over other European languages, including French.) Nigeria is, of course, by a long way the most populous African country. But there are further factors contributing to the preponderance of 1960s and 1970s Nigeria. Lagos and Ibadan in the early years after Nigerian independence (1960) are often singled out for their remarkable cultural activity.[5] The rich literary, in particular dramatic, traditions of Nigerian peoples, the continuing influence and presence of the English colonisers and the general sense of change caused by independence created the surroundings for, among much else, a number of poets, novelists and dramatists whose work continues to be remembered, read and performed. The English influence is particularly relevant to works using ancient material. The English had set up and maintained schools and universities in Nigeria and elsewhere in West Africa that taught Latin, and sometimes also Greek. The University of Ibadan (formerly University College, Ibadan, linked to the University of London) continues to teach classics today. Unsurprisingly, Greek tragedy was spread in Africa initially by Europeans and European institutions.

In the same context, a look at the biographies of the authors listed above shows that many of them have contacts with Europe or America: born between the 1920s and 1940s, their education started before independence, often along traditional British lines, and their degrees in domestic universities were often complemented by studies abroad, in Leeds (Soyinka), Cambridge (Sutherland), Paris (Osofisan), Boston (Rotimi) and Princeton (Clark, but after writing *Song Of A Goat*). Jacqueline Leloup was even born in Europe, in France, and four of the plays were first performed, and several published, in Europe or America.

However, it would be a mistake to suggest total uniformity. Not all plays were written by Nigerians, not all were written in the 1960s or 1970s, not all were ever performed in Europe or America, and not all were written by authors with particularly strong European or American links. As we will see throughout this paper, generalisations about the context of West African adaptations of Greek tragedies share the fate of most generalisations: they are both helpful and limited.

(2) West African playwrights adapting Greek tragedy

(a) Canonical counter-discourse

With this in mind, it is possible to turn to the question of the attraction of Greek tragedy to West African writers. A first answer may be found in the section on 'Classical Greek influences' of Helen Gilbert's and Joanne Tompkins' textbook *Post-Colonial Drama*. The section starts:[6]

> While classical Greek theatre has undoubtedly exerted less influence on post-colonial drama than has Shakespeare, it is nevertheless an important target for canonical counter-discourse, especially in African countries, such as Nigeria, where contemporary theatre practices maintain strong roots in ritual and festival.

Gilbert and Tompkins interpret various plays (all West or South African) as changing the classical canonical sources, so as to, as they put it, 'interrogate' them.

The general background to this analysis is a range of discourses in the former colonies, establishing identities for the newly independent countries, including their cultures and literatures. The partially overlapping discourses of Negritude, pan-Africanism and Afrocentrism all attack, at least at times, the imposition of practices and values by the former colonisers, and their failure to engage with African culture or cultures.[7] This failure has been well documented. What it might look like in the particular case of classicists is illustrated by a passage from the proceedings of a conference 'on Classics' held at University College Ibadan, two years before Nigerian independence:[8]

> From the foregoing brief analysis of classical literature it would not be absurd to suggest here that while West Africa looks up to the West for science and technology, her source of moral and literary inspiration should and must be Greece and Rome ... West Africa is a 'young' territory still largely controlled by France and Britain ... Just as infant Europe greedily sucked the spirit of Hellenism and of Rome long after the civilisation of the latter had withered in a winter of barbarism, and bloomed forth in literary and artistic splendour during the Renaissance, so West Africa is at present digesting and ready to digest all the best that the West can offer.

With hindsight, it is unsurprising that many African (and indeed African-American) writers have protested in many ways against the superiority of European classical antiquity and its function as a model. Most classicists know these protests best through Martin Bernal's *Black Athena*, but they go back several decades. Probably the most influential figure was the Senegalese historian Cheikh Anta Diop, who started publishing in the 1950s.[9] In many cases, protests focused specifically on literature. For instance, Wole Soyinka complained in an interview in the late 1980s:[10]

6. Greek Tragedies in West African Adaptations

I remember my shock as a student of literature and drama when I read that drama originated in Greece. What is this? I couldn't quite deal with it. What are they talking about? I never heard my grandfather talk about Greeks invading Yorubaland. I couldn't understand. I've lived from childhood with drama. I read at the time that tragedy evolved as a result of the rites of Dionysus. Now we all went through this damn thing, so I think the presence of eradication had better begin. It doesn't matter what form it takes.

As Gilbert and Tompkins and others point out, West African adaptations of Greek tragedy, as much other postcolonial literature, reflect such concerns. In their different ways, they make their source texts African, appropriating the canonical paradigm as something of their own. All of them are plays about African issues, with African characters, using African performance styles, and so on. Canonical counter-discourse is a way of using plays associated with the colonial powers as a space for building West African (or other) identities and literatures.

Such counter-discourse is particularly obvious where the modifications to the source introduced by the West African writer explicitly protest against European imperialist actions or ideology. The two plays to look at in this respect are Soyinka's *Bacchae of Euripides* and Osofisan's *Tegonni. The Bacchae of Euripides* is probably the West African play most widely known among classicists, and the one Gilbert and Tompkins focus on.[11] As the title suggests, the play follows in general the plot of its source text. However, Soyinka introduces numerous modifications. Perhaps the most obvious among them is an emphasis on slavery that is not in the ancient play. In line with the often marginal identities of Greek tragic choruses, he adds a chorus of slaves of mixed ethnicity with a black leader, suppressed by the royal house. Pentheus has more tyrant-like features than in Euripides, as becomes clear already in the initial stage directions, which ask for 'a road ... lined by the bodies of crucified slaves mostly in the skeletal stage' (235). In the early parts of the play there is much emphasis on an annual scapegoat ritual in which one of the slaves is selected for flogging. Dionysus' conflict with Pentheus, the central event in the plot, is at the same time a liberation of the slaves, and in the end the chorus of now ex-slaves unites with the chorus of Bacchants to celebrate Dionysus. Apart from anything else (and we will need to come back to this 'anything else'), Soyinka presents to his audience, which at least at the first performance, at London's *Old Vic*, was mostly European, a play from the European canon into which he has written reminders of white exploitation.

Osofisan's *Tegonni*[12] is considerably less well known among classicists than *The Bacchae of Euripides*. The plot centres on Tegonni, a Yoruba princess during the European conquest of West Africa. Like her almost-namesake Antigone, she defiantly buries her brother's body. The British Governor, Lt. Gen. Carter-Ross, had forbidden burial because Tegonni's brother had died fighting on the enemy side. Tegonni, who was about to marry the local British District Officer, is first imprisoned and eventually dies. Throughout the play injustices of the British rule in West Africa are exposed, mostly through the unsympathetic Carter-Ross. Arrogant and high-handed, he mistreats all Africans he has dealings with, whether they oppose or welcome him. He issued the ban on burying Tegonni's brother because that is 'what these niggers respect' (65), and hankers after the good old days when 'you knew you were right, because you were white, and you believed in the Cross and in the Empire' (131). Like *The Bacchae of Euripides*, *Tegonni* was first performed outside Africa (in the US). For both authors, one attraction of Greek tragedy is its privileged position in the European canon, which can be used as a high-profile platform for protest against the former colonisers.

(b) Modes of adaptation

At this point, it is important to avoid an easily made mistake. It would be misleading to use *The Bacchae of Euripides* and *Tegonni* to generalise about the entire body of West African adaptations of Greek literature. The variety among this group of plays will be a running theme of this essay. For now, I want to concentrate on the issue of protest against the former colonial powers. One of my central arguments is that this kind of explicit protest is only one of several modes in which West African writers have adapted Greek tragedy to Africa. A quick look at each of the plays is therefore in order now.

Odale's Choice by Kamau Brathwaite, who worked as an Education Officer in Ghana for eight years, after growing up in the Caribbean, was first performed in a secondary school.[13] The play follows the plot of *Antigone* quite closely. The largest changes are the absence of a Haemon character, the absence of the closing scene with Creon, and Creon's pardoning of the Antigone-character Odale, rejected by Odale as Creon upholds the ban on her brother's burial. All of these changes further enhance Sophocles' focus on Antigone / Odale and her defiance of Creon. The theme clearly struck – and still strikes – a chord with the young audiences and readers of the play. Since its first publication, the text has been reprinted twelve times.

Ola Rotimi's *The Gods Are Not To Blame* sets in Yorubaland the story of Odewale's (= Oedipus') search for the murderer of his predecessor, which turns out to be a quest for his own identity, leading to his self-mutilation and the suicide of his queen.[14] The time is non-specific, and there are no references to any European presence in Africa. A good way into the play is through its richly allusive title, which adumbrates key themes of the play. I will pick out three, all showing Rotimi developing various elements of Sophocles' *Oedipus Rex* for his context and purpose.

First, the title points to the question of divine responsibility. The shrine of the Yoruba god Ogun is visible throughout, and oracles initiate parts of the action, as they do in *Oedipus Rex*. When killing his father, whom he fails to identify, Odewale seems to act as the god Ogun (the scene is re-enacted in a haunting flash-back sequence). As he brandishes his hoe, he screams (III.1): 'This is ... Ogun / and Ogun says: flow! / flow ... let your blood flow'. But then immediately he realises what he has done: 'Ogun ... I have used your weapon, and I have killed a man'. The shift in responsibility from god to man is a creative adaptation of a similar sequence in Sophocles, where Oedipus blames first Apollo, but then himself (after his self-mutilation: 1329-36). But Rotimi makes this shift more explicit, and perhaps less ambiguous, than Sophocles. Near the end (III.4), Odewale teaches his people 'do not blame the gods. The powers would have failed if I did not let them use me ... '. Odewale should have resisted the gods. In an interview, Rotimi points to the notion in Yoruba culture 'that a person chooses his own destiny from 'a sort of *tabula rasa* mind, before he descends to the world to practicalize the choice' and is, therefore, fully responsible for his actions.[15]

This leads to the *second* aspect of the title. Like Sophocles, Rotimi motivates the action in terms of character. Throughout, he stresses his lead character's quick temper. Several people come under fire as Odewale loses his calm, and his history of irascibility is documented in his long-standing nickname 'scorpion'. 'Not to blame the gods' is made easier by Odewale's disposition. *Thirdly*, Rotimi motivates human behaviour further by developing Sophocles' emphasis on Oedipus' origins in a different *polis*. Odewale is a man who is haunted by the fact that he belongs to a different tribe. Again and again, he expresses his fear that the people he governs will mistreat him because he is an outsider, and the murder itself is preceded by an altercation over Odewale's 'funny' dialect. In the end, of course, these differences turn out to be partly unreal, as Odewale finds out who his biological parents are, and the speech to his people quoted in the previous paragraph continues: '... they (= the gods / the powers) knew my weakness: the weakness of a man easily moved to the defence of his tribe against others'. The references to tribal conflicts should be seen in the context of the civil wars in Nigeria in the late 1960s. Some of the responsibility lies with the European powers, whose actions both as colonisers and as neo-colonial forces contributed to the war. However, like Ogun, these powers are not easily blamed. In the interview quoted above, Rotimi stresses 'our own failings': as he puts it, 'ethnic jingoism was at the bottom of it all'.[16] *The Gods Are Not To Blame* is a rich play, weaving together multiple themes like fate, responsibility, leadership, and tribal politics and identity into a complex texture.

Efua T. Sutherland's *Edufa* is set in the home of Edufa, a successful contemporary Ghanian. Edufa's wife Ampona is ill and eventually dies. In the course of the play, it becomes clear that the illness is brought upon her by a charm. Edufa, worried about a prophecy that death is hanging over him, consulted a diviner and acquired a charm whose consequences he did not fully understand. He knew that the charm would kill the first person to swear an oath that they would die for him. What he did not know is that his wife would be the one to swear the oath. In the play we see him struggling to make her oath invalid through counter-magic, but still unprepared to admit the full truth and publicly renounce the charm.

Clearly, *Edufa* is based on Euripides' *Alcestis*, but more loosely than *Odale's Choice* and *The Gods Are Not To Blame* are based on *Antigone* and *Oedipus Rex*. The wife dying for her husband is the most obvious parallel, and further aspects add to the effect: Edufa's angry altercations with his father Kankam, full of mutual accusation, raising questions about the morality of Edufa's actions (questions much more developed by Sutherland than by Euripides); Edufa's friend Senchi, who like Heracles arrives full of banter but tries to help once he understands the situation; and, in general, a tone that (not least thanks to Senchi) shifts between the solemn and the light-hearted. Yet Sutherland adds much that is not there in *Alcestis*. Most important, at the heart of the play there is the question of the status of magic in the modern world. Edufa finds it difficult to reconcile his self-perception as an 'emancipated' man with the apparent power of the charm – an issue I will come back to.

J.P. Clark Bekederemo's *Song Of A Goat* centres on an Izon family living at one of the Niger estuaries.[17] Zifa, a fisherman, is the head of the household. At the time of the story, he is impotent; his wife Ebiere is driven to have sex with his younger brother Tonye. Zifa's rage, as he finds out, drives Ebiere to miscarry the child and Tonye to commit suicide. As Zifa realises the effects of his wrath, he drowns himself. Neither the plot nor the key theme of the dire consequences of upsetting the laws of nature is taken from a Greek play. The relation of *Song Of A Goat* to its Greek source text is even looser than that of *Edufa*, and one could reasonably argue that the play should be struck from my list. Clark himself was uncomfortable with the notion of Greek (or any other) influence: 'The influences may be there, but there are coincidences, too, because we are all human beings with the same basic emotions and experiences.'[18]

Influence in the sense of derivation or imitation is clearly an inappropriate term to use for *Song Of A Goat* (as indeed for any of the other plays I discuss). However, similarities with Greek material are probably too obvious to be *purely* coincidental. I will concentrate here on Aeschylus' *Agamemnon*, which is likely to be one of several source texts (in the widest sense) that went into the making of this play. To begin with, there is a family curse, as in *Agamemnon*. Zifa's impotence, which sets off the catastrophic events, was ultimately caused by his father's killing of a fellow clansman. A sense of ruthless inevitability permeates the play. The character set is also reminiscent of *Agamemnon*. The focus is entirely on one family, with the chorus representing the neighbours who take a concerned interest. Apart from Zifa, his wife and his brother, there is his son Dode, the (thoroughly un-Greek) Masseur, and Zifa's aunt Orukorere. Orukorere is a Cassandra figure. She is half-possessed, and prophesies the catastrophic events well before the end. However, nobody understands her prophecy; the chorus discussing her visions (2.1-169) sound much like the uncomprehending chorus of *Agamemnon* (1072-1330).

More important than any of these motifs is Clark's rich poetic language, which is reminiscent of the *Agamemnon* in several ways. One of its most striking aspects appears already in the title (which itself, of course, alludes to Greek tragedy). Like Aeschylus, Clark uses metaphors of goats and sacrifice throughout the play, weaving them into a continuous ever-intensifying theme. In the first movement, Ebiere seeks the advice of the Masseur on how to deal with Zifa's impotence. The Masseur advises that she should sleep with Tonye, but only after the proper sacrifice, starting with 'blood of a goat' (1.80). She rejects the advice, only to end up having sex with Tonye without trying to assure divine goodwill through sacrifice. Then, at her first appearance, Orukorere shouts (2.6-7) 'I say come out here, all you people. / A goat, a goat, I hear the cry of a goat'. Later, as Tonye and Ebiere are having sex, she assures the uncomprehending Dode (3.175) 'Why, boy, these are no leopard and goat / interlocked between life and death, but

/ two dogs at play'. As Zifa, who finds Tonye in his bed after the event, tries to confirm his suspicions and to avenge himself, the metaphors become reality. He slaughters a goat, and demands that Tonye put the head in a pot which is too small and will break. Ebiere faints, and Zifa comments (4.254) 'Brother, you see the pot is broken!', and Tonye exclaims 'This was a trap, a trap … ', and runs off to kill himself. Wilfully, Zifa has generated a metaphor of destruction to unmask his brother and wife, thus causing further destruction. This interplay of sacrificial language and stage action has strong Aeschylean overtones.

So where do these brief discussions of the plays leave us? It appears, I would say, that protest against European economic, military or cultural domination (which is so prominent in *The Bacchae of Euripides* and *Tegonni*) is not at the heart of all the plays on my list. Elements of such protest may well be present in Rotimi's gods and powers or in Brathwaite's Creon, but they are certainly not stressed. The diversity among the plays is obvious. To a considerable degree, the answer to the question 'what is the attraction of Greek plays to West African writers?' is different for each playwright. Clark 'translated' Aeschylus' language of goat sacrifice, Sutherland found new potential in the story of the wife sacrificing herself for her husband, Rotimi applied the question of guilt from the Oedipus myth to a Nigerian cultural and political framework, and Brathwaite realised that the values, characters and simplicity of the story of Antigone's defiance would inspire his young audiences.

Going back to Soyinka and Osofisan one realises that in their plays, too, not all is protest against the former colonial powers. *The Bacchae of Euripides* will be the focus of later sections. As for Osofisan, he writes in the introduction to the printed edition of *Tegonni* (11):

> In the final decade of the last century, European nations began to scramble to establish colonies in Africa. Through brute force, cunning, and dubious 'agreements', European adventurers seized control over most of suburban Africa, subjugated the local rulers, and established new forms of government in the name of 'civilising' the 'Dark Continent'. *Tegonni, an African Antigone* is situated in the era of imperialist expansion, and the main confrontation is between a princess of Yorubaland, in present-day Nigeria, and one of the British colonial governors.

Clearly, Osofisan would agree that *Tegonni* is literature of protest against the European rulers. Then he continues:

> But my concern in writing is more than that. Using the well-known format of Sophocles' *Antigone*, I have constructed a play that re-examines the issue of race relations and personal courage. But above all, my

concern is also to look at the problem of political freedom against the background of the present turmoil in Nigeria – my country – where various military governments have continued for decades now to thwart the people's desire for democracy, happiness, and good government.

Tegonni is also a play about present-day Nigeria. It is still literature of protest, but protest also against current governments. There are large questions about the degree to which the failure of these governments is ultimately the responsibility of the former colonial powers. But it is clear that *Tegonni*, like *The Gods Are Not To Blame*, points fingers also at the Nigerian rulers of his time.

It appears, then, that what is true for Clark, Sutherland, Rotimi and Brathwaite is true also for Osofisan. In their different ways, all West African dramatists regarded the plots, form, language, characters and themes of Greek tragedy as, to some degree, readily available material for their dramas, their audiences and their issues. These issues included engagement with colonialism, but also with the postcolonial situation and indeed with topics such as pride, selfishness or courage, which have significance beyond the context of colonialism or postcolonialism. In this respect (with heavy stress on 'this'), their plays are similar to recent European or American adaptations of Greek tragedies. This conclusion, uninspiring as it may be, is important. It is important because it warns us against one-dimensional interpretation. I will now try to make it more inspiring.

(c) *Greek tragedy as a model*

My argument so far has ducked some important questions. On the one hand, I have introduced the notion of 'canonical counter-discourse' and pointed to the way some of the plays under discussion use the European connotations of Greek tragedy as a platform for protest against European imperialism. On the other hand, I have pointed to the frequently observed adaptability of Greek tragedy to local contexts, and have argued that protest against the practices of the former colonisers is only one aspect of the plays. The two points are not mutually exclusive, but they call for further discussion of what exactly it means for West African writers to use Greek material. In what sense is it alien, in what sense is it not? And in what sense, exactly, is or isn't refiguring this material an act of 'counter-discourse'? I will try to answer these questions in three steps (sections c, d, e).

Perhaps the first thing to realise is that not all African writers who have stressed that Europe in general or ancient Greece in particular is different or even alien to modern Africa have phrased this contrast as antagonistically as Soyinka did in the quotation above (p. 123). Léopold Sédar Senghor, president of Senegal, poet, cultural theorist and much else, made the frequently cited statement that 'emotion is completely Negro as reason is Greek'. It is clear why statements like this have immediately been criticised.[19] Such statements may not accept that Africans are inferior to Europeans but they take over a traditional dichotomy which classified Africans as inferior to Europeans. Nevertheless, they show that, at least in the 1960s and early 1970s, some West African thinkers were still prepared to analyse aspects of Africa and its cultures in terms originally set by Europeans.

One particular aspect of this tendency is the use of Greek tragedy as a vantage point for thinking about African drama. For example, Michael Echeruo, a Nigerian theatre historian, concluded a 1973 article on ritual and theatre with the suggestion:[20] 'The Igbo should do what the Greeks did: expand ritual into life and give that life a secular base. That way, we may be able to interpret and reinterpret that serious view of life which is now only so divinely manifested in our festivals.' Here and elsewhere, the Greeks serve as an object of comparison, and even an example held up for imitation. This view among several West African scholars in the 1960s and 1970s of Greek tragedy as a kind of model of what drama should be like supports the evidence from the plays. The canonical status and European association of Greek tragedy provided opportunities for demarcating African drama. This demarcation could take the form of anti-colonialist protest, but also of imitation and blending. The two modes are two sides of one coin.

(d) Greek myths for West African plays

The paradigm for discussions of postcolonial adaptations of European literature is usually plays using material from Shakespeare. Gilbert and Tompkins in the quotation above compare postcolonial adaptations of Greek tragedy to postcolonial adaptations of Shakespeare. They point out that the former are less frequent than the latter. Yet frequency is not the only difference. Understanding some of the other differences will help us understand better why and how West African playwrights sometimes found Greek tragedy attractive, and in what sense exactly it is counter-discourse.

One such difference is the type of material used for the plots. Where many (though by no means all) of Shakespeare's plots are about historical subjects, Greek tragedy almost exclusively dramatises myth. The mythological subject matter carries notions like universality, timelessness and archetypes. These associations offer an opportunity for non-European playwrights to extract Greek tragedy from a European context and claim its applicability to their own culture in a way that a historical subject matter does not.

Universality is of course a problematic concept, not just because its anthropological, psychological or literary underpinnings can be challenged (in what sense, if any, is myth universal?), but also, and more important in this context, because of its associations with colonialism. The European powers made European literature a cornerstone of the education of their colonial subjects. European literature was assumed to be the literature the whole world should read, often with little reflection about the implications of transferring literatures between cultures. Both the superiority and applicability of European literature was simply assumed. As G. Viswanathan puts it in a book on literary study under British rule in India, 'the self-justification of the literature curriculum – its use as both method and object of moral and intellectual study – remained the central problematic of British ideology'.[21]

This is where myth is interesting. On the one hand, universalist notions of myth have their fair share of imperialist connotations. For anthropologists like Edwin Smith and Andrew Dale, for instance, collecting tales in then-Rhodesia in the 1910s, the universality of human nature expressed in the myths of different peoples was essential, and yet tied up with notions of primitivism: 'it may be said in conclusion, that man's common human-heartedness is in these tales. Grief and joy are shown to touch the same chords in their hearts as in ours. How simply, yet how touchingly, are the fundamental human emotions described ... Separated by deep gulfs as they are from ourselves in many things, yet across the abysses we can clasp hands in a common humanity.'[22] On the other hand, myth, unlike literature, has no author. Greek myth is not a European 'achievement' in the way Greek (or Shakespearean) tragedy is. The notion of the universality of myth is not directly linked to the canon. It is, therefore, interesting to ask how West African playwrights approach the notion of the universality of Greek myths.

The editor of *Odale's Choice* writes in the first paragraph of his introduction: 'The story and tone of the play is that of *Antigone*, the classic Greek drama. Here it is modernised (though to an indefinite period) and made to apply to an African country, but no country in particular. The theme is timeless: the defiance of tyranny, a situation full of conflict and natural drama'. *Antigone* is a Greek drama, but its story is timeless. We cannot know whether Brathwaite would agree with his editor but at least the reception of the play seems to be driven by notions of 'timelessness'. Brathwaite's play itself (and the same is true for *The Gods Are Not To Blame* and *Edufa*) would be consistent with this reading, but by no means calls for it.

By contrast, *Tegonni* explicitly engages with the issue of transporting Greek myth to West Africa. Femi Osofisan is the most overtly self-conscious of the playwrights I am concerned with. In the case of *Tegonni*, there are various scenes interrupting the main action, in which a divine or semi-divine figure called Antigone talks to some of the characters including princess Tegonni. Repeatedly, the dialogue in these scenes is meta-theatrical: Antigone knows, and instructs others, about the plot and the characters of what is, at one level, her own story. She comes, she says, 'from the Greek and other mythologies' (26). She is a figure of hope who shows the value of fighting oppression, since she has done it so famously elsewhere.

As a figure of myth, Antigone has a somewhat vague status. Her world is not really that of the other characters. This is particularly clear when Osofisan poses the question of whether she and all she stands for is myth in the sense of 'just a myth'. Near the end, Antigone and Tegonni are given the following dialogue (125-6, my italics):

Antigone: *I'm just a metaphor. From the past –*
Tegonni: So why didn't you just stay where you were, *a relic in the memory of poets*?
        ...
Antigone: Listen, if you had insisted, there was only one advice I could have offered you ... Give up, I would have said. Because I've learnt from history, and I have grown wise. Freedom is a myth which human beings invent as a torch to kindle their egos. In the end, it all comes to the same thing, men and women slaughtering one another to the applause of deluded worshippers.
Tegonni: I don't believe this! You cannot have been a victim of tyranny, and believe such things. You cannot have lived among the oppressed, and *say that their suffering is a myth*!
Antigone: I told you I've learnt from history! Go and look down the ages, my dear ...

However, this dialogue should not be looked at in isolation. True, never is Antigone a character like the others; but that is not to say that she is unreal, a 'metaphor' or a 'relic in the memory of poets'. In other scenes, Antigone's universal scope and historical depth are stressed: she has seen many fights against oppression and thus gives meaning to Tegonni's struggle. At one point she says 'the script is the story we rehearsed, as it's happened at other times, in other places' (30), and similarly 'It's not our story, we're from other times. It's just history about to repeat itself' (29), or 'this Gomina [= governor], this Carter-Ross, he will fade away like all oppressors before him' (93). She makes it explicit that her black skin doesn't sever connection with the Antigone of myth: 'what colour is mythology?', she asks (27). And when Tegonni, in the dialogue just quoted, continues to resist Antigone's interpretation of her own status, Antigone eventually admits that she only meant to test Tegonni's resolve to die for her ideals. Myth is not 'just' myth.

We do not know whether universality of myth is a notion that mattered to all the writers under discussion. Quite possibly some of them would reject any such notion. But at least at times, it appears, Greek tragedy has been attractive to West African writers and their audiences and readers because the mythical material behind its plots has associations of temporal and spatial universality that give a general frame to their culturally specific plays. Some, like Brathwaite's editor, seem to be comfortable with accepting these associations more or less directly. Others, like Osofisan, carefully negotiate the tensions between universality and specificity. Others again, like Clark in the quotation above, appeal to the shared 'basic emotions and experiences' of all human beings that lead to similarities between plays of different authors in different cultures. All these are ways of saying that their source material is not just Greek or European. Greek tragedy is some-times appropriated as European in an exclusive sense: Greece is the origin of the 'European tradition', Greek tragedy is part of the 'European canon', for others to copy. Osofisan explicitly, and Brathwaite's editor perhaps implicitly, reject any notions of European privileged access to Greek material. The story of Antigone or the house of Atreus belongs to them as much as to any European author. It begins to emerge that Greek tragedy plays a complicated role in canonical counter-discourse. Greece appears not to be the same as Britain. Let us pursue this path.

(e) Similarities between Greek and African theatre

I shelved until now discussion of one of the most crucial issues for studying West African adaptations of Greek tragedy: the similarities between Greek and West African theatre in general. As will become clear, these similarities are extensive. They are no doubt a further attraction of Greek tragedy to West African playwrights, and indeed a further difference between Shakespeare and Greek tragedy.

West African writers themselves have stressed parallels between African and Greek drama. Clark, for instance, points to shared origins in religion and shared use of masks.[23] Soyinka goes one step further, contrasting medieval and modern European theatre with 'the beginnings of theatre, Greek or African'; through successive stages 'cosmic representation has shrunk into a purely moral one, a summation in terms of penalties and rewards'.[24] His argument about the shift from cosmic or ritual theatre to moral or ethical theatre is complex, but the point to note here is that statements aligning Greek with African against later European are closely related to engagement with 'timeless' Greek myth. They oppose the classification of Greek tragedy as a European genre by appropriating it as, partly, African; and they help us sharpen our understanding of exactly how Greek plays inspired West African adaptations, and exactly how these adaptations are 'counter-discourse'.

The power of Soyinka's argument derives from the considerable evidence one can marshal to support it. Very obviously, ancient Greek and various African theatre traditions share numerous characteristics. The most striking are: choruses and the presence of some kind of public; performance spaces in the open, with spectators sitting on more than one side of the acting area, and plays often set outside buildings; the importance of music and of dance, the use of masks; and – perhaps most important – contact with the supernatural, be it through performance in the context of festivals, through gods appearing on stage or through the enactment of rituals.

Unsurprisingly one finds many of these shared characteristics in those plays in which West African (and other African) drama adapts Greek tragedies. All the plays under discussion have choruses, though often speaking in individual voices. These choruses add a public dimension to the plays, which is sometimes reinforced through a setting outside buildings. In three plays, *The Gods Are Not To Blame*, *Edufa*, and *Song Of A Goat*, this public dimension is played out in the interaction between representatives of the community and a lead character, who is intensely aware of his reputation and role in this community. All the plays, moreover, use song, and some dance, and in all of them supernatural forces play a role.

A thorough discussion of these issues would need to be based on African *performances* of both the plays in question and of 'straight' Greek tragedies. The current state of research makes this project impossible. However, examination of the *texts* will allow us to draw at least initial conclusions. I will concentrate on one example: ritual. In one definition or another, ritual is isolated by many writers as the oldest form of theatrical art in Africa. As such it is drawn upon frequently also in the secular African theatre of the second half of the twentieth century. Moreover, in particular in the late 1960s and 1970s there has been considerable discussion among West African writers over the function and relevance of traditional ritual in new drama.[25] (And in view of the extensive connections that many of the playwrights in question had with Europe and America, it is worth remembering that ritual was highly popular also in European and American theatre during the 1960s and early 1970s.)

Ritual in (as we will see) the widest sense of the word appears in all of the plays under discussion. In some of them it plays a subordinate role. As discussed, the god Ogun looms large in *The Gods Are Not To Blame*. However, this divine influence is not played out through rituals beyond a few references to oracles and ritual song. Similarly, in *Odale's Choice* the title refers to the lead character's decision to give her brother a makeshift burial, and eventually to die for this choice, but the emphasis is less on the death rites due to the gods than on the Antigone-characters's opposition to Creon and eventual voluntary death. The focus is thoroughly on human action and responsibility. By contrast, ritual in some sense is core to the conception of all of the other plays, as ever with great variation. To illustrate the point, I will look briefly at two plays, *The Bacchae of Euripides* and *Edufa*.

The Bacchae of Euripides is often cited as a prime example of the syncretism that is so frequent in much postcolonial literature (though by no means confined to it). Soyinka's play blends different traditions at many levels. Ritual is central here. Essential to his conception of the play is his interest in similarities between Dionysus and the Yoruba god Ogun, manifest already in the 1969 essay 'The fourth stage'.[26] Both in the play and in writing about the play, Soyinka stresses various points of contact between the gods: Dionysus' thyrsus, recalling the willowy pole that is an attribute of Ogun's; the theme of dismemberment, which has a place in the mythology of both Dionysus and Ogun; and wine, attribute of both gods, all are prominent in the play.[27] Soyinka even goes so far as to incorporate word-by-word quotations from a poem he wrote about Ogun a few years earlier.[28]

Thus equipped with Yoruba attributes, Dionysus gives Soyinka scope for writing a play which resonates in a Yoruba context. Going even further, Soyinka incorporates Christian material. The result is a play that recalls, more or less closely, a variety of ritual forms from three religious traditions. Most of the material consists of numerous acclamations, invocations, prayers, chants, and dances honouring or beseeching Dionysus-Ogun, some of them also reminiscent of phrasing in the gospels (most obviously 247-8). Again alluding to both ancient Greek and African concepts, there is a scapegoat ritual, which is practised by Pentheus every year to purify Thebes (236-42); there are two wedding ceremonies, one of them associating Dionysus with Christ and recalling both the crucifixion and the marriage feast at Cana (285-7); the play ends with Agave, Cadmus and Tiresias drinking wine that flows like blood from the impaled head of Pentheus, bringing to mind the eucharist and providing the climax to the theme of wine that runs through the play and that resonates in all three traditions. At no stage does Soyinka replicate exactly any specific ritual as it was or is practised by ancient Greeks, Yoruba or Christians, but he works hard to create a heightened religious atmosphere by manipulating and mixing various kinds of patterns that are part, or at least reminiscent, of ancient Greek, Yoruba and Christian beliefs and observances.

Corresponding practices in *Edufa* are best described as magic. Whether magic is ritual is a matter of definition. Ritual is a notoriously ill-defined term;[29] moreover, the relationship between religion (under which rubric 'ritual' is normally filed by classicists) and magic is famously contested.[30] There are both overlaps and points of differentiation between the two. On the one hand, both are often prescribed or repetitive in some sense, and both often try to influence super-human powers; on the other hand, in so far as ritual is understood as 'religious ritual', it tends to be less private and anti-social than much magic. Therefore, however one defines magic and ritual, it is obvious that *Edufa* provides a useful point of both contrast and comparison to the use of ritual in *The Bacchae of Euripides*. Edufa struggles with the charm that he procured when he feared for his life, but which in the event turned against his wife Ampona. Centred on this struggle, the play is full of narrated and enacted attempts by Edufa and others to work counter-magic. The play opens with Edufa's sister collecting dew and spring water at his instruction (prologue), which he then uses to pour over specially selected herbs (act 1.1). Later in the first act, when Kankam confronts Edufa (1.4), we find out about the charm and Ampona's oath. Act 2 opens with the chorus of women from the town appearing (2.1). They are touring the city, driving away evil through chants, and they do the same in Edufa's house. Sam, an 'idiot servant', appears, bringing (2.2) further objects with magic powers, along with instructions. One of the instructions demands that Edufa paint a sun on the doorstep. When Ampona falls on the image of the sun in the final act (3.3), Edufa is panic-stricken, realising that he failed to cure her through Sam's magic. Ampona goes into her room and a little later Edufa re-emerges, having burned the charm – but too late: Ampona is dead. *Edufa* enacts the difficulty of stopping the powers that one has raised. Edufa fails to undo the charm. Between them, chants, burning of incense, pouring of water, painting of symbols and much else suffuse the play with the power of the charm. By contrast to, for instance, *Odale's Choice*, this is a play in which non-human power is present throughout.

At the same time as enacting this power, the play raises questions about it. In his exchange with Kankam, Edufa portrays himself as an 'emancipated' man (1.4), who does not need to take recourse to diviners. This is not necessarily just a lie. In a programmatic mono-logue, he says (1.4):

> Don't ask me why I did it; I do not know the answer.
> If I must be condemned, let me not be charged for any
> will to kill, but for my failure to create a faith.
> Who thought the charm made any sense? Not I.
> A mystic symbol by which to calm my fears – that was
> all I could concede it.
> It still doesn't make any sense.

This sense of insecurity is with him throughout the play. Ampona's illness is therefore doubly trying for him. He not only wants her well and feels guilty, but also struggles to come to terms with the power of magic and his self-perception. This is the play about a man who lives uncomfortably between two worlds, uncomfortably because he has 'failed to create a faith'.

It would be possible to discuss further playwrights, especially Clark and Osofisan. Such discussion would confirm what should already have become clear: there is great variety in the way West African playwrights use ritual or comparable phenomena. Sometimes ritual is low-key, at other times it is central to the play. Sometimes the ritual in question has close parallels in some West African cultures, sometimes the rituals are invented, sometimes ritual is public, sometimes it is private. None of the plays does the same with ritual as does any one Greek tragedy. However, I would argue that even to an author like Sutherland in *Edufa* the widespread use of ritual in Greek tragedy matters. The point is that ritual, and generally speaking contact with the supernatural, sit natu-rally in Greek tragedies. Greek dramatists have characters enact, narrate and discuss ritual in numerous permutations. Playwrights writing in West African traditions, which are so rich in the use of ritual, can to some degree 'feel at home' in Greek tragedy.

I have come to the end of section 2, and it is time to sum up. Writers in West Africa, as in Europe, are comfortable refiguring Greek tragedy for their own purposes. This frequently stressed flexibility of Greek tragedy is underpinned, in the case of West Africa (and no doubt elsewhere), by Greek tragedy's canonical status as a model, by the notion of myth as timeless and colour-blind (to adapt Tegonni's words), and by a range of characteristics shared with local dramatic traditions.

Is all this 'canonical counter-discourse', then? On the one hand, it clearly is. The plays under discussion need to be seen against the backdrop of a world in which the colonisers had tried to establish the paradigm of European literatures, values, and perspectives, and had often even denied that there was such a thing as African literature. Against this backdrop, using plays strongly associated with the colonial powers as a space for creating postcolonial literatures or identities is inherently charged and an act of opposition and emancipation.

On the other hand, 'counter-discourse' could suggest a confrontational mode that is not always there. Thanks not least to the nuanced connotations of Greek tragedy in a postcolonial context, the project of making Greek tragedies into something African adopts a complex range of modes, often all at one time: rejection and protest (against old and new powers or ideologies), alignment, blending, demarcation, and much else. Negotiating what is African against what is Greek and what is European has turned out not a purely oppositional process. Greek tragedy is European in the sense that Greece is part of Europe, but West African writers show that in the dichotomy 'European' vs. 'African', 'Greek' can play a complex role. This complexity is core to understanding West African adaptations of Greek plays.

This leads to a wider point. What is true for all literature is perhaps especially true for postcolonial literature: the risk of reductionism. To classify plays as postcolonial is to prioritise their political dimensions. I hope that my discussion has shown at least in passing that there is much that can be said about, for instance, the characters, the language, the visual aspects or, emphatically, the meaning of these plays that is not, primarily, political. I have stressed variety throughout. These plays deserve what many European adaptations of Greek tragedy have received: individual discussions as works in their own right (and this, of course, can also be framed as a political question).

(3) West African adaptations for European audiences and readers

The leading question in section 2 has been how and why West African dramatists engage with Greek tragedy, and I have tried to place their plays in the context of African debates. In the remaining pages, the vantage point will shift. This is an essay written by a classicist, so I will ask what these plays have to offer specifically to a classicist, or more generally to the person who brings to the plays an expertise and an interest that is, originally, in ancient Greek rather than modern African drama. What do these plays have to offer to those readers and spectators who approach them as a particular group of adaptations of Greek tragedies, rather than as modern West African plays adapting a particular group of earlier plays? Studying the reception of ancient Greek and Roman literature should always be a two-way process. After looking at the engagement of the new plays with the ancient plays, it is now time to see whether the new plays can point us back to the ancient plays. All the more so, one might add, since several of the plays, *The Gods are Not To Blame, Edufa, The Bacchae of Euripides, Tegonni* and *The Trojan Women Or The Women Of Owu*,[31] are currently performed or have recently been performed in Europe or North America, and since they are studied no longer just as African or Black Writing, but increasingly also under the umbrella of Classical Studies. Courses on reception of Greek tragedy are increasingly popular, and African plays are beginning to establish their place on the curricula of European and American classics departments.

The discussion in section (2) sets the framework. It has become clear that, in many ways, West African plays are not in a separate category. They do what all adaptations of Greek tragedy do: they engage spectators by using some of the themes, characters and plot structures that ancient Greek plays use. But it should also have become clear that in other ways, the plays in question are different. They present Greek tragedy differently from the way it is conceived in at least the bulk of adaptations today, certainly in Europe and North America. Many of the characteristic elements of the West African plays that I discussed earlier – choruses and the presence of some kind of public; the extensive use of music and of dance; and the importance of the supernatural – set these plays apart from most European and American adaptations of Greek tragedies. Not that these elements are unheard of in European or American plays (think, for example, of Lee Breuer's *The Gospel at Colonus*). But to find them in combination, as one does in the West African plays under discussion, is the exception, rather than the rule.

This difference, I would argue, is part of the attraction. European and American spectators and readers (classicist or otherwise) are confronted with something they are not familiar with, and novelty can be appealing. The appeal is perhaps felt especially now, during a period of much increased interest in non-European and non-American theatre in Europe and America. Productions incorporating African, Caribbean or Asian elements as well as tours by performances originating outside Europe and America all win audiences who in the past were familiar mostly with theatre standing in, or close to, the European and American theatre tradition.

Beyond the sheer difference, there is the connection with the Greek tradition. As discussed, choruses representing the community, dance, song, gods as characters, or ritual, do not just set the West African plays apart from many European or American plays; they also connect them with the Greek plays. African dramatists and indeed directors are, potentially, better placed than many of their non-African counterparts, and indeed many non-African classicists, to respond to certain characteristics of Greek tragedy. More than many of their European or American counterparts, at least, they are familiar with masks, dances or gods on stage. Generalisations beyond this point are problematic; I will, therefore, once more look at particular examples, and return to the use of ritual and magic in the *Bacchae of Euripides* and *Edufa*.

Most classicists would probably agree that ritual in Greek tragedy does two things at a time.[32] First, by recalling cult practices, it creates, for want of a better term, a religiously charged atmosphere; it involves and affects spectators; it is perhaps not efficacious in the way ritual is in its normal context, but it is highly emotive. On the other hand, secondly, it is part of a play, shaping, and shaped by, the rest of the play. It is just one element of the play, and resonates with the rest of the play, just as other elements do. When the chorus of *Oedipus Rex* beseech Apollo and other gods to put an end to the plague in a song reminiscent of cult paeans, the reminiscences will have created for (classical Greek) audiences a situation resembling and evoking, though not reproducing, that of cult. At the same time the song needs to be seen in the context of Apollo's and Zeus's complex role in *Oedipus Rex*; it introduces the anxious chorus of concerned Thebans; and in various other ways it prompts a full range of analytical or emotional responses, as does every song in the play.

For most Europeans or Americans today, the second kind of response (looking at ritual as it is worked into a play) is easier than the first (reacting to ritual in a play on the basis of one's experience of ritual elsewhere). Ritual is one of those culturally specific aspects of Greek tragedy that take a great effort to translate. Paeans to Apollo are no longer sung today, and it is hard to imagine what singing and hearing a paean was like for the ancient Greeks. By contrast, resonances between different elements of a play are largely accessible without cultural translation. This is no doubt one reason why classicists, including those listed in n. 32, have recently had more to say about the second than about the first kind of response.

Here many of the West African playwrights are interesting. They too use ritual in both functions, the first and the second. I will start with Soyinka and the second function. Should spectators have forgotten that they are watching a play rather than participating in a ritual, the blend of three different traditions, if nothing else, might remind them. Moreover, many details show that Soyinka wants his audience to think about the ritual elements of the play. For instance, at the end of the play, Pentheus' head, streaming with what looks at first like blood, is a terrible token of Agave's attack on her own son, no matter what effect the allusions to Ogun's and Dionysus' wine or to the Christian eucharist and crucifixion may have on the audience. Or, earlier on, Tiresias, who has offered himself as this year's scapegoat, reprimands those carrying out the flogging 'Fools! Blind, stupid, bloody brutes! Can you see how you've covered me in weals? Can't you bastards ever tell the difference between ritual and reality?' (241). Here and elsewhere, it is clear that Soyinka works hard to integrate evocations of ritual into the texture of the play as a whole.

Yet at the same time he goes a long way to make the ritual elements in his play emotive. The syncretism discussed above builds bridges. Soyinka not only makes ancient Greek ritual forms accessible to African spectators; more than that, by drawing on Christian forms, he does the same for all those spectators, in Africa, Europe, America or elsewhere, to whom Christianity is in some sense meaningful. Moreover, going further probably than Euripides' play and Greek tragedy in general, Soyinka makes the entire play a celebration of Dionysus. Apart from changes in the plot such as the liberation of the slaves through Dionysus, the sheer quantity of praise songs, invocations and other such material directed towards Dionysus is an important means towards this end. Even in the final tableau with Agave, Cadmus and Tiresias drinking from Pentheus' head there are not just the horror and the doubts about the justice of what has happened. The crucifixion and eucharist imagery are associated strongly with benevolent divine action. Here as elsewhere, ritual forms are used to involve spectators. Soyinka himself hints at that when he gives the play the subtitle 'A communion rite', and when he writes in the introduction to the first edition:[33]

Its totality: a celebration of life, bloody and tumultuous, an extravagant rite of the human and social psyche. Certainly there is a hint, if not of religious fanaticism, at least of a manic religious inspiration suddenly let

loose. It is therefore this very quality which creates instances of dissatis-
faction in this play. The ending especially, the petering off of ecstasy into
a suggestion of a prelude to another play. But *The Bacchae* is not an
episode in a historical series, and this is not merely because Euripides did
not live to write the next instalment. The drama is too powerful a play of
forces in the human condition, far too rounded a rite of the communal
psyche to permit of such a notion ... . The more than hinted-at cannibalism [in the adaptation] corresponds to the periodic needs of humans to
swill, gorge and copulate on a scale as huge as Nature's on her monstrous
cycle of regeneration. The ritual, sublimated or expressive, is both social
therapy and reaffirmation of group solidarity, a hankering back to the
origins and formation of guilds and phratries. Man re-affirms his indebt-
edness to earth, dedicates himself to the demands of continuity and
invokes the energies of productivity. Re-absorbed within the communal
psyche he provokes the resources of Nature; he is in turn replenished for
the cyclical drain in his fragile individual potency.

Of course, the success of Soyinka's use of ritual is a matter of judge-
ment. For various reasons, the critical reception of the first
performance was mixed.[34] Not everybody will be able engage the same
way with the particular cocktail of ritual elements Soyinka serves up.
Yet, potentially, his play offers European or American readers and spectators a translation of certain aspects of Euripides' *Bacchae* that they
may find hard to engage with in the original. A classicist, Seth Schein,
reviewing the printed edition commented that 'no English translation
conveys so much of the raw power and theatricality of Euripides' play',
a remark which must owe much to the use of ritual forms.[35]
There is, then, a case for saying that the points of contact between
ancient Greek and modern African drama traditions may help spectators and readers to engage with some characteristic and problematic
aspects of Greek tragedy. However, there are of course problems with
this case. I want to end by briefly discussing two of them.
The first is the risk of exoticism. The continually growing body of
work on cross-cultural performance has stressed that there are challenges and conflicts, as much as attractions, inherent in all theatre that
travels between different cultures.[36] Many European and American
theatre practitioners, for instance Artauld, Brook and Wilson, have
tried to tap foreign performance traditions in order to add something to
their productions that they cannot find in the European tradition.[37] The
same is true for directors or translators of Greek tragedies. Richard
Schechner's *Dionysus in 69*, based on the *Bacchae* and other Greek
plays, featured a birth ritual, adapted apparently from a New Guinean
rite of passage. Jean-Louis Barrault worked the Voodoo rites he had

witnessed in Rio into his Paris *Oresteia*. Pier Paolo Pasolini's fascination with African customs is obvious in much of his work based on Greek tragedy.

All these, and many comparable, performances have been successful with their respective European or American audiences, or at least parts of these audiences. The issue of exoticism concerns these audiences' attitudes to the ritual material. The obvious case is tourist art: tourists videotaping rituals invented only for them, or European audiences watching South African dancers in 'ethnic' costumes, performing dances which in this form were not (or at least no longer) practised at home, but were sent touring until the 1980s. Such events have clear imperialistic overtones, and are easily criticised. The audiences do no engage in any meaningful way with African cultures. Rather, the performances exploit, indulge and propagate European stereotypes of 'primitive', 'authentic' or 'exotic' African culture.

But what, then, about Schechner, Barrault or Pasolini? Their aims are certainly different: they were not commercially driven, for instance, and they used the foreign ritual material to enhance new creative performances. However, in the case of *Dionysus in 69*, to take one example, some people have felt that the New Guinean ritual is primarily marked alien, as a wild and emotional import from an unknown culture. Soyinka speaks of a 'search for the tragic soul of the twentieth-century white bourgeois-hippie American culture'.[38] In other words, Europeans or Americans look for some form of authenticity in foreign cultures, but the authenticity they find is a matter of their imagination rather than any knowledge about, or even interest in, the African, South American, or Caribbean source material. Does that matter? Is it Schechner's responsibility to be in any sense 'faithful' to his New Guinean source material any more than Rotimi or Osofisan should be to their Greek texts? Similar questions may perhaps be asked about *The Bacchae of Euripides* or some of the other plays under discussion. Is some of the appeal of these plays that their exotic African origins give some stamp of authenticity to elements such as choruses, ritual or dances? Is the fact that the ritual elements are part of an African play sometimes more important than their actual portrayal by the dramatist and the performers? And if so, does it matter? Different people will take different views. But it is obvious that European or American appropriation of African plays can raise questions.

Moving on from exoticism, a partly related second problem takes us back, for a last time, to the differences between the different West African plays under discussion. *Edufa*, I noted, contains little by way of 'religious ritual'; instead it is rich in magic. Arguably, magic in *Edufa* has a similar dual function to ritual in *The Bacchae of Euripides*. First, the repeated references to magic suffuse the play with a sense of non-human forces at work. This sense is reinforced by rites enacted on stage. Moreover, all the steps Edufa takes to counteract the power of the charm only serve to increase the sense, so familiar from Greek tragedy, that human power reaches its limit. However, the effect for most European or American spectators, I would argue, is less intense than that of ritual in *The Bacchae of Euripides*. The reason is that magic, as portrayed by Sutherland, has little resonance in European or American mainstream culture.

By contrast, the second function is (as so often) more accessible to spectators and readers outside Africa. Magic in *Edufa*, I suspect, will engage European or American spectators more through the conflicts it creates for Edufa. Should he admit to having procured a charm? Can he, 'emancipated' man that he is, allow himself to believe in magic? *Edufa* has less syncretism and fewer (if any) Christian references than *The Bacchae of Euripides*. The point here is, first of all, that *Edufa* and *The Bacchae of Euripides* are different plays, and Sutherland and Soyinka different authors – for any audience. A preoccupation with the power of ritual is characteristic of Soyinka's work in a way it is not of Sutherland's, and has made some Nigerian critics call him reactionary and nativist.[39] Beyond these differences between authors, there are differences between performance contexts. *Edufa* was first performed in Ghana, and only later left Africa. As noted before, *The Bacchae of Euripides* was commissioned and first performed in the UK. Unlike *Edufa*, it is, at least to some degree, a play written for a European audience. West African plays, I argued, can allow European or American spectators to engage with elements of Greek tragedy in a way that European or American plays often cannot. The point is still true, and indeed central to this paper; it could easily be corroborated through discussions of, for instance, the role of the chorus or of song. However, in making this point one has to be aware that, sometimes, what Europeans or Americans, classicists or otherwise, will find attractive in an African play may be what is written partly for them.

Notes

This paper was first published in *PCPS* 50 (2004). I am grateful for helpful comments from audiences in London and Cambridge in 2001, as well as the *PCPS* and Duckworth editors and referees.

1. Armstrong 1976, Costello 1981, Asgill 1980, Brunkhorst 1995, Brunkhorst 1998, Etherton 1982: 102-42, Gilbert and Tompkins 1996: 38-43. Unfortunately,

Wetmore 2002 came to my attention only after submission of this essay. Isidore Okpewho has announced a book *Black Writers and the Western Canon.* Generally, on West African drama, see the relevant chapters in Banham et al. 1994, Graham-White 1974, Rubin et al. 1997 and Jeyifo 2002. Specifically, on drama as an aspect of postcolonial discourse: Balme 1999, Crow and Banfield 1996, Gilbert 1999, King 1992, Olaniyan 1995. Articles on individual works are cited, where relevant, below.

2. The best starting-point is now Hardwick 2004. See also Broich 1997, Dominik 1999, McDonald 2000.

3. I discuss all of these plays except two: Leloup's *Guiedo* is the only play on the list in French, and the only one that I have not been able to find in the British and German libraries in which I researched this essay. My information is derived from the Cameroon entry in the Africa volume of Rubin et al. 1997, where there is also a bibliography which may provide a starting-point for further work. The world premiere of Osofisan's *The Trojan Women or The Women of Owu* at the Chipping Norton (UK) Theatre in February 2004 took place after the completion of this essay; I will discuss it in Budelmann (forthcoming).

4. The editions do not indicate whether the published text is identical with the text of the first (or any other) performance.

5. Wren 1991.

6. Gilbert and Tompkins 1996: 38. Many of the other items in notes 1 and 2 make similar points. The term 'canonical counter-discourse' is originally H. Tiffin's: Tiffin 1987: 17-34.

7. See Appiah 1992, Howe 1998, Masolo 1994.

8. Edgal 1958: 4-5.

9. In general, Howe 1998: index s.v. 'Greece / Greeks'.

10. Appiah 1988: 782.

11. On *The Bacchae of Euripides* see: Bishop 1983, Bonneau 1986, Conradie 1990, Lefèvre 1986, Okpewho 1999, Seanu 1980, Sotto 1985. On Soyinka more generally see: Jones 1988, Katrak 1986, Wright 1993. All citations from the play are from Soyinka 1973b.

12. Published in Osofisan 1999. On Osofisan in general see: Dunton 1992: 67-94 and Richards 1996.

13. Hardwick 2003: 103 has a brief discussion of the play.

14. Rotimi talks about his play in an interview: Enekwe 1985. For brief discussions of the play see Etherton 1982 123-7, Macintosh 2001.

15. Enekwe 1985: 38-9.

16. Enekwe 1985: 40.

17. Banham 1985 discusses *Song Of A Goat*, and prints extracts from the relevant critical literature.

18. Quoted in Banham 1985: 30.

19. E.g. quoted and criticised by Soyinka 1976: 129.

20. Echeruo 1973: 30; other authors are discussed by Balme 1999: 40-4.

21. Viswanathan 1989: 6.

22. Smith and Dale 1920: 345, quoted and discussed in Okpewho 1983: 1-7.

23. Clark 1973, especially 20 and 24.

24. Soyinka 1976: 41. See also 13-14, where Soyinka introduces a further distinction between 'ritual *tragodia*' and the 'pessimistic moralism' from Aeschylus through to Shakespeare.

25. Osofisan 1982; Soyinka 1976, with the review by Jeyifo 1978; Soyinka 1988, chs 6 and 9.

26. Reprinted most recently in Soyinka 1988, ch. 4. Soyinka himself points to the relevance of the essay in the first edition of the play: Soyinka 1973a.

27. Thyrsus: 242, 244, 250, 254-5, 281; dismemberment: 280-1, 299; wine: 255-7, 241, 246-7, 251, 254, 258-9, 264, 268, 270, 273, 277, 279, 281, 285-9, 289-92, 296, 307.

28. The poem *Idanre*, available in Soyinka 1998: 53-84. Quotations from *Idanre* in *The Bacchae of Euripides* are pointed out in Soyinka's preface to the first edition Soyinka 1973a, and are discussed by Sotto 1985: 76-101.

29. Within classics, see: Calame 1991; Bremmer 1998. It would be fascinating to trace the relationship of the term 'ritual' with colonialism.

30. With emphasis on ritual, see Graf 1991 and Mirecki and Meyer 2002.

31. Possibly more: a web search in October 2003 generated six URL hits.

32. Recent important discussions: Easterling 1993, Gödde 2000, Krummen 1998.

33. Soyinka 1973a. The quotation is from pp. xi-xii.

34. See Soyinka's own account in Soyinka 1988, ch. 7 and the reviews listed by Gibbs et al. 1986.

35. Schein 1977.

36. A good starting-point is Fischer-Lichte et al. 1990 and Pavis 1996.

37. See Innes 1981 and Wiles 2000: 26-47.

38. Soyinka 1976: 6-7. The most influential critique of exoticism in the theatre in general is Bharucha 1990.

39. Discussed by Crow and Banfield 1996: 93-5. See also Soyinka's defence in Soyinka 1988, ch. 9 and the other literature cited above n. 25.

Bibliography

Academiæ Cantabrigiensis Luctus in obitum serenissimi Georgii I. Euergetou [graece] *Magnæ Britanniæ, &c. Regis: et Gaudia ob potentissimi Georgii II. patriarum virtutum ac solii hæredis successionem pacificam et auspicatissimam* (Cambridge, 1727).

Academiæ Oxoniensis Comitia Philologica In Theatro Sheldoniano Decimo Die Julii A.D. 1713. Celebrata: In Honorem Serenissimæ Reginæ Annæ Pacificæ (Oxford, 1713).

Academiæ Oxoniensis Gratulatio Pro Exoptato Serenissimi Regis Gulielmi ex Hibernia Reditu (Oxford, 1690).

Ahmad, Aijaz, 1992, *In Theory: Classes Nations Literatures* (Verso).

Appiah, K.A., 1988, 'An Evening with Wole Soyinka', *Black American Literature Forum* 22, 777-85.

Appiah, K.A., 1992, *In My Father's House: Africa in the Philosophy of Culture* (Methuen).

Arendt, H., 1951, *The Origins of Totalitarianism* (Secker and Warburg).

Armitage, D., 1999, 'Greater Britain: A Useful Category of Historical Analysis?', *American Historical Review* 104, 427-45.

Armstrong, R.P., 1976, 'Tragedy – Greek and Yoruba: A Cross-cultural Perspective', *Research in African Literatures* 7, 23-43.

Arnold, W.T., 1906, *Studies of Roman Imperialism*, ed. E. Fiddes (Manchester University Press).

Asgill, E.J., 1980, 'African Adaptations of Greek Tragedies', *African Literature Today* 11, 175-89.

Ashcroft, B., Griffiths, G., and Tiffin H. (eds), 1989, *The Empire Writes Back: Theory and Practice in Post-colonial Literature* (Routledge).

Aspinall, Algernon, 1914, *The Pocket Guide to the West Indies* (new edn, Duckworth).

Baer, W. (ed.), 1996, *Conversations with Derek Walcott* (University Press of Mississippi).

Baldwin, B. (ed.), 1995, *The Latin & Greek Poems of Samuel Johnson* (Duckworth).

Ballhatchet, K., 1980, *Race, Sex and Class under the Raj: Imperial Attitudes and Policies and Their Critics 1793-1905* (Weidenfeld and Nicolson).

Balme, C.B., 1999, *Decolonizing the Stage: Theatrical Syncretism and Post-Colonial Drama* (Oxford University Press).

Banham, M., 1985, *A Critical View on John Pepper Clark's Three Plays* (Collins).

Banham, M. et al. (eds), 1994, *The Cambridge Guide to African and Caribbean Theatre* (Cambridge University Press).

Barker, J.E., 1910, *Great and Greater Britain: The Problems of Motherland and Empire: Political, Naval, Military, Industrial, Financial, Social* (Smith, Elder & Co.).

Baugh, E., 1978, *Derek Walcott: Memory and Vision, Another Life*, Critical Studies of Caribbean Writers (Longman).

Bernal, M., 1987, *Black Athena: The Afroasiatic Roots of Classical Civilization. Vol. 1, The Fabrication of Ancient Greece 1785-1985* (Rutgers University Press).

Betts, R.F., 1971, 'The Allusion to Rome in British Imperialist Thought of the Late Nineteenth and Early Twentieth Centuries', *Victorian Studies* 15, 149-59.

Bharucha, R., 1990, *Theatre and the World: Performance and the Politics of Culture* (Manohar Publications).

Binns, J.W. (ed.), 1974, *The Latin Poetry of English Poets* (Routledge and Kegan Paul).

Birbalsingh, F. (ed.), 1996, *Frontiers of Caribbean Literature in English* (Macmillan).

Bishop, N., 1983, 'A Nigerian Version of a Greek Classic: Soyinka's Transformation of the *Bacchae*', *Research in African Literatures* 14, 68-80.

Bodelsen, C.A., 1960, *Studies in Mid-Victorian Imperialism*, 2nd edn (Heinemann).

Bodelsen, C.A., 1968, *Studies in Mid-Victorian Imperialism* (Gyldendals forlagstrykkeri, 1924; repr. H. Fertig).

Boehmer, Elleke, 1995, *Colonial and Postcolonial Literature: Migrant Metaphors* (Oxford University Press).

Bonneau, D., 1986, 'From Myth to Rite', in A.S. Gérard (ed.) *European-Language Writing in Sub-Saharan Africa* (Akadémiai Kiadó), 1191-1200.

Bradeen, D.W., 1960, 'The Popularity of the Athenian Empire', *Historia* 9, 257-69.

Bradner, Leicester, 1940, *Musae Anglicanae: A History of Anglo-Latin Poetry, 1500-1925* (Modern Language Association of America).

Brandow, J.C., comp., 1983, *Genealogies of Barbados Families: From Caribbeana and The Journal of the Barbados Museum and Historical Society* (Genealogical Publishing Co.).

Brathwaite, K., 1973, *The Arrivants. A New World Trilogy* (Oxford University Press). These poems were first published by Oxford University Press in three separate volumes: *Rights of Passage* (1967), *Masks* (1968) and *Islands* (1969).

Brathwaite, K., 1979, *Barbados Poetry ?1661-1979[;] A Checklist: Books, Pamphlets, Broadsheets* (Savacou).

Brathwaite, K., 1979a, *Jamaica Poetry: A Checklist. Books, Pamphlets, Broadsheets 1686-1978* (Jamaica Library Service).

Bremmer, J.N., 1998, '"Religion", "Ritual", and the Opposition "Sacred vs. Profane": Notes Towards a Terminological "Genealogy"', in F. Graf (ed.) 1998.

Bridenbaugh, C., and Bridenbaugh, R., 1972, *No Peace Beyond the Line: The English in the Caribbean 1624-1690* (Oxford University Press).

Brock, M.G. and Curthoys, M.C. (eds), 2000, *The History of the University of Oxford, vol. 7: Nineteenth-Century Oxford, Part 2* (Clarendon Press).

Broich, U., 1997, 'Postkoloniales Drama und Griechische Tragödie', in H. Flashar (ed.) *Tragödie: Idee und Transformation* (Teubner).

Browning, R., 1987, 'The Parthenon in History', in C. Hitchens 1987.

Brunkhorst, M., 1995, 'Fugard, Soyinka und die Attische Tragödie: Über die Bedingungen der Möglichkeit eines Konzeptes von Weltliteratur', in M.

Schmeling (ed.) *Weltliteratur heute: Konzepte und Perspektive* (Königshausen & Neumann), 29-48.

Brunkhorst, M., 1998, 'Rituale der Grausamkeit – Traditionen des Widerstands: Antikenrezeption bei Ted Hughes, Wole Soyinka und Athol Fugard', in K. Hölz et al. (eds) *Antike Dramen – Neu Gelesen, Neu Gesehen* (Peter Lang).

Brunt, P.A., 1965, 'Reflections on British and Roman Imperialism', *Comparative Studies in Society and History* 7.3, 267-88.

Brunt, P.A., 1978, 'Laus Imperii', in P.D.A. Garnsey and C.R. Whittaker (eds) *Imperialism in the Ancient World* (Cambridge University Press).

Brunt, P.A., 1990, 'Reflections on British and Roman Imperialism', in *Roman Imperial Themes* (Clarendon Press).

Bryce, J., 1897, *The Holy Roman Empire*, 8th edn (Macmillan).

Bryce, J., 1901, *Studies in History and Jurisprudence*. 2 vols (Clarendon Press; repr. Oxford University Press, American Branch & London: H. Frowde).

Bryce, J., 1914, *The Ancient Roman Empire and the British Empire in India. The Diffusion of Roman and English Law throughout the World* (Oxford University Press).

Budelmann, F., forthcoming, '*Trojan Women* in Yorubaland: Femi Osofisan's *Women of Owu*', in L.P. Hardwick et al. (eds), *Classics in Post-colonial Worlds*.

Burnett, P. (ed.), 1986, *The Penguin Book of Caribbean Verse in English* (Penguin Books).

Burris, S., 1995, 'An Empire of Poetry', in Parker and Starkey (eds) 1995. Reprinted from *Southern Review* 27:3 (1991), 558-74.

Burroughs, P., 1973, 'John Robert Seeley and British Imperial History', *Journal of Imperial and Commonwealth History* 1, 191-211.

Cain, P.J. (ed.), 1999, *Empire and Imperialism: The Debate of the 1870s* (Thoemmes Press).

Cain, P.J., 2002, *Hobson and Imperialism: Radicalism, New Liberalism, and Finance 1887-1938* (Oxford University Press).

Calame, C., 1991, '"Mythe" et "Rite" en Grèce: des Categories Indigènes?', *Kernos* 4, 179-204.

Calame, C., 1996, *Thésée et l'Imaginaire Athénien* (Editions Payot).

Callander, T., 1961, *The Athenian Empire and the British* (Weidenfeld and Nicolson).

Campbell, C.G., 1992, *Colony and Nation: A Short History of Education in Trinidad and Tobago, 1834-1986* (Ian Randle Publishers).

Campbell, C.G., 1996, *The Young Colonials. A Social History of Education in Trinidad and Tobago. 1834-1939* (University of the West Indies Press).

Carmina ad nobilissimum Thomam Holles Ducem de Newcastle inscripta, cum Academiam Cantabrigiensem Bibliothecæ Restituendæ causa inviseret prid. kalend. Maias, MDCCLV (Cambridge, 1755).

Carretta, V. (ed.), 1998, *Letters of the Late Ignatius Sancho, An African* (Penguin Books).

Carretta, V. (ed.), 2001, *Complete Writings* of Phillis Wheatley (Penguin Books).

Carretta, V., 2003, 'Who Was Francis Williams?', *Early American Literature* 38, 213-37.

Carretta, V., 2003a, *Olaudah Equiano: The Interesting Narrative and Other Writings* (Penguin Books, revised edn).

Cartledge, P.A., 1993, 'Like a Worm I' the Bud? A Heterology of Classical Greek Slavery', *Greece and Rome* 40, 163-80.

Bibliography

Césaire, A., 1972, *Discourse on Colonialism*. Translated by Joan Pinkham (Monthly Review Press). First published in Paris in 1955 as *Discours sur le Colonialisme*.

Césaire, A., 1983, *The Collected Poetry*. French and English bi-lingual edn. Translated with introduction and notes by C. Eshleman and A. Smith (University of California Press).

Chamoiseau, P., 1998. *School Days*. Translated by Linda Coverdale (Granta). First published in French in 1994.

Childs, P. and Williams, P., 1997, *An Introduction to Post-Colonial Theory* (Longman).

Ciripova, D., 2001, 'Productions of Greek and Roman Drama on the Slovak Stage', *Eirene* 37, Theatralia, 161-76.

Claassen, J.-M ., 1992, 'The Teaching of Latin in a Multicultural Society: Problems and Possibilities', *Scholia* n.s. 1, 102-18.

Claassen, J.-M., 1998, 'Latin for Students with an African Home Language', *Akroterion* 43, 99-111.

Clark, G., 1936, *The Balance Sheets of Imperialism. Facts and Figures on Colonies* (Columbia University Press).

Clark, J.P., 1973, 'Aspects of Nigerian Drama', in G.D. Killam (ed.) *African Writers on African Writing* (Heinemann).

Clarke, G.W. (ed.), 1989, *Rediscovering Hellenism* (Cambridge University Press).

Clifford, J., 1899, *God's Greater Britain: Letters and Addresses* (J. Clarke & Co.).

Collini, S., Winch, D., and Burrow, J. (eds), 1983, *That Noble Science of Politics: A Study in Nineteenth-Century Intellectual History* (Cambridge University Press).

Colomb, J.C.R., 1880, *The Defence of Great and Greater Britain: Sketches of Its Naval, Military and Political Aspects* (E. Stanford).

Conradie, P.J., 1990, 'Syncretism in Wole Soyinka's Play "The Bacchae of Euripides"', *South African Theatre Journal* 4, 61-74.

Cook, B.F., 1984, *The Elgin Marbles* (Harvard University Press).

Copley, S., and Edgar, A. (eds), 1993, *David Hume: Selected Essays* (Oxford University Press).

Costello, M.L, 1981, 'Greek Drama and the African World: A Study of Three African Dramas in the Light of Greek Antecedents', PhD thesis, University of Southern California.

Cramb, J.A., 1900, *Reflections on the Origins and Destiny of Imperial Britain* (Macmillan).

Cromer, Earl of (Evelyn Baring), 1910, *Ancient and Modern Imperialism* (John Murray).

Cross, A.L., 1914, *A History of England and Greater Britain* (Macmillan).

Crow, B. and Banfield, C., 1996, *An Introduction to Post-Colonial Theatre* (Cambridge University Press).

Cudjoe, S. (ed.), 1993, *Eric E. Williams Speaks. Essays on Colonialism and Independence* (University of Massachusetts Press).

Cudjoe, S., 1993, 'Eric E. Williams and the Politics of Language', in S. Cudjoe (ed.) 1993.

Culham, P. and Edmunds, L. (eds), 1989, *Classics: A Discipline and Profession in Crisis* (Rowman & Littlefield Publishers).

Bibliography

Davis, G. (ed.), 1997, *The Poetics of Derek Walcott: Intertextual Perspectives. The South Atlantic Quarterly*, Spring 1997 vol. 96, no. 2 (Duke University Press).

Davis, G., 1997, '"With No Homeric Shadow": The Disavowal of Epic in Derek Walcott's *Omeros*', in G. Davis (ed.) 1997.

Davis, G., 1997a, *Aimé Césaire* (Cambridge University Press).

Davis, S., 1953, 'The Study of the Classics: Inaugural Address Delivered at Pietermaritzburg 1st October 1953', n.p.

Deudney, D., 2001, 'Greater Britain or Greater Synthesis? Seeley, Mackinder, and Wells on Britain in the Global Industrial Era', *Review of International Studies* 27, 187-208.

Dilke, C.W., 1880, *Greater Britain: A Record of Travel in English-Speaking Countries during 1866 and 1867*, 7th edn (Macmillan).

Dilke, C.W., 1890, *Problems of Greater Britain* (Macmillan).

Dilke, C.W., 1899, *The British Empire* (Chatto & Windus).

Dominik, W.J., 1999, s.v. 'Africa', in *Der Neue Pauly* vol. 13.

Donnell, A. and Welsh, S.L. (eds) 1996, *The Routledge Reader in Caribbean Literature* (Routledge).

Dougherty, C., 1997, 'Homer after *Omeros*: Reading a H/Omeric Text', in Davis (ed.) 1997.

Dougherty, C., 2001, *The Raft of Odysseus. The Ethnographic Imagination of Homer's Odyssey* (Oxford University Press).

Dunton, C., 1992, *Make Man Talk True: Nigerian Drama in English since 1970* (Hans Zell Publishers).

Easterling, P.E., 1993, 'Tragedy and Ritual', in R. Scodel (ed.) *Theater and Society in the Classical World* (University of Michigan Press).

Echeruo, M.J.C., 1973, 'The Dramatic Limits of Igbo Ritual', *Research in African Literatures* 4, 21-31.

Edgal, S.F., 1958, 'Why and How the Classics should be Taught in West Africa', in J. Ferguson (ed.) *Nigeria and the Classics: Papers Read at the Second Conference on Classics Organised by the Department of Extra-Mural Studies in Collaboration with the Department of Classics and the Classical Association of Nigeria ...* (University of Ibadan).

Edwards, C. (ed.), 1999, *Roman Presences: Receptions of Rome in European Culture 1789-1945* (Cambridge University Press).

Egerton, H.E., 1920, *The Origin and Growth of Greater Britain: An Introduction to Sir C.P. Lucas's Historical Geography*, new edn (Clarendon Press), founded on Sir C.P. Lucas' *Introduction to a Historical Geography of the British Colonies* (Clarendon Press, 1887).

Enekwe, O.O., 1985, 'Interview with Ola Rotimi', *Okike* 25, 36-42.

Etherton, M., 1982, *The Development Of African Drama* (Hutchinson).

Farred, G. (ed.), 1996, *Rethinking C.L.R. James* (Blackwell Publishers).

Farrell, J., 1997, 'Walcott's *Omeros*: The Classical Epic in a Postmodern World', in G. Davis (ed.) 1997.

Ferguson, W.S., 1913, *Greek Imperialism* (Houghton Mifflin).

Finley, M.I., 1973, *Democracy Ancient and Modern* (Rutgers University Press).

Finley, M.I., 1978, 'The Athenian Empire: A Balance Sheet', in P.D.A. Garnsey and C.R. Whittaker (eds) *Imperialism in the Ancient World* (Cambridge University Press). Reprinted in M.I. Finley, B.D. Shaw and R.P. Saller (eds) *Economy and Society in Ancient Greece* (Chatto and Windus, 1981).

Fischer-Lichte, E. et al. (eds), 1990, *The Dramatic Touch of Difference: Theatre, Own and Foreign* (Narr).

Flashar, H., 1991, *Inszenierung der Antike: Das Griechische Drama auf der Buhne der Neuzeit, 1585-1990* (C.H. Beck).

Ford, P.J., 1982, *George Buchanan: Prince of Poets* (Aberdeen University Press).

Fornara, C.W., 1971, *Herodotus. An Interpretative Essay* (Clarendon Press).

Fornara, C.W., 1977, 'IG I² 39.52-57 and the "Popularity" of the Athenian Empire', *CSCA* 10, 39-55.

Fornara, C.W. and Samons, L.J., 1991, *Athens from Cleisthenes to Pericles* (University of California Press).

Forrest, W.G., 1975, 'Aristophanes and the Athenian Empire', in B. Levick (ed.) *The Ancient Historian and his Materials. Essays in Honour of C.E. Stevens* (Gregg).

Foster, J. (ed.), 1887-92, *Alumni Oxonienses: The Members of the University of Oxford ... 8 vols* (Parker).

Francois, H.J., 1978, 'Latin in Schools Should be Compulsory', *Voice of St. Lucia*, 20 June 1978, 5-6.

Frank, T., 1914, *Roman Imperialism* (Macmillan).

Freeman, E.A., 1886, *Greater Greece and Greater Britain* (Macmillan).

Freeman, P.W.M., 1996, 'British Imperialism and the Roman Empire', in J. Webster and N. Cooper (eds) *Roman Imperialism: Post-Colonial Perspectives* (University of Leicester, School of Archaeological Studies).

Froude, J.A., 1879, *Caesar: A Sketch* (Longmans, Green & Co.).

Froude, J.A., 1888, *The English in the West Indies. The Bow of Ulysses* (Longmans, Green & Co.).

Gainor, J.E. (ed.), 1995, *Imperialism and Theatre* (Routledge).

Gaisser, J.H., 1994, 'The Roman Odes at School: the Rise of the Imperial Horace', *Classical World* 87, 443-56.

Gandhi, L., 1998, *Postcolonial Theory: A Critical Introduction* (Edinburgh University Press).

Gandhi, M.K., 1997, *Hind Swaraj and Other Writings*, ed. A.J. Parel (Cambridge University Press).

Garnsey, P.D.A. and C.R. Whittaker, 1978, 'Introduction', in P.D.A. Garnsey and C.R. Whittaker (eds) *Imperialism in the Ancient World* (Cambridge University Press).

Garvey, M., 1967, *Philosophy and Opinions of Marcus Garvey. Or Africa for the Africans*. Compiled by A.J. Garvey. 2nd edn (two volumes in one). (Frank Cass). Vol. 1 was first published in 1923; vol. 2 was first published in 1925.

Garvey, M., 1977, *More Philosophy and Opinions of Marcus Garvey*, vol. 3. Selected and edited by E.U. Essien-Udom and A.J. Garvey (Frank Cass).

Gibbon, E., 1884, *History of the Decline and Fall of the British Empire* (Leadenhalle Presse).

Gibbs, J. et al., 1986, *Wole Soyinka: A Bibliography of Primary and Secondary Sources* (Greenwood Press).

Gilbert, H. (ed.), 1999, *(Post)colonial Stages: Critical & Creative Views on Drama, Theatre & Performance* (Dangaroo).

Gilbert, H., and Tompkins, J., 1996, *Post-colonial Drama: Theory, Practice, Politics* (Routledge).

Gilmore, J., 1979, 'Bishop Coleridge: A Bibliography of his Printed Works', *Journal of the Barbados Museum and Historical Society* 36, 50-65.

Bibliography

Gilmore, J., 1987, *The Toiler of the Sees: A Life of John Mitchinson, Bishop of Barbados* (Barbados National Trust).

Gilmore, J., 1996-7, review of Andrew White, *Voyage to Maryland*, in *Journal of the Barbados Museum & Historical Society* 43, 143-6.

Gilmore, J., 1998, '*Nullus in arte color*: Francis Williams and Other Caribbean Writers of Latin Poetry'. Unpublished paper presented at the 22nd Annual Conference of the Society for Caribbean Studies, University of Warwick, 7-9 July.

Gladstone, W.E., 1999a, 'Our Colonies' (1855), in B. Harlow and M. Carter (eds) *Imperialism and Orientalism: A Documentary Sourcebook* (Blackwell).

Gladstone, W.E., 1999b, 'England's Mission' (1878), in P. Cain (ed.) *Empire and Imperialism: The Debate of the 1870s* (Thoemmes Press).

Glissant, E., 1989, *Caribbean Discourse. Selected Essays*. Translated with an introduction by J. Michael Dash (University Press of Virginia). Originally published in French as *Le Discours Antillais* (Paris, 1981).

Glissant, E., 1997, *Poetics of Relation*. Translated by Betsy Wing (University of Michigan Press). Originally published as *Poétique de la Relation* (Paris, 1990).

Gödde, S., 2000, 'Zu einer Poetik des Rituals in Aischylos' *Persern*', in S. Gödde and T. Heinze (eds) *Skenika: Beiträge zum antiken Theater und seiner Rezeption: Festschrift zum 65. Geburtstag von Hans-Dieter Blume* (Wissenschaftliche Buchgesellschaft).

Golder, H., 1996, 'Geek Tragedy? – Or Why I'd Rather Go to the Movies', *Arion* 3rd series 4.1, 174-209.

Goldhill, S., 2000, 'Greek Drama and Political Theory', in C. Rowe and M. Schofield, *The Cambridge History of Greek and Roman Political Thought* (Cambridge University Press).

Goldhill, S., 2002, *Who Needs Greek? Contests in the Cultural History of Hellenism* (Cambridge University Press).

Gould, E.H., 1999, 'A Virtual Nation: Greater Britain and the Imperial Legacy of the American Revolution', *American Historical Review* 104, 476-89.

Gow, A.S.F., 1928, 'Notes on the *Persae* of Aeschylus', *JHS* 48, 132-58.

Graf, F. (ed.), 1998, *Ansichten Griechischer Rituale: Geburtstags-Symposium für Walter Burkert* (Teubner).

Graf, F., 1991, 'Prayer in Magic and Religious Ritual', in C. Faraone and D. Obbink (eds) *Magika Hiera: Ancient Greek Magic and Religion* (Oxford University Press) 188-213.

Graham-White, A., 1974, *The Drama of Black Africa* (French).

Green, T.H., and Grose, T.H. (eds), 1964, *David Hume: The Philosophical Works* (facsimile reprint of the 1882 edn. 4 vols, Scientia Verlag Aalen).

Greenfield, J., 1995, *The Return of Cultural Treasures* (Cambridge University Press)

Greenlee, J.G., 1976, '"A Succession of Seeleys": The "Old School" Re-examined', *Journal of Imperial and Commonwealth History* 4, 266-82

Greenwood, E., 2004, 'Classics and the Atlantic Triangle: Readings of Greece and Rome via Africa', in L. Milne (ed.) *Caribbean Connections. Forum for Modern Language Studies* 40:4, 365-76.

Grégoire, H., 1991, *De la Littérature des Nègres* (Perrin). Facsimile reprint of the 1808 edn with new introduction by Jean Lessay.

Griffith, G.T., 1978, 'Athens in the Fourth Century', in P.D.A. Garnsey and C.R.

Whittaker (eds) *Imperialism in the Ancient World* (Cambridge University Press).

Grigg, E., 1924, *The Greatest Experiment in History* (Yale University Press).

Haig Brown, William (ed.), 1870, *Sertum Carthusianum floribus trium seculorum contextum* (Deighton Bell).

Haley, S.P., 1989, 'Classics and Minorities', in P. Culham and L. Edmunds (eds) 1989.

Hall, C., 2002, *Civilising Subjects: Metropole and Colony in the English Imagination 1830-1867* (Polity).

Hall, E., 1997, 'Talfourd's Ancient Greeks in the Theatre of Reform', *IJCT* 3, 283-307.

Hall, E., Macintosh, F. and Wrigley, A. (eds), 2004, *Dionysus since '69: Tragedy at the Dawn of the Millennium* (Oxford University Press).

Halliwell, S., 1998, *Aristophanes: 'Birds' and Other Plays* (Clarendon Press).

Hamilton, William, 1811, *Memorandum on the Earl of Elgin's Pursuits in Greece* (W. Miller).

Hammond, M., 1948, 'Ancient Imperialism: Contemporary Justifications', *HSCPh* 58-9, 105-61.

Hamner, R.D. (ed.), 1997, *Critical Perspectives on Derek Walcott* (Lynne Rienner Publishers).

Handler, J.S., 1971, *A Guide to Source Materials for the Study of Barbados History* (Southern Illinois University Press).

Handler, J.S., 1991, *Supplement to a Guide to Source Materials for the Study of Barbados History* (John Carter Brown Library and Barbados Museum and Historical Society).

Hardwick, L., 1992, 'Convergence and Divergence in Reading Homer', in C. Emlyn-Jones, L. Hardwick and J. Purkis (eds) *Homer: Readings and Images* (Duckworth).

Hardwick, L., 2000, *Translating Words, Translating Cultures* (Duckworth).

Hardwick, L., 2000a, 'Women, Translation and Empowerment', in J. Bellamy, A. Laurence and G. Perry (eds) *Women, Scholarship and Criticism c. 1790-1900* (Manchester University Press).

Hardwick, L., 2000b, 'Theatres of the Mind: Greek Tragedy in Women's Writing in England in the Nineteenth Century', in L. Hardwick et al. (eds) 2000.

Hardwick, L., 2001, 'Who Owns the Plays? Issues in the Translation and Performance of Greek Drama on the Modern Stage', *Eirene* 37, Theatralia, 23-39.

Hardwick, L., 2003, *Reception Studies* (*Greece & Rome New Surveys in the Classics* No. 33) (Oxford University Press).

Hardwick, L., 2004, 'Greek Drama and Anti-colonialism: De-colonising Classics', in E. Hall et al. (eds) 2004.

Hardwick, L., 2005, 'Staging Agamemnon: The Languages of Translation', in F. Macintosh, P. Michelakis, E. Hall and O. Taplin (eds) *Agamemnon in Performance 458 BC – 2002 AD* (Oxford University Press).

Hardwick, L., Easterling, P.E., Ireland, S., Lowe, N., Macintosh, F. (eds), 2000, *Theatre Ancient and Modern* (Milton Keynes and electronically available at http://www2.open.ac.uk/ClassicalStudies/GreekPlays/conf96/ccfrontpage.htm).

Harlow, V.T., 1990, *Christopher Codrington, 1668-1710* (St. Martin's Press). First published by the Clarendon Press, 1928.

Bibliography

Harrison, T., 1986, *Theatre Works 1973-1985* (Penguin).

Harrison, T., 2000, *The Emptiness of Asia. Aeschylus' Persians and the History of the Fifth Century* (Duckworth).

Hartog, F., 1996, *Mémoire d' Ulysse: Récits sur la Frontière en Grèce Ancienne* (Gallimard). Translated by Janet Lloyd as *Memories of Odysseus. Frontier Tales from Ancient Greece* (Edinburgh University Press, 2001).

Henderson, J., 1987 *Aristophanes 'Lysistrata'* (Clarendon Press).

Hennessy, A. (ed.), 1992, *Intellectuals in the Twentieth-Century Caribbean. Volume 1 Spectre of the New Class: The Commonwealth Caribbean* (Macmillan).

Hingley, R., 2000, *Roman Officers and English Gentlemen: The Imperial Origins of Roman Archaeology* (Routledge).

Hirst, F.W., Murray, G., and Hammond, J.L.,1998, *Liberalism and the Empire: Three Essays* (R. Brimley Johnson, 1900; repr. Routledge/Thoemmes Press).

Hitchens, Christopher, 1987, *The Elgin Marbles: Should They be Returned to Greece?* (Chatto & Windus).

Hobson, J.A., 1905, *Imperialism: A Study* (Archibald Constable).

Hobson, J.A., 1965, *Imperialism: A Study*, 3rd edn (G. Allen & Unwin, 1938; repr., University of Michigan Press).

Holland, B., 1901, *Imperium et Libertas: A Study in History and Politics* (E. Arnold).

Hölscher, T., 1998, 'Images and Political Identity: the Case of Athens', in D. Boedeker and K. Raaflaub (eds) *Democracy, Empire and the Arts in Fifth-Century Athens* (Harvard University Press).

Hornblower, S., 1983, *The Greek World 479-323 BC (Methuen)*.

Hornblower, S., 1983a, 'Introduction: the Archaic Background to the Fifth-century Empire', in S. Hornblower and M.C. Greenstock (eds) *The Athenian Empire* (London Association of Classical Teachers).

Hornblower, S., 1991-6, *A Commentary on Thucydides* (Clarendon Press).

Howard, R.M. (ed.), 1925, *Records and Letters of the Family of the Longs of Longville, Jamaica, and Hampton Lodge, Surrey*. 2 vols (Simpkin, Marshall, Hamilton, Kent and Co.).

Howe, S., 1998, *Afrocentrism: Mythical Pasts and Imagined Homes* (Verso).

Hughes, E.A., 1919, *Britain and Greater Britain in the Nineteenth Century* (Cambridge University Press).

IJsewijn, Jozef, 1990, *Companion to Neo-Latin Studies: Part I, History and Diffusion of Neo-Latin Literature,* 2nd edn (Leuven University Press and Peeters Press).

Innes, C., 1981, *Holy Theatre: Ritual and the Avant Garde* (Cambridge University Press).

Jamaica, Parish of St Catherine [Jamaica] Copy Register No. 1 (microfilm at Hyde Park Family History Centre of the Church of Jesus Christ of Latter-Day Saints, London).

James, C.L.R., 1971, *Minty Alley* (New Beacon Books). First published by Secker and Warburg, London, in 1936.

James, C.L.R., 1977, *The Future in the Present* (Allison and Busby). Contains 'The Atlantic Slave-Trade' (essay 12), orig. 1956; and 'The Artist in the Caribbean' (essay 14), orig. 1959.

James, C.L.R., 1980, *Spheres of Existence. Selected Writings* (Allison and Busby).

Bibliography

James, C.L.R., 1984, *At the Rendezvous of Victory. Selected Writings* (Allison & Busby).

James, C.L.R., 1994, *Beyond a Boundary* (Serpent's Tail). First published in 1963.

James, C.L.R., 1996, 'Discovering Literature in Trinidad: the Nineteen-Thirties', in Donnell and Welsh (eds) 1996. From *Journal of Commonwealth Literature* (1969), 73-80.

Jenkyns, R., 1980, *The Victorians and Ancient Greece* (Basil Blackwell).

Jenkyns, R., 1992, *The Legacy of Rome* (Oxford University Press).

Jenkyns, R., 1996, 'Late Antiquity in English Novels of the Nineteenth Century', *Arion* 3rd series. 3.2 and 3, 141-66.

Jeyifo, B., 1978, 'Books: some corrective myths for the misguided native and the arrogant alien', *Positive Review* 1.1, 15-16.

Jeyifo, B. (ed), 2002, *Modern African Drama* (W.W. Norton).

Jones, E.D., 1988, *The Writing of Wole Soyinka*, 3rd edn (Currey).

Jose, A.W., 1913, *The Growth of the Empire: A Handbook to the History of Greater Britain*, 3rd edn (John Murray).

Jouguet, P., 1928, *Macedonian Imperialism and the Hellenization of the East* (London).

Kallet, L. 2002, *Money and the Corrosion of Power in Thucydides: The Sicilian Expedition and its Aftermath* (University of California Press).

Kallet-Marx, L., 1993, *Money, Expense and Naval Power in Thucydides' History 1-5.24* (University of California Press).

Katrak, K.H., 1986, *Wole Soyinka and Modern Tragedy: A Study of Dramatic Theory and Practice* (Greenwood).

Keeley, E. and Sherrard, P. (eds), 1995, *George Seferis. Complete Poems* (Anvil Press Poetry).

Kennedy, D.F., 1999, 'A Sense of Place: Rome, History and Empire Revisited', in Edwards (ed.) 1999.

Kiernan, V.G., 1995, *Imperialism and its Contradictions*, ed. H.J. Kaye (Routledge).

Kincaid, J., 1986, *Annie John* (New American Library).

Kincaid, J., 1990, *Lucy* (Farrar, Straus, Giroux).

King, B. (ed.), 1992, *Post-Colonial English Drama: Commonwealth Drama since 1960* (Macmillan).

King, B., 2000, *Derek Walcott: A Caribbean Life* (Oxford University Press).

King, K., 1971, *Pan-Africanism and Education* (Oxford University Press).

Kirkman, F.B.B., 1909, *The Growth of Greater Britain: A Sketch of the History of the British Colonies and Dependencies* (Blackie & Son).

Knorr, K.E., 1944, *British Colonial Theories 1570-1850* (University of Toronto Press).

Krise, T.W. (ed.), 1999, *Caribbeana: An Anthology of English Literature of the West Indies, 1657-1777* (University of Chicago Press).

Krummen, E., 1998, 'Ritual und Katastrophe: Rituelle Handlung und Bildersprache bei Sophokles und Euripides', in F. Graf (ed.) 1998.

Lazarus, N., 1999, *Nationalism and Cultural Practice in the Postcolonial World* (Cambridge University Press).

Lefèvre, A., 1986, 'Changing the Code: Soyinka's Ironic Aetiology', in A.S. Gérard (ed.) *European-Language Writing in Sub-Saharan Africa* (Akadémiai Kiadó), 1201-10.

Lefkowitz, M., 1990, 'Bringing Him Back Alive.' Rev. of Derek Walcott's *Omeros. New York Times* Book Review 7 Oct. 1990: 34-5. Reprinted in R.D. Hamner (ed.) 1997.

Lefkowitz, M. and MacLean Rogers, G., 1996, *Black Athena Revisited* (University of North Carolina Press).

Lefkowitz, M., 1996, *Not Out of Africa* (BasicBooks).

Lenin, V.I., 1965, *Imperialism: The Highest Stage of Capitalism*, new rev. trans. (International Publishers).

Levine, M.M., 1989, *The Challenge of Black Athena. Arethusa* Special Issue (New York).

Lindo, L., 1970, 'Francis Williams – A "Free" Negro in a Slave World', *Savacou*, vol. 1, no. 1 (June) 75-80.

Long, E., 2002, *The History of Jamaica* (Ian Randle Publishers). Facsimile reprint with new introduction by Howard Johnson. First published in 3 vols in London in 1774.

Loomba, A., 1998, *Colonialism/Postcolonialism* (Routledge).

Lucas, C.P., 1912, *Greater Rome and Greater Britain* (Clarendon Press).

Macintosh, F., 2000, 'Medea Transposed: Burlesque and Gender on the Mid-Victorian Stage', in E. Hall, F. Macintosh, O. Taplin, *Medea in Performance 1500-2000* (Legenda)

Macintosh, F., 2001, 'Oedipus in Africa', *Omnibus* 42, 8-9.

Mackail, J.W., 1925, 'The Place of the Classics in Imperial Studies', in *Classical Studies* (John Murray).

Mackail, J.W., 1925a, *James Leigh Strachan-Davidson, Master of Balliol: A Memoir* (Clarendon Press).

MacKechnie, Paul, 1992, 'In the Schools: Kamuzu Academy, Mtunthama, Malawi', *Scholia* n.s.1, 142-3.

Maine, H., 1871, *Village-Communities in the East and West* (John Murray).

Maine, H., 1883, *Ancient Law*, 9th edn (John Murray).

Majeed, J., 1999, 'Comparativism and References to Rome in British Imperial Attitudes to India', in Edwards (ed.) 1999.

Major, J., 1892, *A History of Greater Britain as well England as Scotland*, ed. A. Constable (Scottish Historical Society).

Mandela, N., 1995, *Long Walk to Freedom* (Abacus).

Mandler, P., 2000, '"Race" and "Nation" in mid-Victorian Thought', in S. Collini, R. Whatmore, B. Young (eds) *History, Religion, and Culture: British Intellectual History 1750-1950* (Cambridge University Press).

Marlowe, J., 1970, *Cromer in Egypt* (Elek Books).

Masolo, D.A., 1994, *African Philosophy In Search Of Identity* (Indiana University Press).

McCarthy, S., 1991, 'An Interview with Derek Walcott', *Outposts: Poetry Quarterly* 171. Special issue. *Derek Walcott: A Celebration*, 4-24.

McDonald, M., 2000, 'Black Dionysus: Greek Tragedy from Africa', in L. Hardwick et al. (eds) 2000.

McMurtrie, Douglas C., 1942, *The First Printing in Jamaica* ... (privately printed).

Meiggs, R., 1972, *The Athenian Empire* (Clarendon Press).

Miles, G.B., 1990, 'Roman and Modern Imperialism: A Reassessment', *Comparative Studies in Society and History* 32, 629-59.

Mills, E.E., 1905, *The Decline and Fall of the British Empire. A brief account of those causes which resulted in the destruction of our late Ally, together with a comparison between the British and Roman Empires. Appointed for use in the National School of Japan* (Alden & Co.).

Mills, S., 1997, *Theseus, Tragedy and the Athenian Empire* (Clarendon Press).

Mirecki, P. and Meyer, M. (eds), 2002, *Magic and Ritual in the Ancient World* (Brill).

Moles, J., 1996, 'Herodotus Warns the Athenians', *Papers of the Leeds International Latin Seminar* 9, 259-84.

Mommsen, T., 1862-75, *The History of Rome*. 4 vols, translated by W.P. Dickson (R. Bentley).

Money, D.K., 1998, *The English Horace: Anthony Alsop and the Tradition of British Latin Verse* (Oxford University Press, for the British Academy).

Moore-Gilbert, B., 1997, *Postcolonial Theory* (Verso).

Mosley, O., 1932, *The Greater Britain* (British Union of Fascists).

Moumouni, A., 1968, *Education in Africa*. Translated by Phyllis Nauts Ott (Deutsch).

Murray, O., 2000, 'Ancient History, 1872–1914', in M.G. Brock and M.C. Curthoys (eds) 2000.

Musarum Anglicanarum Analecta: sive Poëmatum quorumdam melioris notae, seu hactenus Ineditorum, seu sparsim Editorum, vol. III. (Oxford, 1717).

Nettleford, R., 1992, 'The Aesthetics of Négritude: A Metaphor for Liberation', in Hennessy (ed.) 1992.

Ngugi wa Thiong'o, 1986, *Decolonising the Mind* (James Currey).

Ngugi wa Thiong'o, 1993, *Moving the Centre: The Struggle for Cultural Freedom* (James Currey).

Nicholls, D., 1995, *The Lost Prime Minister: A Life of Sir Charles Dilke* (Hambledon Press).

Ogg, F.A., 1902, 'The Making of Greater Britain', *The Chautauquan* 36, 126-37.

Okpewho, I., 1983, *Myth In Africa: A Study of its Aesthetic and Cultural Relevance* (Cambridge University Press).

Okpewho, I., 1999, 'Soyinka, Euripides, and the Anxiety of Empire', *Research in African Literatures* 30, 32-55.

Olaniyan, T., 1995, *Scars of Conquest / Masks of Resistance: The Invention of Cultural Identities in African, African-American, and Caribbean Drama* (Oxford University Press).

Oliver, V.L. (ed.), 1894-9, *History of the Island of Antigua*. 3 vols (Mitchell and Hughes).

Oliver, V.L. (ed.), 1909-19, *Caribbeana*. 6 vols (Mitchell, Hughes and Clarke).

Oliver, V.L. (ed.), 1915, *The Monumental Inscriptions in the Churches and Churchyards of the Island of Barbados, British West Indies* (Mitchell, Hughes and Clarke).

Oliver, V.L. (ed.), 1927, *The Monumental Inscriptions of the British West Indies* (F.G. Longman, The Friary Press).

Orderson, J.W., 2002, *Creoleana: Or, Social and Domestic Scenes and Incidents in Barbados in Days of Yore* (Macmillan Education). New edn with introduction and notes by John Gilmore. First published in London in 1842.

Osofisan, F., 1982, 'Ritual and the Revolutionary Ethos: the Humanistic Dilemma in Contemporary Nigerian Theatre', *Okike* 22, 72-81.

Osofisan, F., 1999, *Recent Outings: Comprising Tegonni, An African Antigone And Many Colours Make The Thunder-King* (Opon Ifa Readers).

Bibliography

Oxaal, I., 1968, *Black Intellectuals Come to Power. The Rise of Creole Nationalism in Trinidad and Tobago* (Schenkman Pub. Co.).

Padel, R., 1985, 'Homer's Reader: A Reading of George Seferis', *Proceedings of the Cambridge Philological Association* 211, 74-132.

Parker, M. and Starkey, R. (eds), 1995, *Postcolonial Literatures. Achebe, Ngugi, Desai, Walcott* (Macmillan).

Parker, R., 1996, *Athenian Religion. A History* (Clarendon Press).

Pavis, P. (ed.), 1996, *The Intercultural Performance Reader* (Routledge).

Price, S. and Nixon, L., 1990, 'The Size and Resources of Greek Cities', in O. Murray and S. Price, *The Greek City from Homer to Alexander* (Clarendon Press).

Quinn, T.J., 1964, 'Thucydides and the Unpopularity of the Athenian Empire', *Historia* 13, 257-66.

Quinn, T.J., 1981, *Athens and Samos, Chios, and Lesbos 478-404 BC* (Manchester University Press).

Ramazani, J., 1997, 'The Wound of History: Walcott's *Omeros* and the Post-Colonial Poetics of Affliction', *Proceedings of the Modern Literature Association* 112 (3), May, 405-15.

Ramsay, J., 1784, *An Essay on the Treatment and Conversion of African Slaves in the British Sugar Colonies* (J. Phillips).

Ravenshaw, T.F., 1878, *Antiente Epitaphes (From AD 1250 to AD 1800) Collected and sett forth in Chronologicall order* (London, n.p.).

Raychaudhuri, T., 1988, *Europe Reconsidered: Perceptions of the West in Nineteenth Century Bengal* (Oxford University Press).

Reece, J.E., and Clark-Hunt, C.G. (eds), n.d. (c. 1927), *Barbados Diocesan History* (West India Committee).

Reid, D.M., 2002, *Whose Pharaohs? Archaeology, Museums, and Egyptian National Identity from Napoleon to World War I* (University of California Press).

Rhodes, P.J., 1985, *The Athenian Empire, Greece and Rome New Surveys* 17 (Classical Association at the Clarendon Press).

Richards, S.L., 1996, *Ancient Songs Set Ablaze: The Theater Of Femi Osofisan* (Howard University Press).

Robertson, J.M., 1899, *Patriotism and Empire* (G. Richards).

Robertson, N., 1986, 'The True Nature of the "Delian League" 478-461 BC', *AJAH* 5, 64-96, 110-137.

Romilly, J. de, 1963, *Thucydides and Athenian Imperialism*. Translated by P. Thody (Blackwell).

Rood, T., 1998, *Thucydides. Narrative and Explanation* (Clarendon Press).

Rubin, D. et al. (eds), 1997, *The World Encyclopaedia of Contemporary Theatre: Africa* (Routledge).

Said, E., 1978, *Orientalism* (Routledge and Kegan Paul).

Said, E., 1993, *Culture and Imperialism* (Vintage).

Sainte Croix, G.E.M. de, 1954/5, 'The Character of the Athenian Empire', *Historia* 3, 3-41.

Sainte Croix, G.E.M. de, 1972, *The Origins of the Peloponnesian War* (Duckworth).

Schein, S., 1977, 'Wole Soyinka: *The Bacchae of Euripides. A Communion Rite*', *CW* 70, 403.

Seanu, K., 1980, 'The Exigencies of Adaptation: The Case of Soyinka's

Bacchae', in J. Gibbs (ed.) *Critical Perspectives on Wole Soyinka* (Heinemann).

Seeley, J.R., 1971, *The Expansion of England*, ed. J. Gross (University of Chicago Press).

Seeley, J.R., 1870, 'Roman Imperialism I-III', in his *Lectures and Essays* (Macmillan).

Seeley, J.R., 1909, *The Expansion of England: Two Courses of Lectures* (Macmillan, 1883; repr. Little, Brown).

Seferis, G., 1994, *Poiêmata*. 18th edn (Ikaros).

Sherlock, P. and Nettleford, R., 1990, *The University of the West Indies: A Caribbean Response to the Challenge of Change* (Macmillan).

Smith, E.W. and Dale, A.M., 1920, *The Ila-Speaking Peoples of Northern Rhodesia* (Macmillan).

Sommerstein, A., 1990, *Aristophanes* Lysistrata (Warminster).

Sotto, W., 1985, *The Rounded Rite: A Study of Wole Soyinka's Play The Bacchae of Euripides* (Gleerup).

Souza, P. de, 1999, *Piracy in the Graeco-Roman World* (Cambridge University Press).

Soyinka, W., 1973a, *The Bacchae of Euripides* (Eyre Methuen).

Soyinka, W., 1973b, *Collected Plays 1* (Oxford University Press).

Soyinka, W., 1976, *Myth, Literature and the African World* (Cambridge University Press).

Soyinka, W., 1988, *Art, Dialogue & Outrage: Essays on Literature and Culture* (New Horn).

Soyinka, W., 1998, *Early Poems* (Oxford University Press).

Spratlin, V.B., 1938, *Juan Latino, Slave and Humanist* (Spinner Press).

Stadter, P., 1992, 'Herodotus and the Athenian Arche', *ASNP* 22.3-4, 781-809.

Stéhlíková, E., 2001, 'Productions of Greek and Roman Drama on the Czech Stage', *Eirene* 37, Theatralia, 71-160.

Stray, C., 1998, *Classics Transformed: Schools, Universities and Society in England 1830-1960* (Clarendon Press).

Stuchtey, B. and Wende, P. (eds), 2000, *British and German Historiography, 1750-1950: Traditions, Perceptions, and Transfers* (Oxford University Press).

Symonds, R., 1991, *Oxford and Empire: The Last Lost Cause?*, corr. edn (Clarendon Press).

Symonds, R., 2000, 'Oxford and the Empire', in M.G. Brock and M.C. Curthoys (eds) 2000.

Taplin, O., 1991, 'Derek Walcott's *Omeros* and Derek Walcott's Homer', *Arion* 3rd series 2, 213-25.

Taylor, M., 1991, 'Imperium et Libertas? Rethinking the Radical Critique of Imperialism during the Nineteenth Century', *Journal of Imperial and Commonwealth History* 1-23.

Thomas, J.J., 1969, *Froudacity. West Indian Fables by James Anthony Froude Explained by J.J. Thomas.* With an introduction by C.L.R. James (New Beacon Books). Reprint of the 1889 edn.

Thompson, A.S., 2000, *Imperial Britain: The Empire in British Politics c. 1880-1932* (Longman).

Thornton, A.P., 1965, *Doctrines of Imperialism* (Wiley).

Tietze Larson, V., 1999, 'Classics and the Acquisition and Validation of Power in

Bibliography

Britain's "Imperial Century" (1815–1914)', *International Journal of the Classical Tradition*, 185-225.

Tiffin, H., 1987, 'Post-colonial Literatures and Counter-discourse', *Kunapipi* 9, 17-34.

Todd, J., (ed.), 1992, *The Works of Aphra Behn*, I (William Pickering).

Trautmann, T.R., 1997, *Aryans and British India* (University of California Press).

Turner, F.M., 1981, *The Greek Heritage in Victorian Britain* (Yale University Press).

Turner, F.M., 1993, *Contesting Cultural Authority: Essays in Victorian Intellectual Life* (Cambridge University Press).

Van Binsbergen, W. (ed.), 1997, *Black Athena: Ten Years After, Talanta*, 28-9.

Van Binsbergen, W., 1997a, 'Black Athena Ten Years After: Towards a Constructive Re-assessment', in van Binsbergen (ed.) 1997.

Van Binsbergen, W., 1997b, 'Rethinking Africa's Contribution to Global Cultural History', in van Binsbergen (ed.) 1997.

Vance, Norman, 1997, *The Victorians and Ancient Rome* (Blackwell Publishers).

Venn, J., and Venn, J.A., 1922-7, *Alumni Cantabrigienses: A Biographical List of All Known Students, Graduates and Holders of Office at the University of Cambridge; Part I, from the Earliest Times to 1751*. 4 vols (Cambridge University Press).

Venn, J.A., 1940-54, *Alumni Cantabrigienses ... Part II, from 1752 to 1900*. 6 vols (Cambridge University Press).

Veyne, P., 1975, 'Y a-t-il eu un impérialisme romain?', *MEFRA* 87, 793-855.

Viswanathan, G., 1989, *Masks of Conquest: Literary Study and British Rule in India* (Columbia University Press).

Walcott, D., 1970, *Dream on Monkey Mountain and Other Plays* (Farrar, Straus and Giroux).

Walcott, D., 1973, *Another Life* (Farrar, Straus and Giroux).

Walcott, D., 1974, 'The Caribbean: Culture or Mimicry?', *Journal of Inter-American Studies and World Affairs* 16, 3-13.

Walcott, D., 1974a, 'The Muse of History', in D. Walcott, 1998.

Walcott, D., 1988, *The Arkansas Testament* (Faber). American edn published in 1987 by Farrar, Straus and Giroux.

Walcott, D., 1990, *Omeros* (Faber). American edn published in 1990 by Farrar, Straus and Giroux.

Walcott, D., 1992, *Collected Poems 1948-1984* (Faber). American edn published in 1986 by Farrar, Straus and Giroux.

Walcott, D., 1993, *The Antilles: Fragments of Epic Memory*, The Nobel Lecture (Farrar, Straus and Giroux).

Walcott, D., 1993, *The Odyssey: A Stage Version* (Faber). American edn published in 1993 by Farrar, Straus and Giroux.

Walcott, D., 1996, 'The Sea is History', in F. Birbalsingh (ed.) 1996. Text taken from a recording of a talk given at York University, Toronto, 18 January 1989.

Walcott, D., 1997, 'Reflections on *Omeros*', in G. Davis (ed.) 1997. Edited transcript of a talk given at Duke University in the Spring of 1995, ed. G. Davis.

Walcott, D., 1997a, *The Bounty* (Faber). American edn published in 1997 by Farrar, Straus and Giroux.

Walcott, D., 1997b, 'Society and the Artist', in Hamner (ed.) 1997. First published in *Public Opinion* (Jamaica) 4 May 1957, 7.

Bibliography

Walcott, D., 1998, *What the Twilight Says: Essays* (Faber). American edn published in 1998 by Farrar, Straus and Giroux.

Walder, Dennis, 1998, *Post-colonial Literatures in English: History, Language, Theory* (Blackwell).

Waquet, Françoise, 2001, *Latin, or, The Empire of a Sign: from the Sixteenth to the Twentieth Centuries.* Translated by John Howe (Verso).

Wetmore Jr., K. J., 2002, *The Athenian Sun in an African Sky* (McFarland and Co.).

White, A., 1995, *Voyage to Maryland (1633) Relatio Itineris in Marilandiam.* Translated and edited by Barbara Lawatsch-Boomgarden (Bolchazy-Carducci).

Wiles, D., 2000, *Greek Theatre Performance: An Introduction* (Cambridge University Press).

Williams, E., 1969, *Inward Hunger: the Education of a Prime Minister* (Andre Deutsch Ltd).

Wilson, D., 1987, *Gilbert Murray, OM. 1866-1957* (Clarendon Press).

Wise, C., 1956, *A History of Education in British West Africa* (Longmans, Green).

Wormell, D., 1980, *Sir John Seeley and the Uses of History* (Cambridge University Press).

Wren, R.M., 1991, *Those Magical Years: The Making of Nigerian Literature at Ibadan: 1948-1966* (L. Rienner).

Wright, D., 1993, *Wole Soyinka Revisited* (Macmillan).

Wright, P., 1966, *Monumental Inscriptions of Jamaica* (Society of Genealogists).

Wyke, M. and Biddiss, M. (eds), 1999, *The Uses and Abuses of Antiquity* (Peter Lang).

Wynne, G.R., 1901, *The Church in Greater Britain. The Donnellan Lectures Delivered before the University of Dublin, 1900-1901* (Kegan Paul & Co.).

Young, R.J.C., 2001, *Postcolonialism: An Historical Introduction* (Blackwell).

Index

Author

Walcott, Derek, 65, 68, 71-3, 79-
    85, 112, 113
Walder, Dennis, 3, 5
Wheatley, Phillis, 92
Williams, Eric, 66, 77-8, 96

Wordsworth, William, 71
Wyke, Maria and M. Biddiss, 12-
    13

Young, Robert, 59